TANIKA GUPTA

POLITICAL PLAYS

TANIKA GUPTA

POLITICAL PLAYS

GLADIATOR GAMES

SANCTUARY

SUGAR MUMMIES

INTRODUCTION BY ALEKS SIERZ

OBERON BOOKS
LONDON

WWW.OBERONBOOKS.COM

First published in 2012 by Oberon Books Ltd
521 Caledonian Road, London N7 9RH
Tel: +44 (0) 20 7607 3637 / Fax: +44 (0) 20 7607 3629
e-mail: info@oberonbooks.com
www.oberonbooks.com

A catalogue record for this book is available from the British Library.

PB ISBN: 978-1-84943-247-4
Digital ISBN: 978-1-84943-521-5

Cover design by James Illman

Printed, bound and converted
by CPI Group (UK) Ltd, Croydon, CR0 4YY.

Contents

Introduction by Aleks Sierz 9

Gladiator Games 17

White Boy 99

Sanctuary 159

Sugar Mummies 253

To hold a pen is to be at war

– Voltaire

Introduction

Traditionally, British political theatre tramps over a narrow stretch of ground between two gestures: one is of a failure of nerve and the other of a discovery of articulacy. As political playwright David Edgar once pointed out, Jimmy's speech about 'no good brave causes' in *Look Back in Anger* is followed not by him giving his friend Cliff a radical pamphlet, but by his lover Helena giving Cliff a clean shirt. Somehow, the political is constrained by the domestic. By contrast, in Arnold Wesker's *Roots*, there is the second kind of gesture: Beattie finds her own voice in the final scene. By the 1990s, when Tanika Gupta began her writing career, both of these traditions had faded like sepia photographs, and other potential gestures were there, lying quietly hidden, or waiting to be invented. If the 1990s is often seen as an unpolitical decade, in which most plays were 'me and my mates' flatshare dramas and deeply domestic stories, then Gupta's work both challenges this cliché and deconstructs both poles of the personal and political divide. It also adds other, new theatrical gestures to the tradition of British political drama.

The first play in this collection, *Sanctuary*, was originally produced at the National Theatre in July 2002. By that time, Gupta had already written a variety of plays. From the start, her interest in political theatre was apparent. For example, her early play, *Voices on the Wind* (which had a couple of rehearsed readings at National Theatre Studio in 1995) explored a family story about her great-uncle Dinesh Gupta who was a fighter against British imperialism. In 1930, along with two other comrades, he shot and killed Colonel N.S. Simpson, the notoriously brutal Inspector General of prisons, in Dalhousie Square in Calcutta. It was a suicide mission which was part of the violent struggle against British rule in India. But although two of the men committed suicide by shooting themselves in the head, Dinesh Gupta botched his attempt. He was arrested, cured in hospital, and then hanged by the British. While in prison, he wrote letters to his family and these formed the basis of the play, which implicitly questions the myth that the whole anti-imperialist struggle was non-violent. It wasn't. Politics also came into play when Gupta was researching about her great-uncle. She went to the British Newspaper Library but couldn't find any mention of him. So she asked her father. He said, 'What are you looking for?' She said, 'Freedom fighter.' He said, 'Try terrorist.' So she went back to the library, looked up 'terrorist', and there he was. Interestingly, Gupta has returned to the subject of this family story in her new play, *Lions and Tigers.*

In *Sanctuary*, Gupta explores that most political of issues, national identity. The play is set in a church graveyard, whose greenery and flowers evoke the idea of England as a garden, a place that is both Eden-like (with its biblical suggestion of evil lurking among the beautiful plants) and in decline: '*A few bits of rubbish litter the otherwise beautiful garden.*' Like some other artists of Asian heritage, the British-born Gupta has made the journey from writing about subjects close to the life experience of her parents to writing about British life today. This can be seen in the characters of *Sanctuary*, only one of which is Asian. He is Kabir, the Muslim gardener. The church is run by Jenny, a liberal vicar in her thirties whose grandmother, Margaret, represents both traditional English colonial views as well as being tolerant in terms of her sexual and religious ideas. At the end, she also takes the right moral decisions. But the main drama of the play is carried by the clash between Kabir and the characters Michael, an African man, and Sebastian, who comes from the Caribbean. In this English Eden, all of the characters are, in different ways, running away from life. For all of them, it is a sanctuary. But the safety of the place enables other less safe messages to be wrought. Challenging the stereotype that Asians and Africans don't get on, Gupta shows the friendship between Kabir and Michael. But this is also a play with a wider political agenda, which illustrates how a genocide in one distant country (Rwanda) or atrocities in another (Kashmir) can have a dramatic impact on lives lived in this more peaceful land. As Gupta tells Kabir and Michael's painful stories, she implicitly asks the audience to think about difficult ethical issues: how would any of us behave if we were caught up in a genocidal situation? And how is personal friendship affected by knowing the truth about someone's politics? Yet the play is much more than a simple battle for the truth: it is a very rich text which cultivates many different issues with wit and clarity. For example, the character of Ayesha, a half-Turkish fifteen-year-old, illustrates the complexity of cultural heritage in Britain today. At one point she says, 'Dad wasn't really English. His Dad was Scottish – that's my grandfather and my grandmother's half Irish and a quarter Norwegian and a quarter something else...' Yes, there's no such thing as racial purity. Likewise, in contemporary British theatre, the stage image of the mixed-race child usually has an optimistic connotation, and at the end of the play Ayesha clearly symbolises hope for a better future. The image of a mixed-race teenager bravely going forward is a new and refreshing political gesture.

Some plays act as campaigning tools. *Gladiator Games* was written as an openly political project, but its politics resonate far beyond the immediate reasons for its creation. It is based on the case of Zahid Mubarek, a nineteen-year-old Asian who was put in Feltham Young Offenders Institution for six weeks for stealing some razor blades. Soon after his arrival, he was made to share a cell with Robert Stewart, a known racist with severe mental problems. During the night before Mubarek was due for release, Stewart beat him unconscious with a chair leg. The young man died seven days later in hospital on 28 March 2000. Clearly, there was something badly wrong with an institution whose authorities put these two men together, and soon stories began to circulate about a practice known as Gladiator Games, which involved warders putting mismatched prisoners together in order to see who would win their inevitable fights. Rumours suggested that prison officers laid bets on who would win in such conflicts. The political scandal was that it took Mubarek's family more than four years to persuade the government to hold a public inquiry into what exactly was going on at Feltham. After being approached by Sheffield Theatres, Gupta wrote the play at the time the inquiry was sitting and it was staged in October 2005, several months before the inquiry reported. The gestation of the play was not unproblematic. The menfolk of the Mubarek family, from a working-class Pakistani background in the East End of London, were initially suspicious of Gupta and the idea of a play. But when she told them she had written for BBC television's *EastEnders*, they perceived her as a 'proper writer', and so gradually she could win their trust, and tell their story.

But although *Gladiator Games* has some verbatim material based on interviews carried out by Gupta, it is not a simple verbatim drama. She chose to focus on Zahid Mubarek and to use his perspective, rejecting the idea that the drama should be balanced and tell both sides of the story. For her, it was a play that could give voice to a young man who had been the victim of outrageously bad treatment and a horrific crime. Since he was already dead, she had to invent his dialogue. But invention is what playwrights do. The resulting mixture of fact and fiction is typical of contemporary British theatre, and in this case works to strengthen the politics of the play. It is chilling to watch the scenes in prison when Stewart dominates the stage, plainly a disturbed young man. But the play also asks other questions with a wider political edge: what is the reason for incarceration in our society? How can locking people up help to rehabilitate them? What are the best policies for making society safe, and criminals better people? Certainly no British government has managed to answer these questions, preferring instead to lock up individuals, who are then put at the mercy of prison officers. It is also a play about the cancer of institutional racism.

Gladiator Games was remounted more than once as the inquiry process limped along, and it served both as a publicity tool for the campaign for justice for Zahid Mubarek and as a public forum for audiences. When I saw the play at the Theatre Royal Stratford East, there was a typically poignant moment at the very end when Zahid says that he loves his mum. It was very emotional, and somebody in the audience shouted out, 'Tell her again mate.' You could have heard a pin drop. Likewise, the actor Ray Panthaki, who played Zahid, had also played Ronnie from *EastEnders*, so every time he came on stage, someone in the audience would intone, 'Alright Ronnie…' Humorous reactions apart, the play should be commended as both a denunciation of institutional racism in the criminal justice system and a tribute to the Mubarek family and their long struggle for justice.

In *Sanctuary*, the teenager Ayesha has a robust attitude to studying, summed up by her final joy at finishing her exams:

'Last bloody time I have to write anything, ever about kings or queens or bloody useless, fucking novels.' In 2007, Gupta returned to the subject of schools in *White Boy*, which was first put on by the National Youth Theatre at the Soho Theatre in August 2007. The background to the play was the distressing number of teenage stabbings which suddenly seemed to break out all over Britain in 2006 and continued over subsequent years. In London, for example, 23 teenagers were stabbed to death in 2008. But the issue of teenage violence is only one element of the story, which centres on Ricky, a seventeen-year-old white youth. As in *Sanctuary*, Gupta represents the rainbow nation familiar to any inner-city dweller: Victor is Afro-Caribbean, Zara a black Briton, Shaz wears a hijab, Kabir is Asian, Sorted is Sudanese and Flips, the school bully, is white. He also deals drugs. Most of the characters are fifteen years old, and there's also a chorus of other kids. Gupta examines the friendships, and rivalries, within this diverse group of 'breddas'. Ricky, whose parents are white working class, imitates the streetwise language of Victor, whose aim in life is to become a footballer. By showing Ricky as confused about his identity – at one crucial point he cries out: 'Me, what have I got?' – Gupta raises the political issue of the status of the white working class in contemporary Britain. Under the New Labour governments of the 2000s, there was a widespread feeling among people in this class that they had been betrayed by multicultural policies and excluded from council housing and local authority jobs. Historically, the British National Party has attempted to exploit these feelings of disenfranchisement by blaming immigrants and, in Gupta's play, Flips symbolises these kinds of attitudes. He also is guilty of anti-Muslim prejudice and casual racism.

White Boy is both an account of a rapidly changing social landscape and an intervention which stresses that the responsibility for success in life lies with individuals. It's a play that asks urgent questions about how much we are formed by the cultures of our parents, and what we really think about our friends: at one point, Ricky is driven to ask Sorted: 'Is it my fault your kin murdering each other? So you come here and mek me feel shame of what I am. Is it the white boy's fault?' The emotional truth comes from convincing characters, and convincing characters are never politically correct. The play makes a strong case against carrying 'a blade' for self-defence, but Gupta also sympathises completely with the way that teenagers think and feel. She understands young sexuality and teen loyalties. From the street language to the body language of the characters, this is one of the most empathetic teenage plays in the canon. Just after the climax of the play, there is a moment when the school gates that dominated the set in the first production become a shrine to the accidental victim of a knife crime. On stage, this was a powerful visual moment that asked audiences to bear witness to what was going wrong with their children, and by implication to do something about it. As political theatre, the play was, and remains, an incitement to make change happen.

If *White Boy* was a response to a number of highly publicised knife crimes, *Sugar Mummies* was a play commissioned by the Royal Court to look at a subject that lurks in the dark corners of taboo: sex tourism by women in the Caribbean. The idea came from a newspaper article and the theatre sent Gupta to Jamaica to research the piece. It was then successfully staged as part of the theatre's 50th anniversary in August 2006. Set on and around an idyllic beach in Jamaica, it looks at the relationships of three female sex tourists with local men: the British middle-aged women Maggie and Kitty, and the American Yolanda (in the original production, Maggie was played by Linda Bellingham, famous as a television Oxo Mum, and Yolanda by a black actor, Adjoa Andoh). The local men are Sly, Antonio and Andre (who refuses to become a gigolo and wants to train and work as a chef). Andre's mother, Angel, works on the beach as a masseuse and hair braider; her contemporary, Reefie, is an experienced gigolo and Yolanda's long-term lover. Last but not least, the mixed-race twenty something Naomi is a holiday-maker who accompanies her aunt Maggie: she has no need to pay for sex and her priority is to find her biological father (she was conceived and born on the island although she was brought up in Britain).

With enormous wit, pace and style, *Sugar Mummies* explores gender politics in a post-imperial context. It is brilliantly written, very funny and acerbic, but at the same time it takes very seriously the issue of the exploitation of black men. Although Gupta never moralises, the play implicitly condemns the tourist industry which ships women across the world for cheap sex; in an ironic take on feminism, women now have the economic power to buy sex in exactly the same way that men have done for centuries. But, as Gupta makes clear, the exploitation is mutual: the local men are looking not only for money, but also for a ticket to escape the poverty of the island. So the play examines the idea of shopping and fucking in a Jamaican context from a whole variety of angles: Sly represents the young gigolo, Reefie the old hand who has regular customers who return every year, Antonio a young potential gigolo and Andre the critic of the whole industry. In fact, one of the emotional highpoints is Andre's anguish at realising that all relationships are mediated by the dollar – most of the characters experience various aspects of the poverty of consumer society. For while newcomer Maggie knows the score, and Yolanda is a regular sex tourist, Kitty has illusions that she could develop a loving relationship with Sly. She has to learn painfully the justice of Maggie's comment that 'Truth always hurts'. This is the core of the politics of a play in which a black man tells the truth to a white woman. But its overall politics are much more complex, with one dramatic scene in which an older white woman, in a savage echo of the history of slavery, ferociously whips a young black man. It is an appalling and powerful theatrical moment. By the end of the play, although truth has been told to economic power, Reefie is finally unable to tell the truth to Naomi. Yet, as in *Sanctuary*, the image of a mixed-race woman starting out on a new life is a strong gesture of hope for the future.

As is abundantly clear, Gupta has written intensely political plays that have successfully avoided the clichés of narrowly defined Asian theatre (she doesn't write about arranged marriages, racial discrimination or set her stories in exclusively Bengali contexts). Her work is inflected by her heritage, but not bound by it. As all of these plays conclusively demonstrate, she writes with equal perception about white, black and Asian characters, which in itself is a gesture of liberation. In some plays, there are no Asian characters at all, and her writing is equally convincing when it takes Jamaican patois for its base as when it communicates in teen-speak. The point about her political writing is its sheer variety of subject matter, ranging over a series of subjects and social relationships with equal confidence and equally passionate engagement. Her depictions of the tensions between characters that are either idealists or pragmatists, or a mixture of both, combine to create a picture of Britain as a vibrant multicultural society beset with severe problems, not all of which have simple political solutions. Indeed, some of these problems feel as if they are deeper than politics. But her brand of political theatre not only uses new gestures that go well beyond the traditional ones of British theatre, it also challenges audiences to see behind the story and to think about the political choices being posited on stage. That is what great theatre is all about.

Aleks Sierz
London, March 2012

GLADIATOR GAMES

A dramatisation of the events surrounding the death in custody of Zahid Mubarek in Feltham Young Offenders Institute in March 2000.

With verbatim text from evidence given to the Zahid Mubarek Inquiry and interviews.

Foreword

I remember reading about the horrific racist murder of Zahid Mubarek in the papers a few years back. I recall seeing a picture of his handsome, youthful face and the tattooed but equally youthful face of his murderer Robert Stewart. The story affected me, and the fact that Zahid was an Asian youth serving a sentence for minor offences was not lost on me. Beyond my initial reaction, I'm afraid the story slid back into the recesses of my mind.

Over the following years I worked on a project with Clean Break and spent some time in HMP Winchester running writing workshops for the female inmates. I had never stepped inside a prison before then and the research for the play I subsequently wrote for Clean Break also took me to HMP Holloway. I kept thinking: 'There but for the grace of God go I'. The inmates that I met were for the most part women who had lost their way and turned to crime, who through poverty, lack of education, family trauma, broken homes, lack of opportunities, bad legal representation or simply through getting in with the wrong company, had ended up in prison. In HMP Winchester, my writing group of fifteen women were mainly black, mixed-race or foreign nationals, and all of them were desperate to change, to live better, more productive lives once they were back on the outside. Some of them were serving disproportionately long sentences for seemingly minor offences. Education was virtually non-existent, the prison library had very little reading material except for soft porn and the odd Jane Austen novel, and some of the prison officers seemed to resent the women having opportunities to educate themselves. After I'd finished my writing workshop, the group hand-made me the most beautiful card and each signed their names writing at the end 'remember me'.

When the director Charlie Westenra approached me to write about Zahid Mubarek, the same questions I had asked before came back. Does prison work? What are we doing as a society when we are sending children and young people to prisons without giving them the means to change, to educate themselves, to rehabilitate? In interviews with Zahid's uncle Imtiaz, he brought up this very question – saying that, surprisingly, during the whole Zahid Mubarek Inquiry, there was hardly any mention of the word 'rehabilitate'. In my interview with Colin Moses, Chair of the Prison Officers' Association, he pointed out that UK inmates don't have the right to vote, which meant that as far as Governments were concerned, it was a proportion of society that didn't need to be represented. Who cares about prisoners as long as they are 'safe behind bars', away from the community, unable to harm law-abiding citizens? Money was supposedly better spent on public services such as hospitals and schools. But Moses added that we forget that prisons are also a public service.

As I worked through the vast piles of evidence from witnesses for the Zahid Mubarek Inquiry and looked at the way prison had failed to protect Zahid or keep him 'safe behind bars', the systematic failures of the Prison Service at every level were astounding. The incredible story of Robert Stewart's long-standing mental illness which was never addressed or recognised, his racist views and his long history of self-harm tell another story of a young man who has also been failed by society. It is easy to say that this is liberal posturing but one has to try and work out how we deal with the Stewarts of this world. He said of himself to the Commission for Racial Equality:

'Somebody should have thought I was a time bomb waiting to explode'.

In his various Chief Inspectorate reports on Feltham, Sir David Ramsbotham wrote:

'Feltham contains what my very experienced Chief Medical Inspector described as the most seriously mentally disturbed group of young men he has come across in his career, the majority of whom should be in medical rather than custodial accommodation. This report is without doubt the most disturbing that I have had to make during my three years as HM Inspectorate of prisons. I have to disclose to the public...that conditions and treatment, of the 922 children and young prisoners...are in many instances totally unacceptable...'

Beyond the obvious mental illness, however, were the chillingly racist letters written by Stewart from his various prison cells. The fact that these went unnoticed and unmonitored by the Prison Service has prompted many to question whether prisons are safe for black inmates.

Zahid Mubarek came from a strong, loving and close-knit family, and whilst they were shocked at the harshness of Zahid's sentence they hoped that a short spell in prison would help him see the error of his ways. Indeed, his letters to his family show a young man who was keen to move away from petty crime. The way in which Zahid died was horrific beyond belief but the family kept asking: 'How did this happen?' They had to fight for four and a half years to persuade the Government to conduct a Public Inquiry into Zahid's death and the-then Home Secretary, David Blunkett, refused to meet or speak to them. The Law Lords forced Blunkett's hand and the family won their quest – although, sadly, the question of sentencing was left outside the remit of the Inquiry. Whilst the family's bravery and determination is astonishing, what I did see through meeting them was a broken-hearted family still grappling with their grief. As a parent myself, I can't imagine how you move on from the terrible death of a child, but the Mubarek family's doggedness to hold the Prison Service accountable and open to scrutiny is matched only by Stephen Lawrence's family's determination to expose institutional racism in the Metropolitan Police Service. Regardless of the recommendations of the Zahid Mubarek Inquiry, it seems obvious to me that institutional racism exists in the Prison Service and as such, by exposing it, the Mubarek family have done us all a favour. Who can say with complete certainty that it won't be their son or daughter forced to share a cell with a Robert Stewart in the future?

Tanika Gupta
September 2005

I'd like to thank the following people for their help and support in writing this play: Colin Moses; Suresh Grover; Imtiaz Amin; Amin Mubarek and Sajida Mubarek; Imran Khan.

Timeline of events

23 October 1980	Zahid Mubarek born at Whipps Cross Hospital, London.
17 January 2000	Zahid is sent to Feltham Young Offenders' Institute after being found guilty of stealing razors and interfering with a motor vehicle.
8 February 2000	Robert Stewart, a prolific offender from the Manchester area, is moved into the same cell as Zahid. Stewart's odd behaviour is noted by other inmates.
21 March 2000	Hours before Zahid's release, Stewart batters him with a table leg as he sleeps. Stewart then presses the cell alarm button.
28 March 2000	Seven days later, Zahid dies in hospital from his injuries. Stewart is charged with his murder.
November 2000	Stewart is found guilty of murder and sentenced to life. He is found to be a psychopath and the trial uncovers evidence of his racist tendencies. Three weeks after his jailing, the Commission for Racial Equality announces it will hold its own investigation into the events.
4 September 2001	The family go to the High Court to force the Home Secretary, David Blunkett, to hold an independent public inquiry. Mr Justice Hooper agrees with the family, saying David Blunkett has failed in his duty to take into account his obligations under the Human Rights Act.
March 2002	The Court of Appeal throws out the earlier decision, siding with the Home Secretary. The judges say there is no need under Human Rights law to hold an inquiry because it has been proven the Prison Service has been at fault, an internal inquiry has investigated and Robert Stewart has been jailed for the murder.

October 2002	The prisons watchdog sends a team inside Feltham. It concludes that the jail had fundamentally changed and was 'off the critical list'.
July 2003	The CRE publishes its report into Zahid's death, amid criticism over its conclusions and the time taken to reach them. CRE chairman Trevor Phillips says he is convinced Zahid would not have died had he been white. The report says there was a 'shocking catalogue of failure' within the Prison Service. The family reject the report, saying it is flawed and leaves them none the wiser as to why Zahid was sharing a cell with Stewart.
October 2003	The family turn to the House of Lords. Lord Bingham, sitting with Lords Slynn, Steyn, Hope and Hutton, overturns the Court of Appeal and sides with the family. They order the Home Secretary to hold an Inquiry.
28 April 2004	David Blunkett announces 'The Zahid Mubarek Inquiry'.
30 August 2004	The Inquiry begins. Phase One investigates the events leading up to Zahid Mubarek's death.
April 2005	Closing submissions, Phase One.
19 September 2005	Phase Two of the Inquiry begins. It holds the first of six seminars. The events will help chairman, Mr Justice Keith, to assess what recommendations he should make to the Home Secretary to minimise the chances of a tragedy such as Zahid's murder happening again.
5 October 2005	Phase Two of the Inquiry ends.

Mr Justice Keith hopes to deliver his report to the Home Secretary in April 2006.

(Sources: BBC, Monitoring Group, The Zahid Mubarek Inquiry)

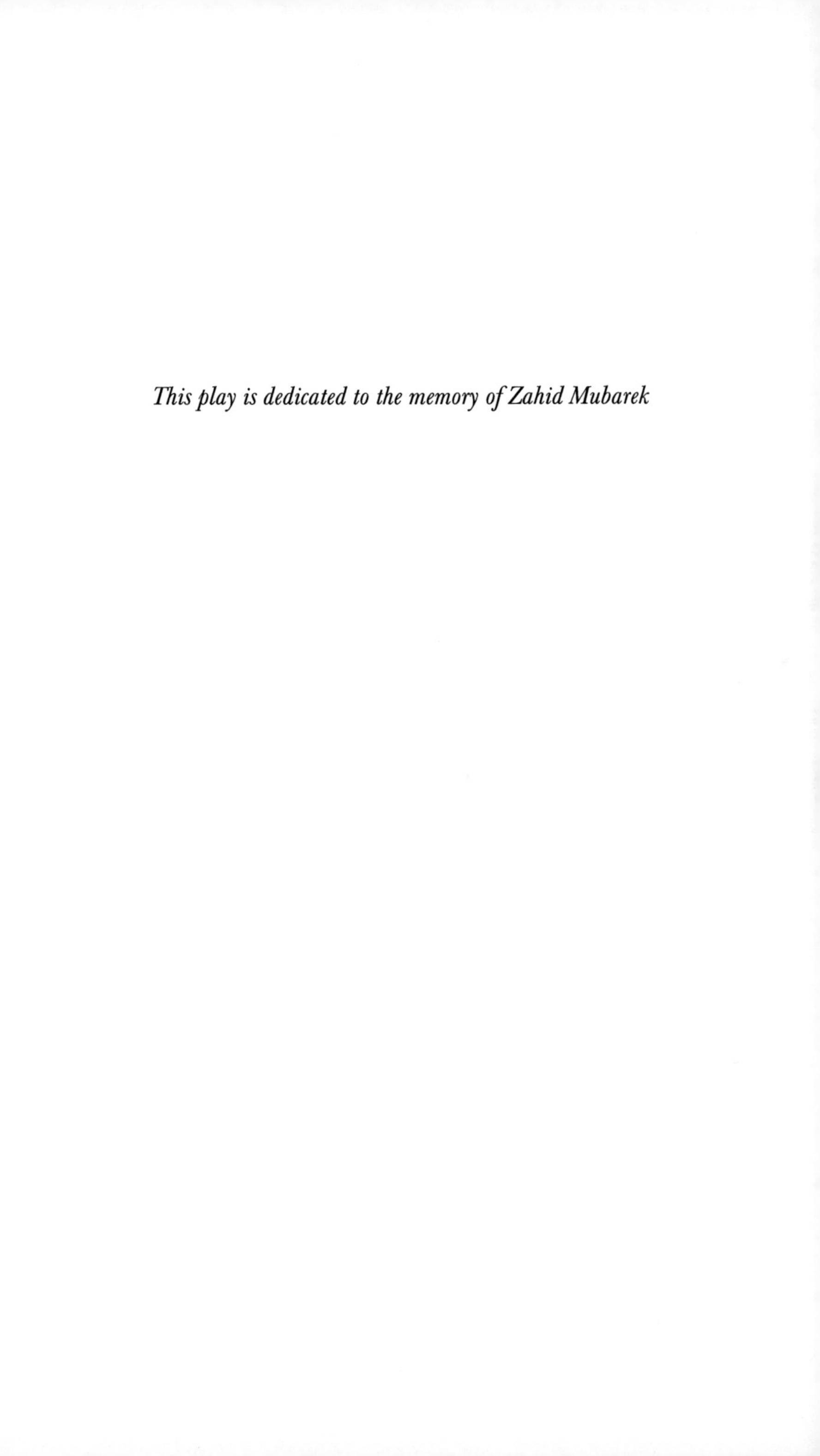

This play is dedicated to the memory of Zahid Mubarek

Gladiator Games had its World Premiere performed at the Crucible Studio from 20–29 October 2005; then performed at Theatre Royal Stratford East from 2–12 November 2005.

Restaged at Theatre Royal Stratford East from 2–25 February 2006.

Cast in order of speaking:

IMTIAZ AMIN, ZAHID MUBAREK	Ray Panthaki
ROBERT STEWART, DUNCAN KEYS	Kevin Trainor
MAURICE TRAVIS, JAMIE BARNES	Paul Keating
MUBAREK AMIN, SURESH GROVER	Shiv Grewal
SAJIDA MUBAREK, SATWANT RANDHAWA	Claire Lichie

All other parts played by members of the company

Writer	Tanika Gupta
Director	Charlotte Westenra
Designer	Paul Wills
Lighting Designer	Hartley T A Kemp
Composer	Niraj Chag
Sound Designer	Nick Greenhill
Casting	Leila Bertrand
Assistant Director	Zahra Ahmadi
Dialect Coach	Jeannette Nelson
Fight Director	Bret Yount
Production photographer	Johann Persson

For Sheffield Theatres:

Stage Manager	Donna Reeves
Deputy Stage Manager	Helena Lane-Smith
Assistant Stage Manager	Julie Davis

For Theatre Royal Stratford East:

Stage Manager	Julia Crammer
Deputy Stage Manager	Altan Reyman
Assistant Stage Manager	Rebecca Clatworthy

Characters

ZAHID MUBAREK

AMIN, his father

SAJIDA, his mother

IMTIAZ, his uncle

MARTIN NAREY, Director General, HM Prison Service

COLIN MOSES, Chair, Prison Officers' Association

DUNCAN KEYS, Assistant Secretary, POA

NIGEL HERRING, Branch Chairman, POA

STEVEN MARTINDALE, Feltham prison officer

DEBBIE HOGG, Feltham prison officer

IAN MORSE, Feltham prison officer

STEPHEN SKINNER, Feltham prison officer

MALCOLM NICHOLSON, Feltham prison officer

SATWANT RANDHAWA, Feltham prison officer

ROBERT STEWART, prisoner

MAURICE TRAVIS, prisoner

JAMIE BARNES, prisoner

JUSTICE KEITH, Judge at Inquiry

DEXTER DIAS, barrister at Inquiry

NIGEL GIFFIN, barrister at Inquiry

PADDY O'CONNOR, barrister at Inquiry

SURESH GROVER, Monitoring Group, Institute of Race Relations

PROFESSOR GUNN, Institute of Psychiatry, KCL

LUCY BOGUE, Independent Monitoring Board, Feltham

JUDY CLEMENTS, Race Equality Adviser, HM Prison Service

DOCTOR, PRISON OFFICERS, INMATES, POLICE OFFICERS, SPOKESPEOPLE

List of sources

1 Verbatim evidence from the Zahid Mubarek Inquiry – witness statements, oral and written **[V1]**
The Inquiry includes evidence from:
   a MPS – Metropolitan Police Service **[V1a]**
   b Butt Inquiry/Feltham Murder Report **[V1b]**
   c Closing statements **[V1c]**

2 Interview – three taped interviews taken with:
   a Imtiaz Amin and Suresh Grover at the Monitoring Group, Institute of Race Relations **[V2a]**
   b Colin Moses, Chair of the Prison Officers' Association **[V2b]**
   c Sajida Mubarek and Mubarek Amin (Zahid's parents) at their home in Walthamstow **[V2c]**

3 Channel 4 documentary: 'Prison Works: the death of Zahid Mubarek' **[V3]**

4 *Panorama* documentary, BBC: 'Boys Behind Bars' **[V4]**

5 CRE (Commission for Racial Equality) Inquiry: witness statements **[V5]**

6 Correspondence:
   a Zahid Mubarek's letters from Feltham **[V6a]**
   b Robert Stewart's letters from prison **[V6b]**
   c Letters to the Mubarek family **[V6c]**

7 'Colour Bar' leaflet **[V7]**

8 Justice Hooper's judgement **[V8]**

9 Justice Bingham's statement **[V9]**

Verbatim text reproduced from these sources is marked with an asterisk in square brackets [*]; the references are given at the end of the reproduced text in the form shown above (**[V1a]**, **[V3]**, etc).

Anything unmarked is a dramatisation based on events / hearsay.

Act One

SCENE 1

An Asian man in his mid-thirties – IMTIAZ – steps forward and addresses the audience.

IMTIAZ: My name's Imtiaz Amin, Zahid was my eldest brother's son.

[*] I'm ten years older than Zahid. There were lots of things we had in common – like cricket, certain music, dare I say it 'gangsta rap'. Zahid used to play regularly at Vestry Park round the corner from where we live. A group of him and some lads used to congregate there regularly. Start playing with a tennis ball and cricket bat. He was very close to his cousins and had a group of friends. He was very athletic. He did a year on this Prince's Trust army training thing. It was a confidence-building thing. It was just to gear people up for work, people who may suffer from, erm – low esteem, motivational problems – whatever. And it was very military orientated. Zahid wanted to go into the army. He also used to help his dad working on his car – doing up the Cosworth – loved that car he did.

He had a sense of humour, always joking with us – made us smile.

But he got into trouble. Ended up serving a short custodial sentence of ninety days at Feltham for stealing six pounds' worth of razor blades and interfering with a car. Nobody understood why he got sent down for what he did. It was, it was a shock. **[V2a]**

Two BARRISTERS step forward.

DIAS: [*] Dias. Closing Submissions on behalf of the Mubarek family.

It is absolutely true that no one could have forecast with mathematical certainty that on 20th March 2000 Robert Stewart would club to death Zahid in cell 38 at Feltham, Swallow Wing. But how far does this truly absolve the prison service, especially when one considers the obvious risks that Stewart presented? **[V1c]**

GIFFIN: [*] Giffin – Counsel for the Zahid Mubarek Inquiry. Closing statements.
I pose the question: a disaster waiting to happen or a prisoner who did not stand out? There seems to have been a radical disconnection between the perception of Stewart and the risks which he posed. The submissions which the Prison Service now makes to you come very close indeed to saying that in terms of handling, nothing really went wrong in this case and Zahid's murder was a dreadful but essentially random occurrence. **[V1c]**

DIAS: [*] In simple terms, what do we think might happen when we lock up a dangerous, severely mentally disordered, psychopathic racist in a cell for 20-plus hours with a young Asian who is in prison for the first time? The opportunities to avert this tragedy lie scattered across the prison records and in the collective knowledge of Stewart that the Prison Service had gained over his criminal career. **[V1c]**

GIFFIN: [*] There is, I think, for the Mubarek family at the end of these hearings no simple answer to the question: 'How did this happen?' There are questions as to whether some witnesses have told the truth to this Inquiry.

You will also have to decide how far the question of racial discrimination and the effectiveness or ineffectiveness of the Prison Service and of Feltham in dealing with racism at this time enters into the equation. I suggest, for my part, that it is impossible not to conclude that there were very serious problems on a greater scale, certainly at Feltham, than anyone had succeeded in identifying before Zahid was killed.

What price is society prepared to pay in terms of how many people it sends to prison and what resources it provides to the Prison Service in order to avoid future occurrences of this kind? **[V1c]**

DIAS: [*] Sir, ultimately this Inquiry documents the story of two young men from different backgrounds, one white and one Asian. They were both born in 1980 and because of the deep-seated failures in our prison system, they were locked together behind the door of cell 38 at Feltham. On a March night in 2000, Robert Stewart, who was known to the Prison Service to be violent, dangerous and a racist, clubbed Zahid to death with a table leg while Zahid slept. The family want to say that the murder of Zahid Mubarek was a terrible injustice. His family believes that it is one which in differing ways affects us all. As Dr Martin Luther King once wrote from a cell in another prison: 'Injustice anywhere is a threat for justice everywhere. We are caught in an inescapable network of mutuality tied in a single garment of destiny. What affects one directly affects all indirectly.' This was a murder that could and should have been prevented. As such, it is part of the story of our troubled times. **[V1c]**

SCENE 2

Sounds of a busy hospital as lights go up. We see a body on a stretcher being brought in (we cannot see the face but just see a shape beneath the sheets). A doctor and a nurse busy themselves working on the patient: a drip is set up, etc.

An Asian man (AMIN) and woman (SAJIDA) stand by and watch helplessly. SAJIDA is weeping continuously but not making any noise. A younger Asian man (IMTIAZ) enters. He looks equally distraught. AMIN and SAJIDA approach him. The two men embrace briefly.

IMTIAZ: *(East London accent.)* How is he?

AMIN: *(East London accent.)* He's just come out of the operating theatre. He's still unconscious.

IMTIAZ: How long have you been here?

AMIN: We waited over an hour before they brought him here.

IMTIAZ: Why'd it take them so long to get here?

AMIN: I dunno. Something about them going to another hospital…Ashford…that's what they said…when they first phoned. Then, they came round…the Police…gave us an escort and said they were bringing him here. We were waitin' and waitin'.

He looks…he looks…they said there'd been a fight in the cell.

IMTIAZ: Did he speak?

SAJIDA: *(Pakistani accent.)* His face.

IMTIAZ: Amin, did he speak?

AMIN: How can he speak? He's unconscious.

IMTIAZ looks upset.

SAJIDA: *(In Punjabi.)* What happened, Imtiaz?

IMTIAZ: I phoned the prison. Phoned loads. Kept me waiting…kept passing me on to someone else. No one knew anything. Eventually spoke to the Governor number two. Said he didn't know what happened, first he said there'd been a fight, then he said something about that Zahid'd been attacked by his cellmate – probably through jealousy.

AMIN: Jealousy?

IMTIAZ: 'Cos Zahid was being released today.

SAJIDA: How could this happen? I don't understand.

IMTIAZ: He's in a bad way?

AMIN nods.

He's gonna make it though – right?

AMIN looks at SAJIDA anxiously.

AMIN: His head looks…swollen…like a huge balloon. Three times the normal size. Face is full of blood – bruises all over it…

SAJIDA: He's just a boy.

Beat.

IMTIAZ: Anyone from the Police here? The prison?

AMIN: A policeman was here…didn't tell me nuthin' though.

SAJIDA: Just a few more hours…he would've been home.

AMIN: He was so happy, last time I saw him, at the last visit, you know? He was so excited that he was getting out.

SAJIDA: We have to pray for him.

SAJIDA starts to cry more. AMIN and IMTIAZ watch her helplessly. AMIN takes IMTIAZ aside, away from SAJIDA.

AMIN: Go and see him Imtiaz. See for yourself.

IMTIAZ: What do the doctors say?

AMIN shakes his head.

AMIN: Is my boy gonna… For what? Why?

AMIN breaks down. IMTIAZ looks distraught. He helps his brother back into the chair. He watches SAJIDA and AMIN for a moment as he sits next to them. The hospital is still busy with people rushing around.

They're supposed to be safe in prison. They're supposed to look after 'em. He's just a kid. Why Zahid? Why'd this happen to him? He's a good lad…never got into fights before…

A DOCTOR comes forward.

DOCTOR: Mr and Mrs Mubarek, would you like to come through now?

As SAJIDA and AMIN follow the DOCTOR to ZAHID's bedside, IMTIAZ steps forward and addresses the audience.

IMTIAZ: By the time I got to the hospital that morning of the 21st they'd already operated on Zahid. And – he was just unconscious, lying down – they had him there naked. One quandary was that here was this perfectly formed man here. But you just looked at his head and it was just horrendous. You know. He was in intensive care for seven days. His skull had been cracked in several places. He had these holes and these pipes coming out – kind of fluid stuff coming out. You couldn't imagine that someone in that condition could survive.

IMTIAZ looks back at AMIN and SAJIDA.

[*] Anyway, we were at the hospital, yeah, for the next seven days, basically hoping for some sort of a recovery. It was very disheartening. It was every emotion you can think of, you just went through anger, you wanted to cry, you wanted to hug him.

After three days people from the prison came to the hospital. They included the Muslim adviser and Martin Narey who was the Director General of the Prison Service. **[V2a]**

MARTIN NAREY enters. He approaches AMIN and SAJIDA.

NAREY: *(Posh Northern.)* Mr Mubarek?

AMIN looks up.

Martin Narey.

NAREY puts his hand out to AMIN. AMIN hesitates before taking it.

How is Zahid doing? Have the doctors spoken to you?

AMIN: Yes. The prognosis isn't good.

NAREY looks upset. AMIN stares blankly at NAREY.

What 'appened in that cell?

NAREY: I don't honestly know.

AMIN: Was there a fight?

NAREY: We're not sure.

AMIN: He was so excited about coming home. He was being released later this morning.

NAREY: Yes…

AMIN: Who was this cellmate?

NAREY: I'm afraid I don't have any more information…

It's a Police investigation now and they're doing everything they can to get a clear picture of events.

AMIN turns away.

[*] You had a right to expect us to look after Zahid safely and we have failed. I am very, very sorry. **[V6c]**

AMIN: 'Sorry' doesn't come into it, does it?

AMIN exits, leaving NAREY looking after him anxiously. SAJIDA never even looks up.

IMTIAZ: [*] We didn't really appreciate Martin Narey's visit. We just wanted to know if our nephew or son was going to make it through.

I was just running around trying to find some kind of representation. I was just really angry that something like this happened, you know what I mean? I was particularly pissed off that something like this could happen in a prison and I wanted it to be highlighted. It could be anyone's kid. And this is what prisons are like. It was a real shock for us. A solicitor friend of mine gave me the web-link for the Institute of Race Relations. I was looking at the web for that and there was a link to the Monitoring Group from that and I just got in touch with them and Suresh Grover came to the hospital. **[V2a]**

SURESH enters.

SURESH: [*] *(Indian accent.)* I met Imi before Zahid died. There was a lot of anxiety in the family. Firstly would Zahid survive? Secondly how did he end up in this situation? Thirdly – who would be held responsible? **[V2a]**

IMTIAZ: [*] We kept asking these questions which no one would – like – no one could answer. There was this thing about this…prison adviser, which was that he was actually leaking some information to us regarding this individual who had done this crime. It was him who first told us that this guy – Stewart – Zahid's cellmate had been – has got a history – of violence – and that he's done this to other people before. Later on you know they wanted to go for an out-of-court settlement – which we outright refused. **[V2a]**

SURESH: [*] Let's put it this way, it wasn't the prison service that offered. The adviser was told to approach the family to tell them to take some money and forget about it. That's what the adviser said to Imtiaz.

IMTIAZ: Yeah.

SURESH: It's as blunt as that. I think you are being polite. The adviser said to the family, why are you doing this? You could get a lot of money – take the money. We never kept in contact with him after that. Why was he doing that? It isn't his job. He shouldn't be put in that position. After the attack there was nobody there from the prison service whatsoever. **[V2a]**

IMTIAZ: [*] The Imam from the prison – he visited. He wasn't there officially. He was actually giving us some information as well. He was telling us about – this individual – Stewart, Zahid's cellmate – and about the regime and the failings about what was going on there and stuff. It was then that we started to get this picture that it was bigger than Robert Stewart. Two main things for us were not only Robert Stewart – his record – but the negligence caused by the prison officers. **[V2a]**

SAJIDA enters.

SAJIDA: [*] We'd been at the hospital all day, we came home at about 11.30 in the evening – had a phone call at about one and when we got there, he'd already died. That was exactly a week after he'd got to the hospital. **[V3]**

The DOCTOR pulls a sheet over ZAHID's body.

SURESH: [*] The family wanted the body of Zahid quite quickly after his death – for religious purposes – but in order to convict the person they needed the brain so we were negotiating. In the end we agreed that the body could be released without the brain. The brain had to be analysed for another six weeks. **[V2a]**

We hear the unmistakable sound of a life support machine's beep. ZAHID's body is wheeled out.

MARTIN NAREY re-enters and approaches IMTIAZ. IMTIAZ is lost in thought for a moment while NAREY stands awkwardly. Eventually IMTIAZ looks up at NAREY.

NAREY: Mr Amin…

IMTIAZ: Yes?

NAREY: I was thinking of planting a tree…in honour of Zahid's memory…in the grounds of Feltham.

IMTIAZ looks at NAREY, incredulous.

IMTIAZ: I'd rather you flattened the place.

NAREY looks uncertain and exits.

A few days after Zahid's death DCI McLeenan…

SURESH: The guy who interviewed Stewart…

IMTIAZ: Yes…he showed us these letters that Stewart had written in prison. There was this one in particular that he'd written a month before Zahid was attacked.

IMTIAZ reads STEWART's letter.

IMTIAZ: [*] '23RD FEB 2000

CANNOT SEE IT STICKIN' IN ERE.

IF I DON'T GET BAIL ON THE 5TH, I'LL TAKE XTREME MEASURE TO GET SHIPPED OUT, KILL ME FUCKIN' PADMATE IF I HAVE TO; BLEACH ME SHEETS AND PILLOWCASE WHITE AND MAKE A KLU KLUX KLAN OUTFIT AND WALK OUT ME PAD WIV A FLAMING CRUCIFIX AND CHANGE THE CROSS ON MY HEAD TO A PLUS AND THEN A SWASTIKA WIV A BIRO.

…SIGNED STEPHAN LAWRENCE.' **[V6b]**

It was disgusting. I mean, I've experienced petty racism all through my life but this…this was on another level. I felt angry at Stewart – I mean you're getting an insight into someone's mind and you don't wanna be there.

SURESH: That was the moment for me. When I first met Imi, we didn't talk about racism. It didn't even occur to us that this was a racist attack.

IMTIAZ: No, not at all. Not at all. But Stewart's letters changed all that. I couldn't understand how someone could kill Zahid for the colour of his…bloody skin.

IMTIAZ exits.

SURESH steps forward.

SURESH: [*] Not many people would go through a death in a prison, come across the person who murdered their son, totally psychotic… I mean we saw Stewart at the murder trial. He was giving 'V' signs to the father and Imtiaz and everybody, shouting at the jury members, he was absolutely barmy. His defence was that he's so racist he didn't know what he was doing. You don't come across those kind of things. It's one of the few times when I've sat in a court and thought, 'My God what am I doing in this country?' You fight on the Lawrence case, you think there's a sea change in this kind of attitude and then you see something like that, someone like Stewart. And you think your whole energy and time has been wasted. And he has no remorse about the thing. He has no respect for the family. Okay, you killed the person because of whatever but you don't have to be extravagant in killing someone and radiating your racism. This is what he did.

STEWART enters.

In November 2000 – Robert Stewart was found guilty of murder and was sentenced to life. On the same day, we launched the campaign to get a Public Inquiry into the death of Zahid Mubarek. **[V2a]**

SCENE 3

TRAVIS: [*] *(Manchester accent.)* Maurice Travis. I've known Robert for about eight years, we met in a care home when I was about twelve; he's slightly younger than me…we're good mates and still contact each other by letter now. We started committing crime together, all sorts and got locked up together. I would say he follows me, it's like he worships everything I do, he does. **[V5]**

We see STEWART and TRAVIS sat in a cell together. They are laughing and talking together in whispers.

Go on, I dare you, fuckin' wimp.

STEWART: Fuck off Trav.

TRAVIS: Go on, it'll be a laugh. You got the matches. Do it.

STEWART: What's in it for me?

TRAVIS: I'll give you a few burns.

STEWART: How many?

TRAVIS: Four.

STEWART giggles.

PROFESSOR GUNN steps forward.

GUNN: [*] My name is Professor Gunn. I am the Emeritus Professor of Forensic Psychiatry at the Institute of Psychiatry, Kings College London. My work has included research into the mental health and psychiatric needs of prisoners. I'll follow the set of questions set out in writing to me.

Robert Stewart was born on 4th August 1980 and is a recidivist with (in 1999) 18 convictions and 65 offences to his name, including two offences against the person, six offences against property and 45 theft offences. Two of the property offences were for arson. He had by the year 2000 served six prison sentences. **[V1]**

We see STEWART striking a match and setting fire to something.

TRAVIS: Fuckin' ace.

GUNN: [*] Dr Nayani who was instructed by Robert Stewart's defence solicitor concludes: 'the defendant suffers with severe personality disorder. Mr Stewart is a psychopath.'

Robert Stewart told Dr Shapero that he was expelled from a secondary school at the beginning of the second year after setting the sports hall on fire 'for fun'. He did not receive home tuition. He was found a placement at the beginning of the third year of secondary school but 'never went' and only attended 60 days out of 190. At the end of his third senior academic year, Mr Stewart was suspended from school and taken into local authority care. By this time he was 'getting into trouble all the time'. **[V1]**

PRISON OFFICER: *(Offstage.)* Open cell 25.

The two boys watch the fire as it gains strength – mesmerised (lots of smoke). The smoke fills the stage and the two boys leap around the cell yelping and shouting and laughing. We hear an alarm go off and shouting off stage. The fire is quickly put out by a PRISON OFFICER.

PRISON OFFICER: What the hell d'you think you're playing at?

STEWART is giggling.

It ain't funny! You could have hurt yourselves.

STEWART: Just did it for a laugh, guv.

PRISON OFFICER: Whose idea was this? Yours, Travis, I'll warrant.

TRAVIS: Yeah – thought we might burn this place down to the ground.

PRISON OFFICER: Clear this mess up now. I'm giving you a direct order. Clear it up. Out, Travis. See what the Governor has to say about this. You're both on report and segregation.

TRAVIS is led away.

GUNN: [*] Here are some salient events from Mr Stewart's record which suggest mental disturbance.

20th August 1997, flooding cell deliberately; recurrent self-injury; hearing voices come from anywhere.

25th September 1997, RS 'refuses to speak or engage in any form of conversation. I feel this inmate will do harm if removed from strict conditions.' **[V1]**

STEWART sits on his bed and stares weirdly at the audience.

[*] October 1997, it was noted that he exhibited 'bizarre behaviour on wing. Suggest hospitalisation for assessment.' He was admitted to the health centre. He said he felt odd compulsive actions. The nurse noted 'spoke with Stewart about compulsive actions. Whilst denying hearing voices,

feels he must carry out whatever action he feels to do. This happens during quiet periods.'

26th October 1997, relocated in a strip cell having smeared excrement on his wall, covered himself in margarine and flooded his cell. **[V1]**

STEWART ties lots of bits of clothes to himself.

STEWART stands in his cell and screams gobbledygook at the top of his voice. The screaming goes on for a while. Then he sits down again.

[*] November 1997, he was found to be incommunicative: 'all he can say for himself is "I don't know"'.

21st November 1997, it was noted 'RS behaving strangely, eating soap and swallowing screw from doorstop'. He was again moved to the health centre and it was at this time he set fire to his tracksuit bottoms.

The following day Dr Das considered that his behaviour was all an act to be placed in the health care centre along with his friend Travis; however, he was discovered with a ligature around his neck which was tied to the end of his bed and he was noted to be banging his head against the wall and biting his arm.

December 1997, his personal officer said: 'A very strange young man…although he has caused no problems on the unit I feel he may suffer from some sort of psychological illness.'

Later that month he was noted to be 'talking gibberish'.

Two weeks later he was seen by a medical officer who said his state of health was good and his state of mind was 'normal'. **[V1]**

TRAVIS enters.

TRAVIS: At HMP Hindley when we shared a cell together we set the cell on fire, both of us did it, we liked the idea of putting people's lives at risk, even our own, we thought it was funny. I got moved, but eventually we ended up together again. **[V5]**

GUNN: In June 1998 Mr Travis murdered Prisoner A in circumstances which Robert Stewart was to some degree involved.

TRAVIS goes back to the cell with STEWART. They sit and talk together.

STEWART: It's Averill's birthday coming up.

TRAVIS: When?

STEWART: Next week.

TRAVIS: Fucking pig. Let's slice 'im up.

STEWART: Cut his throat.

TRAVIS: I'll stab 'im, you cut his throat.

STEWART: Need a tool.

TRAVIS: Got cookery class next week.

STEWART: Get some blades from the cupboard there.

TRAVIS: Nice one. I fucking hate 'im. He deserves it.

STEWART: Thinks he owns the place.

TRAVIS: Thinks he's a gangsta.

STEWART: Fucking prick, that's what he is.

TRAVIS: Let's give 'im a special birthday present.

STEWART and TRAVIS shake on it.

TRAVIS steps forward again. A POLICE OFFICER leads him to a chair and sticks a tape on to record his statement.

[*] We cooked curry, me and Robert and that…mmmm… me and Robert Stewart…yeah…have cooked a curry… yeah and an apple, no, a jam tart, pie or something like that. I don't know what it was…yeah… We've ate our

curry and that…yeah…the teacher's said, 'Right wash your pots and that'…mmm…so we just put all our pots in the, in the sink…mmm…and then we've ate our jam tart thing… mmm…and then he's started going on saying: 'I want some of this, I want some of that'…yeah…try bullying me for a pie…'cos he's ate his and we took our time with ours, trying to bully us for that…yeah…and then teacher's got some chocolate cakes out, what the teacher's made – yeah – and like 'cos it was Averill's birthday, Averill's saying, 'I'm having your twos. You better say that you don't want none' – yeah – and all this. And then, but I said, 'No you're not having mine', and they're saying, 'Right, you're gonna get battered when you go to the gym. You're going to get leathered', mmm…and it's going on and on. Robert's washing the pots. There's a big carving knife on the side. Averill's coming towards me and then he's just said, 'You're getting knocked out', and stood there staring at me. And then Robert's just passed me a knife and I've just flipped. I didn't mean to kill him or anything like that. Just you know, it was a out of the blue thing, I didn't think what I was doing. Just lost it. I've just freaked out. I've just shut me eyes when I was doing it. **[V1a]**

GUNN: [*] The nature of the involvement is not very clear, but there is some evidence that Robert Stewart knew in advance that Maurice Travis intended to stab A and possibly that Robert Stewart had planned the incident jointly with Travis and/or passed him the knife. There is no record that I am aware of, of a psychological investigation being made on Robert Stewart to determine his mental health, his reasons for the involvement, or an assessment of his future dangerousness. **[V1]**

TRAVIS: [*] After I stabbed Averill I expected Robert to cut his throat as well, but he didn't. That made me angry. We both got arrested. I admitted it. Robert just denied it. He made out he wanted no part in it, but he did and I took the rap for it all. I knew it wouldn't be too long before he killed someone. Eventually he ended up in Feltham and informed me he was in a pad with a Paki. I just told him to do him and he did it… I know Robert has killed his pad mate – somebody whose name begins with 'Z' and I saw it in the papers. There was no discussion as to how he should kill him – but I know he 'battered' him. **[V5]**

The POLICE OFFICER switches off the tape and leads TRAVIS away. As TRAVIS goes, STEWART stands in his cell. He looks devastated that TRAVIS has gone.

GUNN: [*] October 1998, after he had lost contact with Travis who was by then on a murder charge, it was noted that RS 'cannot be trusted for even a minute'.

January 1999, he was reported to have swallowed part of a small battery which he said he 'did' for a laugh.

March 1999, an officer noted: 'I do feel as has been said earlier, that this lad is a disaster waiting to happen, he cannot be trusted and I feel as if we are just waiting for our next problem with him.'

16th November 1999, HMYOI Altcourse. C Kinealy writes: 'I spent quite some time today talking to this boy…in my opinion he has a longstanding deep-seated personality disorder. He shows a glaring lack of remorse, feeling, insight, foresight or any other emotion. In my opinion he has an untreatable mental condition and I recommend no further action.'

The CRE report concluded that Robert Stewart had been seen 29 times by medical or health care staff whilst in prison since 1995 but there was no record that he had ever been seen by a psychiatrist. It is easy with the wisdom of hindsight to say that Mr Stewart needed psychiatric attention at several points in his prison career. I think however I must be stronger in my conclusion and say that there were many pointers to considerable psychiatric disturbance in Robert Stewart.

Racism which may play a role in this case is not generally considered to be a psychiatric matter. It's just possible however that in Mr Stewart's case the racism stemmed from underlying paranoid ideas which may be part of a personality disorder of a mental illness.

If Mr Stewart had been recognised as seriously mentally disordered and had been provided with an appropriate and detailed assessment either within the prison itself or preferably in an NHS hospital, it is unlikely that he would have been sharing a cell with Mr Mubarek. **[V1]**

PROFESSOR GUNN snaps his book closed and exits.

IMTIAZ enters carrying files.

IMTIAZ: We started our campaign to get a Public Inquiry; we organised pickets outside the Home Office and we sent out thousands of leaflets publicising our campaign. We got a lot of support from all sorts of people. In April 2001, we wrote to the Home Secretary.

[*] 'Dear Home Secretary,
I'm writing to express my concern at the tragic and racist murder of Zahid Mubarek in Feltham prison in March 2000. All the evidence and internal reports regarding the incident show that murder could have been avoided.' **[V7]**

This was the reply I got:

[*] 'Dear Sirs,
In view of all that has been done to investigate the circumstances of Zahid Mubarek's death and to learn the lessons from it, I do not believe that a separate inquiry would add anything of substance or that it would be in the public interest to hold one.
Yours faithfully,
David Blunkett' **[V6c]**

STEWART is left in his cell. He is scrawling a letter.

A PRISON OFFICER enters and takes STEWART out.

PRISON OFFICER: You're going for a little trip. Go on, get your stuff.

STEWART picks up a bag.

Down to 'the Smoke' for Court. About that nasty little letter you wrote. Go on, take your stuff.

STEWART: Where they taking me?

PRISON OFFICER: Feltham.

SCENE 4

COLIN MOSES steps forward.

COLIN MOSES: [*] *(Geordie accent.)* Colin Moses, Chair of the Prison Officers' Association. I represent 35,000 members of staff.

I've said this on more than one occasion and it's been disputed by some – but I believe that the effect of the tragic death of this young man – Zahid Mubarek – will be the equivalent of Stephen Lawrence's tragic death in the Metropolitan Police Service. (There are differences yes, we know who the culprit was.) I've been in the Prison Service for twenty years – feel very old saying that – I've worked in prisons where I've been the only black member of staff and I've also served in Feltham in 1986. There's a lot of people in the Prison Service who feel very, very insulted by the term 'institutional racism'. You show me another trade union with a black man heading it. I was put here by appointment. I was elected, but how many black and Asian prison officers are being recruited? We have to change the culture of the organisation.

Every person that dies – it has a massive, massive impact on staff. As a black man I felt touched by that death. Actually Zahid would be the same age now, as my son. You hope you put your children in a safe environment.

Every death in prison affects us. That's one of the reasons I made a personal apology from the Union to the family.

Feltham's a massive area. What you do is you go up to the fence and you listen and the noise is absolutely horrendous. Because you're locking children, 16/17-year-old young men into a cell and telling them to be quiet!

There are rapists, murderers, muggers, child abusers in there. These are very disturbed young men.

Feltham is not a hospital. This is not a boarding school.

When you put that light out – people don't go to sleep.

Imagine it, it's light outside, it's a warm balmy night. I'm scared of the dark, I also have nightmares, I'm also locked in this room by myself. I've told my cellmate all my stories, I want to tell you my stories, *(He points up as if to a cell above him.)* you're stronger than me, you torture me through the windows.

I want to make a noise, I'm bored with the television so I just shout and scream, play my music loud, sing along, I masturbate, I do all these crazy things, there's nearly one thousand young men. I may be up all night talking. I may be unable to sleep, someone's shouting at me to wake up.

If you look at the mirror of society – you'll see that we send more young black men to prison than we do to university. We also send more Asian men to prison than ever before – the fastest growing group in prison, religious group that is, are from the Islamic faith. Same with those of mixed heritage and or foreign nationals, and all of this goes unreported.

Conversely we have prisons which have virtually no black or Asian staff.

We work a prison with 127 public sector prisons (private prisons lock up people for profit) and to do that there must be public investment. When you have the largest or one of the largest YOIs establishment in Western Europe – Feltham – as badly resourced as it is, with lack of investment and lack of staff, what do you expect will happen? There is some excellent unreported work that goes on in some prisons. The vast majority of prison staff are professional, hard-working individuals. There's a lot more to being a prison officer than opening and closing doors.

Seventeen per cent of prisoners are black. In some prisons, it's up to 40/50/60 per cent. Feltham used to run at 55-60 per cent. Pentonville, Brixton, Wandsworth, Wormwood Scrubbs, Belmarsh, Holloway, all with massive ethnic minority populations. Some in excess of 50 per cent. As I said before, in this country, if you're black, you're more likely to go to prison than you are university.

Unfortunately, there are thousands more Stewarts in prison, thousands of mentally-ill young men. There are more than before because we lock more people up.

Don't talk to me about institutional racism of the Prison Service if you aren't going to address the institutional racism of Magistrates' Courts. What sort of sentencing policy have we got when people are being put away for stealing razor blades? In this country there are 75,000 people in prison. That goes up to 83,000 if you include people with tagging. Half a million people pass through the court system. This is a sausage factory industry. There are barristers out there making a lot of money out the system. It's a business. Every night in this country we lock up a small town. **[V2b]**

SCENE 5

IMTIAZ is surrounded by papers, leaflets and files which he is looking at. SAJIDA is there.

IMTIAZ: Can't believe what those prisons are like.

SAJIDA is quiet.

The way they're run!

AMIN enters.

IMTIAZ: We can't let it end like this. They haven't given us straight answers.

Beat.

There's a lot they're not telling us about. Why was Zahid put in a cell with that animal?

AMIN and SAJIDA are silent.

I know they say they're doing enough, this Butt Report and now the CRE Inquiry, but it's not enough. The CRE don't even want us to participate. It's all behind closed doors… If the Prison staff knew this…Stewart…was a racist, why they put him in a cell with Zahid?

Beat.

Suresh says we should carry on. Imran Khan has agreed to represent us. Amin, we gotta fight for justice.

AMIN: Home Secretary won't even meet us.

IMTIAZ: We can do this…

AMIN: How? David Blunkett won't reply to our letters, he won't see us…it's like he doesn't recognise what happened here.

IMTIAZ: Look, what they're doing isn't right. We can do this despite David Blunkett. We don't need his blessing.

IMTIAZ perseveres.

We met Paul Boateng. He agreed there should be a Public Inquiry. People are taking this seriously. We've got the Monitoring Group behind us, we've got a campaign going, these leaflets have gone out to thousands of people, we've had press conferences, MPs have come out in support of us…

SAJIDA: How will it help us? Will it bring Zahid back?

IMTIAZ: No…but…we could stop it from happening to someone else's son. We got nothing to be ashamed about. Zahid deserved another chance.

SAJIDA: On his own, in that cell…no one there to help him… He must have suffered so badly. Locked up with that mad man…tortured…he was hiding things from me because he didn't want to burden me. Always trying to protect me, wasn't he? Maybe if he hadn't been so secretive, so protective…if he'd told us what this…this…man in his cell was like, we could have done something?

IMTIAZ: If we do this, we have to do it as a family.

SAJIDA: We are ordinary people.

IMTIAZ: I don't know if it'll work but we gotta try. It's not enough that Stewart was put away for life. There were more people involved in Zahid's death than just him. The prison staff knew that he was a racist. It came out in the trial! He'd written over two hundred racist letters while he was in prison! Swastika signs all over them.

AMIN makes a decision.

AMIN: We've lost a life. The least they can do is give us an inquiry after what's happened to us. What would happen if it was one of them? How would they feel? And what would they want out of it?

Beat.

Imtiaz. You be our spokesman.

Beat.

You take it on, Imtiaz. It's too much for me and Zahid's mum. We'll be right behind you every step of the way –

but you gotta do it. Liaise between us and the lawyers and stuff.

IMTIAZ: Right.

AMIN: After all, you've always been the one with the gob on you.

IMTIAZ turns to the audience.

IMTIAZ: In September 2001 we went to the High Court to try and force Blunkett to hold an Independent Public Inquiry… Justice Hooper ruled in our favour and said:

[*] 'An effective and thorough investigation can, in my judgement, only be met by holding a public and independent investigation with the family legally represented, provided with the relevant material and be able to cross-examine the principal witnesses.' **[V8]**

SURESH enters.

SURESH: [*] But in March 2002, the Court of Appeal upheld the Home Secretary's appeal. The Judges said there was no need to hold an inquiry because it had been proven that the prison service had been at fault.

IMTIAZ: It seemed like Blunkett had won. It was a real body blow – like everything we'd fought for was in vain. **[V2a]**

SCENE 6

We are now in Feltham Prison. STEWART is showed into a cell.

PRISON OFFICERS – MARTINDALE and DEBBIE HOGG – approach STEWART.

MARTINDALE: Is this your first time in prison?

STEWART: No.

MARTINDALE: Are you expecting contact with your family and friends?

STEWART: Yes.

MARTINDALE: Do you use drugs or alcohol?

STEWART: No.

MARTINDALE: Do you feel like hurting yourself at the moment?

STEWART: No.

MARTINDALE: Are you feeling suicidal?

STEWART: No.

MARTINDALE: Haven't got a file on you. Better start a new one. What you in Court for?

STEWART: Sending abusive letters.

IMTIAZ steps forward.

IMTIAZ: Stewart came down to Feltham a few times because of Court hearings in London. This was to do with those harassing letters he'd sent to a woman in London. A new arrival in a prison is supposed to have four sets of records: a PER form which is a Prisoner Escort Report form giving key details about the prisoner; a flimsy, which reveals the latest state of play with the individual at the previous prison; a F2050 general file which gives full details of the prisoner's prison history; and an Inmate Medical Record (IMR) which should spell out the possible psychological history. When he initially arrived from HM Hindley Prison he came without any records. So, no one knew anything about Stewart, apparently. Just another young prisoner.

STEWART starts writing letters.

MARTINDALE: [*] On initial interview with the lad on induction, it was just one of those gut feelings where something doesn't feel right…all he did was wander around. He had no friends. That's why we watched him all the time. We were uncomfortable with his presence. On the same day Senior Officer Robert Benford contacted me and asked me to come over to the security office and he showed me Stewart's security file. His was the largest security file I have ever seen on a prisoner since I have been in the service. I wrote on the flimsy which had been opened that day, in large red capital letters: 'STAFF ARE ADVISED TO SEE THE SECURITY FILE ON THIS INMATE (HELD IN SECURITY). VERY DANGEROUS INDIVIDUAL. BE CAREFUL.' It was down to each individual member of staff to go and find out what the security file contained… I made one entry when I met Stewart. What happens after that has got nothing to do with me. All I was responsible for was when Stewart was in Lapwing with me and nothing else. **[V5]**

STEWART holds out his letter for DEBBIE HOGG. She takes it and as she walks away, she reads it.

DEBBIE HOGG: Erm…dodgy letter from the new boy in cell 15.

MARTINDALE: Dodgy?

DEBBIE HOGG: Goes on about how many black inmates there are in Feltham in comparison to Hindley.

MARTINDALE: And?

DEBBIE HOGG: It's a bit racist. Goes on about 'niggers' and 'pakis'.

MARTINDALE yawns and stretches.

DEBBIE HOGG: What should I do?

MARTINDALE: Give it back to him. Tell him to rewrite it in an acceptable form. Let's not be heavy-handed.

DEBBIE HOGG takes the letter, walks back to the cell and hands it back to STEWART.

DEBBIE HOGG: Stewart – if I were you, I'd change the terminology. It may be racist, it may not be racist, but I don't like what's in the letter so I'm returning it to you.

STEWART: *(Polite.)* Thank you Miss.

MARTINDALE: I remember saying to Officer Meek what a nasty bit of work Stewart was. I have seen an entry dated 7.3.2000 to say Stewart was received on Swallow.

MARTINDALE exits.

STEWART: [*] Well before they put me in a cell with him, they had put this note in my file saying that 'A letter was sent out by this inmate with racially something material', so they shouldn't have put me there in the first place. If they had done the job properly and put me on a remand wing, then it wouldn't have happened. If they'd read the letters when they were supposed to, they should have thought, 'Get the guy out', and the previous files with all these fights and assaults and that in the past. Somebody should have thought I was a time bomb ready to explode. **[V5]**

SCENE 7

IMTIAZ and SURESH enter.

IMTIAZ: Even though Blunkett had won, we fought on, we lodged an appeal. In October 2003, nearly a year and a half after the ruling against us we took our case to the Law Lords.

SURESH: The Home Office's approach to the Inquiry and to the Mubarek family has been absolutely heartless. If you compare their reaction to the Lawrence family – it's totally different. I think they thought they could get away with this because prisoners are not treated in the same way. The reason why I'm so angry with Blunkett is because I think he prolonged the family's grief.

IMTIAZ: Eventually we won our appeal in the Law Lords. Law Lord Justice Bingham said:

SURESH: *(Reads.)* [*] 'In the light of the House of Lords' judgment in the case of Regina *v* the Secretary of State for the Home Department *ex parte* Amin, to investigate and report to the Home Secretary on the death of Zahid

Mubarek, and the events leading up to the attack on him, and make recommendation about the prevention of such attacks in the future, taking into account the investigations that have already taken place – in particular those by the Prison Service and the Commission for Racial Equality…' **[V9]**

IMTIAZ: [*] It was a remarkable and unanimous decision, asking the Home Secretary to set up an independent Public Inquiry into the death of Zahid Mubarek.

It was the first time ever in judicial history that a family had been able to get such a decision out of the Law Lords.

SURESH: The thing is, what the Stephen Lawrence Inquiry showed us was that you can begin to eradicate racism if you bring it out into the open and the people responsible are held publicly accountable.

IMTIAZ: On the 29th April 2004, over four years after Zahid was murdered, the Home Secretary announced the Public Inquiry into my nephew's death – headed by Justice Keith. Now finally – maybe, we thought, we'd get to the bottom of things. **[V2a]**

JUSTICE KEITH: *(Off.)* [*] Good morning, ladies and gentlemen and welcome to the first day of the full hearings of the Public Inquiry into the death of Zahid Mubarek. The Inquiry's preliminary hearing took place in May. It opened with us observing a minute's silence in memory of Zahid and I know that a remembrance ceremony took place for him this morning.

The initial focus of this Inquiry is on the circumstances which led up to the attack on Zahid, and that will in particular involve an investigation into how he came to share a cell for a number of weeks with someone like Robert Stewart.

The Inquiry will therefore have to address the particular decisions which contributed to that critical cell allocation and any systematic failings associated with them. The Mubarek family believe that race played a part in those decisions. If any evidence emerges which suggests that that could have been the case, or that race could have played a part in any systematic failings, I regard my terms of reference as requiring me to investigate that as well. To that extent, therefore, my terms of reference make it necessary for the Inquiry to focus on issues of race, over and above the racially motivated nature of the attack on Zahid. My distinguished advisors and I are only too aware of how important this Inquiry is: we know how much it means to Zahid's family who fought so long to get it. We will do what we can to get at the truth so that Zahid's family will at least have the satisfaction of knowing that such lessons as can be learnt from his tragic death may make our prisons a safer place in which to be. **[V1]**

SCENE 8

We are now with ZAHID. He is in the cell, lying on his bed.

We hear the sounds of Feltham. JAMIE calls ZAHID from his cell. We don't see JAMIE but hear his conversation.

MORSE: *(Off.)* ABW Mubarek.

ZAHID: What's that mean guv?

MORSE: *(Off.)* Arsehole before wicket.

ZAHID: Thank you.

A woman – LUCY BOGUE – steps forward.

LUCY: [*] Lucy Bogue. Former Chairwoman of the Independent Monitoring Board Feltham – IMB.

My perception of Feltham during my time on the IMB was an establishment in turmoil. Yearly budget cuts, high population, shortage of staff and constant Senior Management turnover created an establishment that was difficult to move forward. **[V1]**

MORSE: *(Off.)* You're taking longer than the test match, Mubarek.

Open cell 38.

LUCY: [*] A key issue during the material time was that Feltham was identified as being a suitable establishment to create a Detention and Training Centre for young men under the age of 18. This meant that a large amount of 'ring-fenced funding' was poured into one side of Feltham, known as Feltham A, which left Feltham B as the poor relation. The knock-on effect of this was that staff left Feltham B to work on Feltham A. During 2000 men on Feltham B were locked up for long periods in disgusting conditions. Those over-18s on Feltham B were left with few if any activities. **[V1]**

JAMIE: *(Off.)* Oy Zahid!

ZAHID is quiet.

Zahid!

ZAHID: Yeah, what?

JAMIE: I talked to the screw, about us sharing and that.

ZAHID: What'd he say?

JAMIE: Said he'd see how I behaved first.

ZAHID: Gotta stop flipping out man.

LUCY: [*] Each cell contained one lavatory bowl with no privacy screen, 12 inches from the foot of the bottom bed. With only one metal seat, welded to the wall and one metal table welded to the wall, the second person would be forced to eat all meals seated on the bottom bunk, in close proximity to the lavatory bowl. **[V1]**

JAMIE: *(Off.)* This place is doing my head in. So bored.

ZAHID: Yeah. Nuthin' to do.

JAMIE: Who's got the box tonight?

ZAHID: Dunno.

JAMIE: When's it your turn?

ZAHID: Next Thursday I think.

MORSE: *(Off.)* Open 35.

A Prison Officer – MORSE – steps forward.

MORSE: [*] Ian Morse. I am employed as a Prison Officer. I knew Robert Stewart as a prisoner based on Swallow Unit. I don't recall reading any documents about Robert Stewart during his time on Swallow Unit. Stewart was a quiet prisoner. Zahid was a bubbly character and never caused any problems. **[V1]**

We hear the howl of an inmate, crying.

A plate of food is pushed through into ZAHID's cell. He picks it up reluctantly.

ZAHID: Oh man. That Caps – always howling.

JAMIE: *(Off.)* He's lost it big time.

ZAHID: Same thing?

JAMIE: Sent a VO for his mum, got all dressed up. She never turned up.

ZAHID: Poor bastard.

JAMIE: Least you get visits. Keep you from going mad – visits.

ZAHID: Caps must know the score by now?

JAMIE: You'd have thought. He's a twat. What's he expect? His mum's a whore. *(Shouts.)* Caps! Shut up! Your mum's a fucking whore!

LUCY: [*] The number of prisoner movements in 1996 was in excess of 38,000. The result of this high turnover was that sentence planning became increasingly difficult as there was a rapid allocation of 18-21 year olds to other prisons. **[V1]**

JAMIE: 'Least you've got a short sentence. How long you been here?

ZAHID: Twenty-three days.

JAMIE: I'm stuck here for years.

ZAHID: Yeah man. Stinks.

LUCY: [*] With the Feltham B prisoner population in constant flux, it became increasingly hard for all members of staff to forge relationships with boys or properly manage their time spent in the establishment. This, added to the existing problems of overcrowding, led to the demise of any fulfilling or substantial regime for boys on Feltham B. **[V1]**

MORSE: [*] I made an entry in Robert Stewart's flimsy when he arrived on Swallow Unit from Reception. I was also responsible for allocating him to cell 38. February 8th 2000. **[V1]**

JAMIE: *(Off.)* 'Least you can read books and stuff.

ZAHID: Like I said. We get to share a cell and I'll teach you.

JAMIE: Maybe if I tell that to the screws they'll move us in together.

ZAHID: Maybe.

LUCY: [*] A common complaint throughout Feltham B was the lack of evening association. Association is the time that prisoners have out of cells in order to socialise with other prisoners. The boys might play pool. **[V1]**

MORSE: *(Hands ZAHID a plate of food.)* Open cell 38.

LUCY: [*] In the rota book, on 16.2.2000 (five weeks before Zahid's death), a Board member noted that whilst boys in Swallow Unit should have two hours of association, there was no sign of any boy being unlocked after 2.45pm. It must be understood that the paucity of the regime would have meant that boys would spend up to 22 hours locked in a cell. Feltham at this time had no in-cell electricity and so there was little for the prisoners to do. **[V1]**

ZAHID: Starvin'.

JAMIE: *(Off.)* Yeah, me too. I could do with some Kentucky Fried Chicken.

ZAHID: Don't…

JAMIE: Finger lickin' good.

ZAHID: Me, I want my mum's chicken biryani.

JAMIE: Sounds good to me. Food here smells like shit.

ZAHID looks at his plate of food and sniffs it. He tries to eat.

ZAHID: Probably is shit.

JAMIE: Euch. Don't say that!

ZAHID laughs.

MORSE: [*] I was on the desk at 7.30pm. I can't recall what cells were vacant in Swallow Unit at the time but the unit was usually very full so often there was very little choice as to where the prisoners would be allocated. I didn't have any concerns about Robert Stewart. **[V1]**

LUCY: [*] It was the opinion of myself and the Board that the impact of 22 hours locked in a very confined space must have had an adverse effect on the behaviour of any adolescent, let alone some of the most damaged and disturbed adolescents in the country. The lack of fulfilling association time was both degrading and disgusting. **[V1]**

JAMIE: *(Off.)* Oy. Zahid.

ZAHID: Yeah.

JAMIE: What d'you miss most from outside?

ZAHID thinks.

You hear me?

ZAHID: Yeah. Miss playing cricket with me brothers in Vestry Park. Yeah man. Miss that the most. You?

JAMIE: Everything.

ZAHID slides his tray of food out along the floor of the cell.

MORSE: [*] On that night I would have had no information about Stewart other than his name and prison number, remand or convicted and how long serving, I would have checked the available spaces on the wing… I had a cell card and one space and one prisoner. **[V1]**

STEWART enters. MORSE leads him towards the cell.

Cell 38, opening doors.

ZAHID sits up on his bed.

Got a new cellmate Mubarek.

STEWART stands before ZAHID. They look at each other.

STEWART: *(To MORSE.)* When's my money coming from Hindley, boss?

MORSE: Don't know. I'll check it out for you.

STEWART sits on the bed.

MORSE glances at them both and then exits.

The scene ends with the two young men wordlessly sat on their beds looking at each other.

INTERVAL.

Act Two

SCENE 1

We hear a tape recording of a very emotional man on the phone speaking.

VOICE: [*] I'm no bleeding heart on this but that kid was murdered for other people's perverted pleasure. The game was called 'Coliseum'. Mubarek was killed because people thought it was funny to see what would happen when they put a young Asian lad in with someone who wanted to kill Asians. Now Mubarek wasn't the only victim in there. He was the victim that died.

DUNCAN KEYS steps forward.

The usual wall of silence has gone up through the Prison Service as you would expect, but they can no longer sit there and hear the question about how Mubarek ended up in a cell with a known racist. That's how he ended up. Because of a game called 'Coliseum' and staff in that wing.

If the right questions had been asked on the Butt Inquiry instead of looking at processes and procedures and all that rubbish and actually found that it was human beings that put those two people together rather than bloody processes and procedures – then there would be a murder inquiry into the staff there. Because it's something that went dramatically wrong. Dramatically wrong. **[V5]**

Tape is switched off.

KEYS: [*] Duncan Keys. I am employed as an Assistant Secretary for the Prison Officers' Association.

I can confirm that it is my voice on this recording and I made this call, having tried and failed to speak to someone at the CRE by telephone the previous day. I made this telephone call as I felt that the information was important and could be relevant to the Public Inquiry. I also felt that it could be relevant to the death of Mr Mubarek. The first time I ever heard of a practice whereby two prisoners were put in a cell together in the expectation that they might fight was when I spoke to Tom Robson after he had visited Feltham Prison. Tom is a member of the National Executive Committee and a good friend of mine. He told me that they were in the Prison Officers' Association office when Mr Herring had started to tell him about a game played by prison officers in Feltham known as 'Gladiator' or 'Coliseum'. **[V1]**

HERRING: [*] Nigel Herring – Branch Chairman of the Prison Officers' Association. I have never instigated or taken part in a practice known as 'Gladiator' or 'Coliseum'. The only committee member from Feltham who had previously heard rumours about 'Gladiator' was Ian Morse. I remember him saying that he had heard these rumours in connection with an investigation. **[V1]**

KEYS: [*] The prisoners could be one black, one white, one big and one small, one bully paired with another bully. Whatever the combination, the intention was to see whether or not the two fell out and came to blows. Tom told me that Mr Herring had told him that the officers were betting on the outcome of such pairings.

Having come to the conclusion that the Union was not going to do anything to draw these allegations to the attention of the authorities, I decided that I had to take some steps to make sure that the information came to someone's attention. I was however extremely nervous about making a direct, open approach to the CRE because I had previously raised the matter with my line manager, Brian Caton, and he had told me that I should do nothing. As a result, I decided to make an anonymous call to the CRE. **[V1]**

HERRING: [*] I would also like to emphasise that I have not witnessed or taken part in banter malicious or otherwise about Mr Mubarek's death. **[V1]**

KEYS: [*] I accept with hindsight that I exaggerated aspects of what I said but did so because I wanted to make the allegations seem strong and plausible, because I thought that the issue should be investigated. In my interview with the Police I was asked by DI Booth about my statement that the practice known as 'Gladiator' was linked to Zahid Mubarek's death. I explained in that interview that I had put two and two together and came up with five. The fact that I did so and the fact that I linked this practice with the death of Zahid Mubarek, when I now appreciate that there was no direct evidence that his being placed in the cell was anything to do with this practice, is a matter of considerable regret to me. I offer my sincere apologies to the Mubarek family for the hurt I have caused by my actions. **[V1]**

HERRING: [*] Any 'Gladiator' practice would have to involve the complicity of many officers. The great majority of officers have complete commitment to the welfare of prisoners and would not shrink from reporting any misconduct of this kind within a short time. No such practice could survive or be kept secret. **[V1]**

KEYS: [*] I, initially thought that the possibility that such a practice was ongoing was unlikely, although I was aware that there had been previous instances of inappropriate behaviour by Prison Officers at Feltham and accordingly, I did not dismiss the possibility that this might have gone on. **[V1]**

HERRING: [*] If you haven't got the staff to even give these guys breakfast, or take them to work, what do you get? 'You're winding us up, you're trying to wind me up.' And we're dealing with very angry people, that go, like that, they will stab you just like that, and that's why they're there. **[V3]**

IMTIAZ and SURESH enter.

IMTIAZ: [*] Unless it's eliminated there's always gonna be an element of doubt. If you're looking at the facts of how Stewart manages to go through two prisons, Hindley first and then Feltham, undetected, the amount of opportunities that they had, the prison officers, to stop this guy – they could see that he was dangerous and hence they should have allocated cells accordingly – it doesn't make sense. It is just so far out there that you've got to think that somewhere along the line somebody had something to do with helping him along… I don't know… I really don't know…the way these two just come together in one cell – it just doesn't really make sense. I mean, you've just gotta take a look at his convictions. **[V2a]**

SURESH: [*] If the 'Gladiator' thing is true, then apart from Stewart murdering, then someone else is responsible for manslaughter or murder – so it became a Police investigation. The Police said they were going to close the investigation on this because it was impossible to determine. But Duncan Keys comes across as an extremely convincing witness. Nigel Herring does not. You can talk to prisoners and they'll tell you about this thing called 'wind ups'. Prison officers say this doesn't exist. **[V2a]**

NIGEL HERRING and DUNCAN KEYS look at each other with hatred and then exit.

IMTIAZ: [*] Originally we weren't sure about whether any of the staff at Feltham knew that Stewart had a history. We just thought that those reports hadn't gone through. This was what I was thinking.

SURESH: Yes, me too.

IMTIAZ: But in the Inquiry I saw there were reports that were read and still they never did anything about it. There were people that knew that Stewart was a handful. They did nothing.

That's where the real 'Gladiator Games' has been, between the family on one hand and the Prison Service and the British Government on the other. It's a shame you have to ask the Government to invest in the truth. **[V2a]**

SCENE 2

In the Association room, STEWART is playing table tennis with INMATE 1. STEWART having lost his game starts smashing the bat against the table repeatedly.

STEWART: Fuck's sake.

INMATE 1: Keep your hair on mate. It's just a game!

STEWART continues to smash his bat up. We hear unseen FELTHAM PRISON OFFICER shout.

FELTHAM PO: *(Off.)* Oy! Inmate Stewart. You break that bat and you'll have to pay for it.

JAMIE: *(Off.)* Oy oy oy oy!

STEWART calms down immediately and goes into a corner.

ZAHID and JAMIE enter. JAMIE looks at STEWART.

ZAHID: Jamie, leave it man, calm down.

JAMIE: What's your new padmate like?

ZAHID: Safe.

JAMIE: Yeah?

ZAHID: Acts a bit weird but seems all right.

JAMIE: Looks weird all right. Where's he from?

ZAHID: Manchester – doing time at Hindley. Sounds like he's been inside forever. Don't like the things on his head. Think he's NF.

JAMIE: Said anything nasty?

ZAHID: Doesn't talk much.

JAMIE: Everyone calls him RIP.

ZAHID: Yeah.

JAMIE: I asked about moving cells again.

ZAHID: Any luck?

JAMIE: Said he was 'too busy'.

ZAHID: Go and ask again.

JAMIE: All right.

SKINNER steps forward.

SKINNER: [*] Stephen Skinner. At the time of the attack on Mr Mubarek my position was that of a prison officer based on Swallow Unit. I knew Zahid Mubarek from working on Swallow Unit. He used to come over and chat to the officers working on the unit when it was association time. During these conversations with Zahid he never expressed any concern to me about his safety or indeed about his cellmate. **[V1]**

STEWART and ZAHID go back to their cell and are locked in.

STEWART: You got a girlfriend?

ZAHID: Nah.

STEWART: I have. She's banged up 'n' all.

ZAHID: Inside?

STEWART: Yeah. Writes to me and stuff. I write back. I love writing – me.

ZAHID: Nice one.

STEWART: Wrote to her last week. Told her I was gonna chop off her head.

ZAHID looks at STEWART as if he's mad. STEWART laughs. ZAHID fiddles with his radio and sticks some music on.

What is that crap you listen to all the time?

ZAHID: It's not crap. It's Biggy.

STEWART: Put something else on.

ZAHID: It's my radio. What kind of music you listen to?

STEWART: Not this shit.

ZAHID: What then?

STEWART: Not this shit.

ZAHID: What rock music?

STEWART: Not this shit.

ZAHID: What pop music?

STEWART: Not this shit.
Not this shit.
Not this shit.
Look at my fucking house.
Look at my fucking car.
Look at my fucking birds.

ZAHID: I like it.

STEWART: Jigaboo, nigger gangsta rap shit.

ZAHID: It's my radio. I'll listen to what I want.

STEWART: I hate it.

ZAHID: Tough.

STEWART: Fuck's sake.

STEWART lies on his bed and covers his ears with his pillow.

JAMIE steps forward.

JAMIE: [*] Jamie Barnes. I am a convicted prisoner and am presently at HMP Wellingborough. Zahid and me were friends and I first asked Prison Officer Skinner some time in February 2000 whether I could move into Zahid's cell. To the best of my recollection I think this conversation took place in the office overlooking Swallow Unit's association area and Zahid was with me when I asked. The only reason I asked was because Zahid and I were friends and I was fed up being in cell 35 on my own. **[V1b]**

STEWART leans forward on his bed and stares weirdly at ZAHID. ZAHID looks unnerved.

ZAHID: What you starin' at?

STEWART: Nuthin'.

STEWART continues to stare.

JAMIE: [*] I don't remember now what Skinner's response was but nothing came of my request so I repeated it to another officer, Morse, a few days later. Again the conversation took place in the Unit office but I don't remember if Zahid was with me this time. **[V1a]**

MORSE steps forward.

MORSE: [*] I have no information about any requests made by Zahid Mubarek to move to another cell. If he wanted to make another request and if he had spoken to an officer then it would have been suggested to him that he should fill in an application form. **[V1]**

STEWART stops staring at ZAHID and lies on his bed.

STEWART: You comin' off drugs?

ZAHID does not reply.

Always lying around, you are. Look like you're comin' off drugs.

ZAHID: Haven't had a shower for days.

STEWART: You fucking stink.

ZAHID: Not my fault. Showers are busted again.

ZAHID gets up and combs his hair. He tries to make himself look presentable and sprays himself with deodorant. He stands by the cell door waiting patiently.

JAMIE: [*] Still nothing came of my request so about two days later I again asked Skinner. This time he said he was busy and no cell moves could happen that day. A day or so later Stewart was moved into Zahid's cell. **[V1a]**

ZAHID leaves the cell and goes to the visitors' room. STEWART stays in the cell and starts to write letters. ZAHID meets his mum and dad, AMIN and SAJIDA. They embrace.

AMIN: How's it going?

ZAHID: Yeah, all right. It's okay.

SAJIDA: You getting enough to eat?

ZAHID: Yeah. Food's great here. No worries Ammi.

SAJIDA: You look thin.

ZAHID: Kind of lose your appetite a bit in here. Not really doing much exercise.

AMIN: Gettin' on all right with the other lads?

ZAHID: Yeah. Some of them are right troublemakers. Make me look like an angel.

AMIN and ZAHID laugh.

STEWART reads out one of his letters.

STEWART: [*] IT'S SHITE IN ERE, PLANET OF THE APES. AV GOT A PADMATE TO COME BACK TO (A PAKI). **[V6b]**

ZAHID: How're me brothers? Okay?

AMIN: Yeah. They're fine. Missing you.

ZAHID: I miss them. Don't bring 'em here again will ya?

AMIN: They want to see you.

ZAHID: It ain't right – them hanging about here. Don't want them to end up like me.

Back in the cell we see STEWART writing a letter. We hear him reading it out.

STEWART: [*] 23RD FEB 2000

CANNOT SEE IT STICKIN' IN ERE.

IF I DON'T GET BAIL ON THE 5TH, I'LL TAKE XTREME MEASURE TO GET SHIPPED OUT, KILL ME FUCKIN' PADMATE IF I HAVE TO; BLEACH ME SHEETS AND PILLOWCASE WHITE AND MAKE A KLU KLUX KLAN OUTFIT AND WALK OUT ME PAD WIV A FLAMING CRUCIFIX AND CHANGE THE CROSS TO A PLUS AND THEN A SWASTIKA WIV A BIRO. (HA) NAH, DON'T THINK I'LL BE THAT HARD, THOSE SCREWS DON'T KNOW ME LIKE THESE AT HINDLEY. I SENT YOU A VO LAST WEEK WITH THE VISITORS NAMES, ADOLF HITLER, CHARLES MANSON, HAROLD SHIPMAN…SIGNED STEPHAN LAWRENCE. **[V6b]**

We see STEWART ripping a leg off the table. He breaks the leg in two and fashions the smaller splint into a dagger. He replaces the table leg to prop up the table.

ZAHID: Grandma and Grandpa?

AMIN: Missing you too.

ZAHID: Spoke to them on the phone last week.

SAJIDA: They are both praying for you to get out early.

ZAHID: Good. Feeling a bit homesick actually. Miss my cricket and you know – the family and that.

AMIN: You haven't got long in here. Take the punishment, learn from it and then you can move on.

ZAHID: Yeah, yeah…

AMIN: You sure everything's okay?

ZAHID: Got a new cellmate. He's a bit weird. Just sits there and stares at me, sometimes for ages. Doesn't say nuthin'. He's got this tattoo on his forehead. Says RIP you know?

AMIN: 'Rest In Peace'?

ZAHID: Yeah. I've asked to change cells.

AMIN: Just keep your head down son and do your time.

JAMIE: [*] Zahid never complained to me about getting racial abuse from Stewart nor did I ever get the impression that he felt threatened by him. Stewart was a quiet guy who tended to keep to himself and he was never abusive or violent to me or anyone else as far as I know. **[V1a]**

ZAHID stands again, hugs his mum and dad and then goes back to his cell. As he enters he sees that STEWART looks cagey.

ZAHID sits on his bed. They sit in silence. ZAHID writes a letter.

[*] However I got the impression he was racist, mainly from his appearance and demeanour and the way he acted. He rarely mixed with other people and would wait to shower until everyone had finished. When he did speak to people it was mainly to members of the white gangs. He would mainly refer to black people in a fairly muted way as 'them', but it was clear to me that he didn't like them. I don't think he realised that I'm half-Indian by birth and, if he had, that he would have made those comments to me. **[V1a]**

We are back in the association room. STEWART and others are playing table football, etc. JAMIE is there chatting etc.

ZAHID comes down the stairs looking a bit pissed off. He approaches STEWART.

ZAHID: The Guvnor found your stuff in the toilet.

STEWART smiles.

STEWART: Don't care.

ZAHID: They did a cell search. I got the rap for it.

STEWART: So?

ZAHID: I got the rap for it!

STEWART: You gonna grass on me? You wanna take this to the showers?

ZAHID: Leave it out. What's happened here?

STEWART: Table's broken, just propped it up. They never found the other one.

JAMIE: What you chattin' about?

STEWART pats his stomach.

What?

STEWART lifts his tracksuit and shows the boys.

You got a tool? Where d'you find that?

STEWART: Made it myself. Protection.

JAMIE: Oy, Zahid, can I have me radio back?

ZAHID: What radio?

JAMIE: The one you borrowed off me.

ZAHID: Gave it back mate.

JAMIE: No you didn't.

ZAHID: Did. Last week. Gave it back.

STEWART joins in the game.

STEWART: He did.

JAMIE: Stop fucking me around…

ZAHID: You're losin' your memory man. Gave it back, didn't I?

STEWART: Hold up. You sold a radio last week didn't you? Was that Barnesy's?

ZAHID: Come to think of it…

JAMIE: Stop winding me up.

JAMIE marches off to ZAHID and STEWART's cell. The other two follow him calling out as they go.

ZAHID: Oy – you can't just walk into our pad.

STEWART: Yeah…need our permission.

JAMIE goes into the cell and starts patting down ZAHID's bed. ZAHID and STEWART continue winding JAMIE up.

ZAHID: Got a fiver for the radio. Could go halves on it if you like.

JAMIE: You're gonna give me two pounds fifty for my radio? You're takin' the piss.

STEWART: Be fair – it was a tenner.

STEWART and ZAHID are now passing the radio between them and winding JAMIE up. JAMIE's furious.

JAMIE: Give it back!

ZAHID: Wasn't your radio anyway, you nicked it off someone else didn't you?

JAMIE: Fuck off.

STEWART is enjoying the wind up. Eventually, ZAHID relents. He gives back the radio. JAMIE snatches it back ungraciously. ZAHID is laughing. JAMIE is pissed off. He makes as if he's going to take a piss.

What a laugh – eh? What a fucking mansion it is in here. Think I'll take a piss in here.

STEWART momentarily looks annoyed. His hand goes to his weapon.

ZAHID, still laughing, pushes JAMIE out of the cell.

ZAHID: Come on man, we were just winding you up.

JAMIE exits, annoyed. ZAHID goes back to his cell.

It is the end of association.

A woman – JUDY – steps forward.

ZAHID and STEWART are in their cell.

JUDY: [*] Judy Clements. Race Equality Adviser to HM Prison Service.

During my regular prison visits, I spoke to Black and Minority Ethnic (BME) prisoners and received countless reports of alleged ill-treatment, believed to be on the grounds of race, as well as accounts of blatant racism, usually in the form of name calling. **[V1]**

ZAHID is lying on his bed whilst STEWART is staring at his belongings.

STEWART: You been nicking my stuff?

ZAHID: What stuff?

STEWART: My stuff.

ZAHID: What stuff?

STEWART: You been usin' me shower gel? Me writing paper?

ZAHID: No.

STEWART: Don't fucking lie to me.

ZAHID: What you on about?

STEWART: It's been moved. I can tell.

JUDY: [*] The main concerns raised by BME prisoners can be summarised.

Frequently being 'shipped out' if they complained that they were being subjected to racist behaviour by fellow prisoners or staff.
Being refused access to telephones.
Being placed in segregation units.
Being located in establishments a long way from their homes and family.
The limited availability of ethnic food. **[V1]**

STEWART stares at his stuff again.

STEWART: It's not where I left it.

ZAHID: It's where you always leave it.

STEWART: I know. It's been moved.

ZAHID: You probably moved it. I got my own things – why would I want to touch your stuff?

STEWART: Can't you understand me accent or somethin'? I said I can tell.

STEWART stares angrily at ZAHID.

ZAHID: Take a chill pill.

STEWART: I know what you lot are like. Fucking robbin' us all the time.

ZAHID: Fuck off.

STEWART continues to stare at ZAHID. ZAHID looks unnerved. He gets up and starts pacing.

JUDY: [*] Most disturbing were allegations of acts of serious violence against BME prisoners and the disparity amongst prison staff in reporting these matters as racist. Prison staff and management at local level were, in most areas, in complete denial that BME prisoners were subjected to any form of racism. Consequently they seldom intervened. **[V1]**

STEWART: I know you took me stuff. Just admit it.

ZAHID: I didn't touch it.

ZAHID calls out to JAMIE.

JUDY: [*] I found in every prison that I visited that BME prisoners were disproportionately over represented in the prison discipline regime and were adjudicated upon far more that the majority white prison population. **[V1]**

ZAHID: Oy! Jamie.

We see JAMIE in his cell smoking a cigarette.

Jamie!

JAMIE: What?

ZAHID: You got a burn?

JAMIE: Nah mate. Given up.

ZAHID: Don't give me that.

JAMIE: Health kick.

ZAHID is more agitated.

STEWART: Look at you. Always so agitated.

ZAHID: I ain't even talkin' to you. I ain't got your shit.

ZAHID lays down again.

STEWART is now standing in the cell. He calls out to JAMIE.

STEWART: Hey! Barnesy.

JAMIE ignores him.

Barnesy! You got a burn?

JAMIE: Fuck off.

STEWART: Me padmate's been nicking me shower gel and writing paper.

JAMIE: Thought he smelt nice. Hey Zahid!

ZAHID ignores them both.

JAMIE: Cool and refreshin' eh mate?

ZAHID: Shut up Jamie.

JAMIE laughs. STEWART sits back down and stares at ZAHID.

STEWART: We'll see who has the last laugh on this one.

SCENE 3

We are back in visiting hours again. SAJIDA and AMIN enter. ZAHID joins them. They embrace.

SAJIDA: Only two more days to go Zahid.

AMIN: You're nearly there lad.

ZAHID: Who's going to be there?

AMIN: Your cousins, your brothers, your uncles. Nothing too big.

ZAHID: Can't wait dad. Can't wait. Be so nice to get out of here. I'm gonna get a job, sort myself out, you'll see, You'll be proud of me.

SAJIDA: We are always proud of you…this is just…

AMIN: You slipped up Zahid. Things are gonna be different. We'll see you right.

ZAHID: What're you gonna cook mum?

SAJIDA: Your favourite – chicken jaal.

ZAHID: Ohhh…feel like I haven't eaten for months.

SAJIDA: You have lost weight.

ZAHID: I'm sorry dad, mum. I'm sorry about all this stuff I put you through.

AMIN: As long as you've learnt your lesson.

ZAHID: I think they're releasing me on Tuesday.

AMIN: I thought they were supposed to be releasing you two days ago?

ZAHID: Yeah – didn't work out 'cos they hadn't done the paperwork. Still haven't moved me. Cellmate's still acting weird.

AMIN: Yeah well, you'll soon be out of there. Then you won't have to worry about him no more.

ZAHID stands up to go back to his cell. He hugs his parents again.

ZAHID: So you'll be picking me up?

AMIN: I'll be here.

They watch him go. ZAHID turns.

ZAHID: Hey dad! Don't be late! Bring the Cosworth. And dad – don't be late.

ZAHID goes back to his cell.

ZAHID: It's our turn for TV tonight.

STEWART: What's on?

ZAHID: Some Russell Crowe film.

STEWART: Which one?

ZAHID: *Romper Stomper.*

STEWART: Shit! That's a great film!

TV is flicked on. Stage goes dark as we hear (or indeed see) the opening violence of the film.

SCENE 4

We are at the Inquiry. GIFFIN steps forward.

GIFFIN: [*] Counsel for the Zahid Mubarek Inquiry – Giffin. Closing statements.

Sir, these submissions are made at the end of a long process of investigation of the events which led to the murder of Zahid Mubarek and of the context in which those events took place. That investigation has extended to the assembling and consideration of more than 15,000 pages of documents, the taking of written statements from some 110 witnesses of fact, reports from two distinguished consultant psychiatrists and the hearing of oral evidence from 60 witnesses spread over some 64 days. That represents an enormous intake of information.

Much public attention has been paid, understandably so, to the suggestion that Zahid might have been the victim of a deliberate practice of officers placing prisoners in shared cells in the hope or expectation of racial violence or other conflict between them: the so-called 'Gladiator' allegations. I do not believe that there is any evidence from which you could conclude that Stewart was deliberately either placed or left with Zahid in the hope that that violence or conflict would occur between them. The true facts are quite sufficiently disturbing without being reduced to that facile form. Nonetheless, there remains alive the suggestion that some such practice did occur at Feltham at some time and on some unascertained scale. **[V1c]**

We see ZAHID and STEWART in their cell. ZAHID is getting ready for release the following morning. STEWART is watching him.

[*] Even if we leave aside the history of events before 1999, there were I think, potentially as many as 15 occasions when individual prison staff, sometimes now identifiable, sometimes not, might have influenced the course of events if they had acted differently in response to the information they had.

1 We know that on 7th March 2000, a fortnight before the attack, a prison officer, Mr Morse, had open before him the wing file warning that Stewart was very dangerous and recording that he had written a racist letter, yet he remained in the cell with Zahid, no action taken.

2 We also know that the next day another officer, Mr Skinner, had the same file in his hand, marked in red on its cover 'See inside', yet Mr Skinner took no action.

3 There is then the important suggestion that a day or two preceding Zahid's death, a piece of wood was found by a prison officer in cell 38 which could and should have led to the identification of the broken table and to the realisation that Stewart had been making weapons.

4 Both of Stewart's personal officers admit they never took any positive steps to find out anything about him or Zahid or to make entries on his wing file. If they had done so, they would have seen the written warnings there.

5 When Stewart came to Feltham for the third time there was no vetting of his security file.

6 When Stewart wrote a racist letter on Lapwing Unit which was intercepted on January 12th 2000 and shown to Senior Officer Martindale, no action was taken.

7 Someone will have checked Stewart's warrants or certainly should have done when he entered Feltham and seen that he was charged with offences under the Harassment Act, yet his correspondence was not monitored and so letters which revealed his violent and racist thoughts were never seen.

8 No warning about Stewart's violence based on his PER (Prisoner Escort Record) was passed onto the wing.

9 The wing file containing Mr Martindale's warning and the information about the racist letter was allowed to go missing at some point between 12th January 2000 and

7th February 2000 and when Stewart was allocated to a cell without any attempt then or later to pursue the missing wing file or seek information about it.

10 At Hindley there were a number of failures in the autumn of 1999 and at the start of 2000 to record incidents properly on Stewart's security record, so conveying to anyone who looked at it the false impression that his record had been clean since January 1999.

11 At Altcourse, Stewart was or may have been assessed as not being dangerous without the individual who reached that conclusion being made aware of the contents of his security file.

12 At Hindley, it is likely in my submission that staff were informed that on 19 September 1999 Stewart had sent a harassing letter from the prison, but no security report was raised and:

13 No action was taken to monitor his correspondence.

14 At Altcourse, the prison was informed that Stewart was to be questioned by police about alleged offences of racial harassment, but nothing was done to find anything more about the circumstances.

15 At Hindley, letters from Stewart were intercepted in August 1999 and January 2000 which led to security reports but not to any further action. **[V1c]**

We see a FELTHAM PRISON OFFICER look into the cell on his night rounds to check they are all right. STEWART is writing letters.

It is now night time and ZAHID is tucking himself into bed. STEWART stands and reads out one of his letters. (Some stagecraft to signify this is all going on in STEWART's head.)

STEWART: [*] DID YOU WATCH ROMPER STOMPER? IT'S MAD. I'M IN IT. HA HA, WISH THEM SKINHEADS WAS IN ERE, NIG NOG WOULD SOON SHUT UP I THINK. AM GONNA MAKE ME OWN BEER IN ME PAD, WATCH ME SOME TV

AND TUMP [thump] UP SOME JIGABOOS. GONNA NAIL BOMB BRADFORD, MOSS SIDE – ALL THE NON WHITE AREAS. **[V6b]**

STEWART sits down to write another letter.

O'CONNOR steps forward.

O'CONNOR: [*] O'Connor. Closing Submissions on behalf of the Mubarek family.

Sir, at the outset may we, on behalf of the Mubarek family, publicly express our appreciation for the sensitivity with which the death of Zahid has now been investigated. The murder of Zahid devastated his family and rightly shocked the nation. It is incomprehensible to the Mubarek family and to the public that he could have been forced to share a cell with Robert Stewart for six weeks. **[V1c]**

STEWART stands up and reads another letter. ZAHID rolls over in bed.

STEWART: [*] WELL DID YOU WATCH ROMPER STOMPER THE OTHER DAY? LET'S GO GET THE GOOK'S. MAD DAT FILM STARRING ME! **[V6b]**

ZAHID: *(Calls out.)* I'm tryin' to sleep, switch the light off.

STEWART ignores ZAHID.

STEWART: [*] DID YOU WATCH ROMPER STOMPER THE OTHER DAY. FAT FILM. I WISH DEM BLOKES WERE IN ERE AND DEM WHAT KILLED STEPHEN LAWRENCE. THE NIGGERS WOULD SOON SHUT UP… AM GONNA CONTACT THE FIVE O AN ADMIT TO SOME SHIT, NICE SPELL UP NORTH WEST, WATCH SOME GRANADA TV, HEAR SOME REAL ACCENTS, SEE SOME WHITE PEOPLE. **[V6b]**

O'CONNOR: [*] It is remarkable how little remorse has appeared from the mouths of witnesses before the Inquiry. A reluctance even to acknowledge collective fault has been shown.

What is the relevance of race discrimination at Feltham to this murder? This provided an institutional context for Stewart's racism to thrive and come to its appalling fulfilment. Ms Clements, in her evidence, said: 'I think there is in my mind no doubt that race and racism had a key part to play', and she has asked in her evidence: 'Could we have been so blind?' The blindness of the threat he posed to ethnic minorities is testament to the blinding power of racist attitudes. **[V1c]**

STEWART paces the cell, writing and reading his letters. He seems to be working himself up into a frenzy.

STEWART: [*] I'M GONNA NAIL BOMB THE ASIAN COMMUNITY OF GREAT NORBURY, ST LUMM RD + THEM AREAS. IT'S ALL ABOUT IMMIGRANTS GETTING SMUGGLED IN HERE. ROMANIANS, PAKIS, NIGGERS, CHINKIES TRYIN' TO TAKE OVER THE COUNTRY AND USING US TO BREED HALF CASTES. **[V6b]**

ZAHID: Switch the light off.

STEWART chucks a pair of his underpants onto the light.

O'CONNOR: [*] Let us engage in a life swap in which Zahid Mubarek and Robert Stewart exchange ethnic origin and religion but nothing else. Zahid is a white Christian and Stewart a black Muslim. The prison officer on duty has been warned that the Muslim Robert Stewart is dangerous to staff. She has several options for cell-sharing. Even on appearance alone, is there any chance she would have allocated that Robert Stewart to share with a white Christian prisoner? The white Zahid Mubarek would never have been subjected to the apparent threat from the black or Muslim Robert Stewart for one night, let alone six weeks. **[V1c]**

STEWART reads one last letter.

STEWART: [*] I LIVE A LIFE OF CRIME, ALCOHOL, VIOLENCE, DRUGS, PRISON, CARS, RACISM + GIRLS. LET ME KNOW YOUR VIEWS ON BLACKS + ASIANS. **[V6b]**

O'CONNOR: [*] The Prison Service and the Prison Officers' Association seek to downplay the role of racism as a motive for this murder and the role of institutional racism as a contributing factor. We venture to submit that very little of what we have learnt about Feltham in the years 1996 to 2000 can be dismissed as entirely irrelevant to the murder of Zahid.

It is right to say that almost every area of life in Feltham which can be assessed or measured by the Inquiry has been shown to have been tainted with race discrimination. If there had not been institutional racism within the prison service, it is more likely that Zahid Mubarek would be alive today. That is why the family believes this issue to be of such importance in their son's death. **[V1c]**

We see STEWART sitting on his bed, staring at the sleeping figure of ZAHID. Eventually he takes the table leg from its hiding place and approaches ZAHID. He stands over ZAHID with the table leg in his hand.

[*] Zahid lost his life on the morning of his due return from Feltham to his family. He had faced up to his problems in a very mature way. They were surely in the past for him. The Inquiry has seen his letters to his family where he apologised directly and openly to his father for letting him down. He was concerned to set a good example for his two younger brothers. The positive hard-working and athletic side of his life would probably have been channelled into an army career. **[V1c]**

ZAHID: Switch the fucking light off.

O'CONNOR: [*] His memory has been frozen at this moment by an act of cruel racist violence. Nothing can bring him back. One of the manifestations of ideological racist hatred over the last century has been the cynical distortion of language. This has the nihilistic power to undermine the rational part of the human spirit which racists know is their enemy. This was the intended effect of the letters 'RIP' on the forehead of Robert Stewart. The simple sentiment of 'rest in peace' to the dead is turned into a threat of murderous violence addressed at whoever looks at his face. That abomination of language remains the message of those letters to the Mubarek family, at least for the moment. This Inquiry can at least reclaim the humanity of that simple sentiment and enable the family to ensure themselves that Zahid does, in the true sense of the words, rest in peace. **[V1c]**

STEWART brings down the table leg onto ZAHID's head. The lights go out.

ZAHID: *(Shouts.)* Ahhh!

STEWART: *(Shouts.)* Shut up! SHUT UP!

We hear the sound of the unmistakable thud of the table leg as it hits ZAHID again and again.

Beat.

Sound of an alarm rings out.

Light on STEWART's eyes.

STEWART: [*] Me cellmate's had an accident guv. **[V1]**

Prison Officer NICHOLSON steps forward.

NICHOLSON: *(Strong Scottish accent.)* [*] Malcom Nicholson. At the time of the attack on Mr Mubarek I was an OSG working permanent nights. On the night of the attack on Mr Mubarek I was on duty on Swallow Unit. At about 0345 hours a cell bell rang. That isn't unusual. They want toilet paper. Normally get up there and they want toilet paper so you have to go back down. Picked up some toilet paper and went up. Went up to the door and opened the flap. **[V1]**

STEWART: Me cellmate's had an accident guv.

NICHOLSON approaches the cell now with toilet paper in his hand. He looks through the flap.

STEWART is standing in the cell holding the table leg. ZAHID is still lying in bed. NICHOLSON backs off and quickly exits, leaving STEWART standing there over ZAHID. We hear the sound of radio requests being made – progressively sounding more and more urgent.

RADIO: [*] Oscar 2 to attend Swallow Unit. Novembers 3, 4 & 5 to respond to Swallow Unit. All available staff to attend Swallow Unit immediately. **[V1]**

FELTHAM PO 2: *(Off.)* Open cell 38.

STEWART remains calm in his cell. ZAHID does not move. It takes a long time but eventually NICHOLSON and a second PRISON OFFICER arrive.

FELTHAM PO 2 opens the door.

FELTHAM PO 2: Drop the stick. Drop the stick Stewart. Now. Do it now.

STEWART drops the table leg. It is covered with blood.

Your back against the wall. Against the wall.

STEWART does as he is told.

NICHOLSON and FELTHAM PO 2 enter the cell and look at ZAHID. They both look horrified.

FELTHAM PO 2: *(To STEWART.)* What have you done?

STEWART: It was an accident.

FELTHAM PO 2: *(Horrified.)* What have you done?

STEWART: [*] It was an accident guv. **[V1]**

NICHOLSON takes STEWART out of the cell and puts him against the wall. Both PRISON OFFICERS go into the cell and peer at ZAHID.

NICHOLSON: Shit, look at his face. Looks really bad. Mubarek!

FELTHAM PO 2: Shit. Shit…better call an ambulance. Where's Nurse Berry? Mubarek! Can you hear me?

An Asian female Prison Officer – RANDHAWA – turns up. There is a flurry of activity as the PRISON OFFICERS phone an ambulance. STEWART remains standing in there.

RANDHAWA: [*] Satwant Randhawa. At the time of the attack on Mr Mubarek, I was carrying out my night shift as a Night Patrol Support officer at Feltham YOI. I received the call to go to Swallow Unit around 0340am and I made my way there as swiftly as possible. As I proceeded into the right hand side of the unit I noticed a prisoner outside a cell, whom I subsequently discovered was Mr Stewart outside cell number 38. I looked at Stewart. He looked at me and looked straight through me. There was no emotion showing in his face. He was still stood quite calm he wasn't restrained. **[V1]**

Is he conscious?

FELTHAM PO 2: Aye.

RANDHAWA walks past STEWART and looks at him. FELTHAM PO 2 leads STEWART away into another cell, where he is locked in.

RANDHAWA enters cell 38 and stands close to ZAHID.

RANDHAWA: [*] Mr Mubarek you've been hurt and we've called the nurse. **[V1]**

As RANDHAWA stays by ZAHID she addresses the audience.

[*] As I walked into the cell I saw blood splattered on the left hand side of the cell wall and to the right of me I recall seeing a table leg which had been removed and covered in blood. I thought then that Mubarek had had a battering

with that. Mr Mubarek was underneath his bed clothes and was very well tucked in and it struck me just how neat and tidy the bed clothes had been made up with him in them.

Mr Mubarek was still alive and his breathing was laboured. He did not look distressed but looked to me as if he was more unaware of what had occurred than anything else. He lifted his hand to his ear where blood was seeping from and he was also bleeding from his nose and had blood upon his face. **[V1]**

She turns to ZAHID.

You'll be okay. The nurse is coming.

She turns to the audience again.

[*] At this stage I was in the cell with him trying to keep him calm and let him know that he was not on his own and that he had someone with him. I could also hear a gurgly noise where he was breathing. He was trying to lift himself, and he was trying to talk but was having difficulty and was incoherent and so I just tried to keep him calm before the nurse arrived. **[V1]**

She turns to ZAHID.

Lay back. Just lay back, we are trying to get the nurse to you.

FELTHAM PO 2 hands STEWART some clothes through the flap.

FELTHAM PO 2: Strip down and change into these. I need your clothes.

STEWART changes obediently.

RANDHAWA turns to the audience again.

RANDHAWA: [*] He lay back and laid down still. At that point I felt helpless as we do a basic first aid course as part of our initial training. We are not issued with disposable gloves and there are none available on the wing. We waited about fifteen minutes for the nurse, which seemed like an eternity at the time. Obviously, with the injury, when I saw the actual injury on his forehead, the length of it, it looked like a really deep cut. Whilst waiting I kept talking to him to reassure him. When Nurse Berry eventually arrived, she tended to Mubarek and she held his hand and she started asking – 'Where's the ambulance?' The ambulance had already been called anyway. She said, 'We are losing him and he is going into shock, we need to raise his feet'. **[V1]**

STEWART hands his old clothes back through to FELTHAM PO 2 who puts them into a bag.

STEWART is calmly washing his hands of the blood in his cell. FELTHAM PO 2 watches him.

FELTHAM PO 2: He's washing his hands. He shouldn't be doing that, should he? Isn't that evidence?

NICHOLSON: Stewart, back against the wall, against the wall.

RANDHAWA: [*] The paramedics arrived and put Mr Mubarek on an oxygen feed and immediately took over the situation. We were moving at a very fast pace to get Mr Mubarek into the ambulance and then off to the hospital. Throughout this time the paramedics were clearly concerned about Mr Mubarek because they were saying, 'We're losing him'. I volunteered to go with the ambulance 'cos Mubarek was still in our custody.

ZAHID is taken out of the cell on a stretcher. STEWART then lies on his bed and goes to sleep.

We arrived at Ashford hospital and Mr Mubarek was taken into the emergency operating room whilst we remained outside. The whole emergency area was in utter mayhem desperately trying to save his life. We were then informed that Mr Mubarek was to be moved to a special head injury unit at another London hospital. Mr Skidmore and myself returned to HMP Feltham. **[V1]**

STEWART takes off his shoe and scrawls on the wall with his shoe.

STEWART: [*] MANCHESTER
JUST
KILLED
ME
PADMATE
[*Swastika symbol.*] RIP
OV
M1CR **[V wall of cell]**

SCENE 5

IMTIAZ and SURESH step forward.

IMTIAZ: [*] Seeing those prison officers, you get the impression they've already sat around and decided on what they're going to say. They just turn around and say 'I don't remember…' That's what they all did, all of them 'I don't remember, I don't remember…' They closed ranks. The Inquiry actually found that there were records that were lost – like the prison cell search records on Swallow Unit when Zahid and Stewart were there. No one could explain where these records had gone. I think it still remains to be seen for us whether this has been a thorough enough Inquiry. I've still got many questions. I would like to have seen those prison officers cross-examined more closely. **[V2a]**

SURESH: [*] The Inquiry has finished now. Justice Keith has told me that he hopes to publish his report around March this year and then deliver his recommendations to the Home Secretary soon after. As for Gladiator Games – there's no direct evidence to prove that it definitely happened in this case but if you're asking me were those prison officers aware Stewart was a racist? I can't honestly see how they missed the signs. And I hope Justice Keith will at least mention it.

I think the Inquiry will be very hard on Feltham as to the circumstances which led to Zahid's death – how his murder should have been prevented. Will they implicate anyone? I don't think so. Will they hold anyone responsible? No. I think the Home Office will say Zahid died in 2000 and since then the Prison Service has improved dramatically – blah, blah, blah. I don't think that the Home Secretary will agree with the recommendations – to clean the Prison Service up from bottom up. It'll be a partial success in the sense that we know much more than we ever did. For us, Zahid is much more than someone who died in a prison cell. We will never forget how he died but we want to remember him for his aspirations and what inspired him to live and I think if there is legacy on Zahid, it should be those hard-hitting structural changes in the Prison Service – a Prison Service that is more open and accountable. If we lived in pre-9/11 days we would see the recommendations being taken up. Post 9/11, I think we live in the dark days. I really believe that. Curtailment of civil liberties, for people white or black, will be serious. **[V2a]**

IMTIAZ: [*] I used to be in computing before and after this case kicked off I found it difficult to be going into work when there was another part of my life that was dedicated to something that was really, really important to me. People say I've changed.

SURESH: He used to go clubbing.

IMTIAZ smiles.

IMTIAZ: Yeah… I just wasn't motivated to be doing what I was doing then. There was a vacancy going here and Suresh knew I was interested in working in this place and he gave me a trial period, it was part-time initially and I did it and I think he's happy with my work here so far and, erm, yeah so here I am. I'm based at the Monitoring Group now. Knowing Zahid I think even though he was going through this patch in his life we were always confident that he would come out – even if was through our efforts, we would get him through this. There was so much that he didn't tell his parents 'cos – I know that he didn't want to burden his mother with his problems or anything like that. **[V2a]**

SAJIDA enters.

SAJIDA: Zahid always used to sit around and tell jokes. He was always happy.

SURESH: [*] What we were told was that Zahid was charged with stealing six pounds' worth of razor blades and interfering with a car. The probation report makes it clear that he has a drugs problem and that he had a few other convictions for petty crimes – shop lifting – that sort of thing but – if you look at Stewart's convictions and see what happens to him and compare that with Zahid – totally different treatment of Stewart. At worst Zahid should have got a probation report, a community service and maybe a suspended sentence. **[V2a]**

SURESH exits.

SAJIDA: [*] He was very playful with his younger brothers. Always joking with them. Mostly in English. He was older. Four and a half years older. The twins were born in January 1985. **[V2c]**

IMTIAZ: [*] Apparently from the court *(Hesitates.)* …Tanzeel told me that when he was there – it was quite poignant looking back on it now – in hindsight because it was like when the Judge said 'take him down' or whatever, Zahid just turned round to his grandad and Tanzeel and said in Punjabi, *'Me jara ow'*, it was his way of saying, 'I'm going again'. He said just the expression on his face was, was, you know, er, it was like…they was never going to see him again. You know…er…

Long pause.

At the time, my nephew and my dad thought it was pretty much the way they deal with things here. And especially dad, he believes in the system. My father's point of view was look – he's going to the Young Offenders Institute – it's not a full-blown prison. They've got to have things in place to rehabilitate er... *(He laughs sadly.)* have things in place to sort them out so that they can lead a more productive life. Had we known this much *(Measures a speck with his fingers.)* of what Feltham was about, really, you know, it would have been different. It would have been different. I was in Holloway Prison a couple of weeks ago, a visit for the prison law course I'm doing and I met a prison officer there. He said to me, 'You look remarkably familiar', and so I told him my name. He put his arm around me and said: 'Look, I'm really, really sorry about what happened. I was working at Feltham at the time and I knew Zahid. He was a smashing lad.' This was just a couple of months ago – it really hit me.

He was very much loved – despite his problems. He was very much loved. **[V2a]**

IMTIAZ exits.

SAJIDA: [*] He would phone every day from the prison. Talk to the brothers, the grandparents. Ask them – what are you eating? He sent a birthday card to the brothers from the prison. He said he was worried, always worried. He just wanted to come home. He wanted to get out. He used to tell the grandfather to pray for him when he went to the Mosque on Fridays. I used to ask him how he was but he never really used to tell me. He would say he was okay but would normally ask after his brothers. I am sure he was avoiding telling me precisely how he felt or how he was coping to avoid upsetting me. **[V2c]**

AMIN enters.

AMIN: [*] We've come a long way from nothing.

We want to see things happen. Basically we wanted to know why it happened, how it happened and why they were sharing the same cell. You know if you see a guy with a tattoo, short haircut, you don't need to be a scientist to work out what he is.

We want to move on. **[V2c]**

SAJIDA: [*] But the memory will be alive all the time. He will never be forgotten. **[V2c]**

[*] When I go to bed I see him in front of me. **[V3]**

SAJIDA and AMIN step back.

ZAHID enters.

ZAHID: [*] Dear Mum and Dad,
How are you? I am fine now. How are Zahir and Shahid? They mean the world to me. Tell them not to turn out like me. I was always hanging around with the wrong people and f–king smoking drugs and that's what f–ked me up. Dad I knew I should've listened to you from the beginning.
Dad when I get out I want you to get me a job.
And how are grandad and grandma? Tell them I love them. Dad, tell mum I have not forgotten about her and tell her I love her so much. Tell my mum not to worry. I am okay.
Love
Zahid. **[V6c]**

End.

Results of the Zahid Mubarek Inquiry

In June 2006, the report of the public inquiry, chaired by Mr Justice Keith, found a 'bewildering catalogue' of both individual and systemic shortcomings at Feltham. The inquiry uncovered a 'catastrophic breakdown in communication' between prisons regarding the history of Robert Stewart and the final report named nineteen staff who were judged to have been at fault.

The inquiry report made 88 recommendations covering risk assessment of mentally ill prisoners, sharing cells, information-sharing, prison staff training, and the disclosure of psychiatric reports by courts to prisons.

It also asked the Home Office to consider introducing the concept of 'institutional religious intolerance'.

'Treating prisoners with decency may not be a vote-winner,' concluded Mr Justice Keith.

'Societies are judged by the way they treat their prisoners, and if more resources are needed to ensure that our prisons are truly representative of the civilised society which we aspire to be, nothing less will do.'

WHITE BOY

Introduction

I asked Tanika to write a relevant current play for the National Youth Theatre, focusing on what it means to be young and British today. After our initial meeting what struck me was just how profound and current Tanika's idea of *White Boy* could potentially be. Her knowledge of adolescent antics and their changing language amidst a multi-cultural urban environment was impressive. The fact that Tanika knew it was now *uncool* to be white in inner-city schools was in one way no surprise, but in another way I knew theatrically the play would be a revelation and an important piece of contemporary drama. This conflict of identity, set against the ever-increasing tragedy of knife crime by young people, most certainly hit the mark and made our packed audiences of all ages see a moving story that will remain with them all for a long time to come.

Four years on from its original commission, *White Boy* continues to hit home with more young casualties to knife crime and an ever-present tribalism still creating conflicts of identity amongst British youth. We can still learn from Tanika's play and I am pleased to see there is still a desire to read it and perform it.

Paul Roseby
Artistic Director of NYT
www.nyt.org.uk

Characters

RICKY

17-year-old white youth. Speaks with Caribbean/street accent. Footballer.

VICTOR

17-year-old black (Afro-Caribbean) youth. Ricky's best friend and school heart-throb. Gifted footballer.

ZARA

15-year-old young black woman.

SHAZ

15-year-old Asian/Hijab-wearing young woman. (Real name: Shazia.)

KABIR

15-year-old Asian youth. Shaz's boyfriend.

SORTED

15-year-old Sudanese youth. Has a strong accent and a stammer. Wheeler-dealer.

FLIPS

16-year-old white youth. Rough. School bully.

Other characters include a CHORUS of school kids who make up the back-drop to some of the scenes

White Boy was first performed on 10 August 2007 at Soho Theatre, in a National Youth Theatre production, with the following cast:

RICKY, Luke Norris

VICTOR, Obi Iwumene

ZARA, Venetia Campbell

SHAZ, Peyvand Sadeghian

KABIR, Haseeb Malik

SORTED, Timi Fadipe

FLIPS, Daniel Ings

CHORUS, Parissa Barghchi, Elliot Burnett, Stuart Conlan, Frances Jackson, Sam McAvoy, Nancy Wallinger

Director Juliet Knight

Designer Lotte Collett

Lighting David W Kidd

The production was revived on 16 January 2008, again at Soho Theatre, with the following changes to the cast:

KABIR, Amiar Kamal

FLIPS, Ciaran Owens

CHORUS, Sita Thomas, Daniel Ward, Pedram Modarres, Stuart Conlan, Frances Jackson, Nancy Wallinger, James Cooke, Isaac Stanmore

SCENE 1

We are outside the school gates. The gates themselves are high, wire mesh fence – almost prison-like but new and still shiny. The overall impression is one of a school where security is important. There is a small bench to one side (covered in graffiti) with a tiny patch of bald grass in front of it. The patch of earth is covered in litter.

As the scene opens, school kids enter from all parts of the auditorium, some in hoodies, walking resolutely towards the wire mesh. Soon, there is a fight in progress and everyone seems to be watching. Although we can't exactly see who is fighting, we can gauge from the reaction of the kids around, that this is a vicious one. Kids are shouting:

YOUTH 1: Go on Mohammed! Gwan!

Whilst others are chanting:

YOUTHS: FLIPS, FLIPS, FLIPS…

Suddenly we hear the sound of a boy screaming in pain. The crowd parts and a youth – MOHAMMED – is crouched on the floor, face bloodied and nursing an arm in obvious pain. A bigger youth, FLIPS stands over him, menacing but triumphant. He grins as a whistle/ school bell sounds and then everyone scatters.

SCENE 2

We hear the sound of school kids leaving school for the day.

SHAZ and KABIR (fifteen-year-old Asian kids) are sitting on the bench snogging away furiously. They are dressed in school uniform (she is in hijab and wears long trousers under her skirt).

RICKY, a white seventeen-year-old youth enters expertly dribbling a football and kicking it up against the fence. It crashes and shakes the wire mesh.

KABIR sticks up his fist, mid-snog. RICKY touches fists with KABIR but KABIR never stops kissing.

ZARA enters, also in uniform, dumps her bag unceremoniously on the floor, slumps on the bench and scowls at SHAZ and KABIR next to her.

RICKY: Dunno how they breathe.

ZARA: *(Shouts at the couple.)* You're gonna suffocate!

RICKY: Nice way to die.

ZARA: *(Laughs.)* Drowned in someone else's spit?

RICKY: Rank.

RICKY continues to dribble the ball around.

SORTED enters. He is a fifteen-year-old Sudanese youth, gawky and awkward. He is also dressed in school uniform, which is at least two sizes too big for him. He tries to tackle the ball off RICKY but is useless and RICKY runs rings around him. Eventually he gives up and approaches ZARA. He looks shifty as he looks about him. He has a bad stammer.

SORTED: *(Sudanese accent.)* W-Wotcha Zara.

ZARA: Yeah – alright.

SORTED: You see the f-f-f…

RICKY: Fight?

SORTED: At school today?

RICKY: Yeah. Stupid fuckers.

SORTED: Moha-Moha-Moha-

RICKY: Mohammed's in hospital. I know. Hope he dies then we can all live in peace.

SORTED: He won't die.

ZARA: Nah. He'll come back with reinforcements and mash up the rest of them. What the fuck was it all about anyway?

SORTED: Moha-Moha-Moha-

RICKY: Mohammed. You gotta learn to say that word Sorted. How d'you cope when you're in Mosque?

SORTED: *(Shrugs.)* His girlfriend gave Flips a b-b-b-b-b-b-low… a shine.

RICKY looks pointedly at ZARA.

ZARA: Nasty.
Must be sick in the head or maybe she owed him money. Euch.

SORTED looks around him shiftily, on the lookout.

ZARA gets out her make-up bag and starts to apply some lippy.

SORTED looks at his watch.

SORTED: V-Victor's late.
Maybe he'll a-a-ask you out today?

ZARA ignores SORTED and continues to put make-up on.

What's he g-g-got…?

ZARA: That you haven't?
Where do I start?

SORTED: *(Smiles.)* J-just need to t-try me out. You'll see.

SORTED tries to snuggle up to ZARA but she pushes him off.

ZARA: I can see well clear from here – fuck face.

SORTED: I'll take you to the c-c-c-candy shop.

ZARA: Sorted. Move from me. One thing you ain't and that's Fifty Cent.

SHAZ: More like Fifty Pence man.

SORTED looks hurt and moves away. He looks at RICKY.

RICKY: Nice try bro.

ZARA relents.

ZARA: Sorted man. You're more like my little brother. I can't go out with you. Wouldn't be right would it?

SHAZ and KABIR finally pull apart.

KABIR: Yeah – what's wrong with you sicko?

SORTED surreptitiously hands KABIR a small bag of grass. KABIR sniffs the contents of the bag and then hands over a tenner, before stashing the bag in his shoe.

SORTED: If you see Flips. Will you s-s-s-

RICKY: You ain't hiding from him again are you? Tell me you ain't?

SORTED starts to sift through ZARA's make-up bag.

ZARA: Oy nosy! That's private property.

SORTED continues to rifle through ZARA's bag.

RICKY: I dunno why you got mixed up with that fucking family in the first place. Shouldn't have nuthin' to do with them. Sorted – you listenin' bredda?

SORTED: Yeah.

RICKY: Pretends he's your kin and then he turns on you – like a snake.

SORTED: Only one who g-gave me the time of day.

RICKY: Give you the time of day 'cos he know you is a soft touch.

ZARA: Tell him how it is. Maybe he'll listen.

RICKY: All this dealin' you do for him. It ain't right. You could get into some serious trouble. Gotta have some self respec' – know what I mean?

ZARA: If you had parents here – they'd tell you.

SORTED: *(Lashes out.)* But my parents aren't here are they?

ZARA: Keep your hair on.

SORTED: I gotta l-l-look out for myself.

ZARA backs off. SORTED calms down.

What's this?

SORTED holds up a contraption.

ZARA: Eye lash curlers.

SORTED: H-h-how…?

ZARA: How they work? Look. …

ZARA places the eye lash curlers carefully on SORTED's eye lashes.

Hold it for a few seconds and then…

ZARA takes the eye lash curlers away.

Look at that!

ZARA shows SORTED his reflection in her hand mirror.

SORTED: C-c-c-curly. It works!

RICKY laughs at SORTED.

KABIR: Oy Sorted – you wanna put some make-up on?

SHAZ giggles.

SHAZ: You'd make a very pretty girl.

ZARA: Leave him alone.

KABIR: Zara got the hots for Sorted?

ZARA: You're so predictable Kabir.

KABIR: You're just jealous. Need to get yourself a proper boyfriend Zara.

SHAZ: *(To KABIR.)* Shut up.

KABIR: What?

RICKY: You two should be careful. One day, you're gonna get caught red handed. Someone's gonna see you, grass on you and that's it Shaz. One-way ticket to Malaysia – married off to a man with a tash and a huge belly.

SHAZ: Leave it out.

ZARA: Lipsin' is definitely against your religion.

KABIR: Where's it say that?

ZARA: Dunno, but I bet it does.

RICKY: Look at you, all hijab and trousers – bit fucking hypocritical innit?

SHAZ: What the fuck would you know – white boy?

RICKY: I know what I'm talking about.

SHAZ: It ain't against our religion to love.

KABIR: Yeah man.

SORTED pulls out something else from ZARA's bag. It is a kitchen knife. He lays it on his lap and stares at it in awe.

SORTED: C-o-o-l.

RICKY does a double take.

ZARA: For fuck's sake Sorted…

ZARA quickly scoops the knife up and sticks it back in her bag.

RICKY: Zara?!

ZARA: Protection innit.

RICKY: Shouldn't be wandering 'round with a blade… What you gonna do with it?

KABIR: Well out of order.

ZARA: There's this girl in my year…doin' my head in…keeps threatening me and stuff. Thought, if I carried this…

RICKY: Get rid of it.

ZARA: Everyone does it.

RICKY: That make it right?

KABIR: He's got a point.

SHAZ opens her little dinky handbag and shows the boys a knife in her bag too.

SORTED: Cool.

KABIR look at SHAZ in horror. RICKY sucks his teeth.

RICKY: You're all fucking mad. Shouldn't be messin' round with blades. You get caught or worse…

SORTED suddenly scoots.

VICTOR, a black seventeen-year-old youth, carrying his school bag saunters out of the gates, texting on his phone. He stops and touches fists with RICKY. SHAZ snaps shut her bag. Everyone else tries to cover up talk about knives.

VICTOR: Yo Ricky what's going on. Sorted on the run again?

RICKY: Probably thought you were Flips.

VICTOR takes the football from RICKY and plays keepie uppie with it. He virtually ignores ZARA who is desperately trying to gain his attention by walking seductively up and down.

VICTOR: You going training?

RICKY: Yeah.

VICTOR: Reckon you'll make it to the squad for Saturday?

RICKY: Hope so. Don't fancy another game on the bench. Couldn't face my dad. Gives me so much grief when I don't play.

ZARA: Victor! Hi!

VICTOR suddenly sees ZARA.

VICTOR: *(Cool.)* Hi.

He turns and nods at KABIR and SHAZ.

ZARA: You see the fight today?

VICTOR: Nah. I keep away from that kind of shit.

ZARA: How've you been Victor?

VICTOR: Alright.

ZARA: Me too – Revising – you know.
End of term exams…mocks…

VICTOR: I feel for ya… GCSEs…nightmare. Parents and teachers all go into overdrive.

ZARA: Yeah?

VICTOR: Keep saying crap like 'No pressure but these are the most important exams of your life'.

ZARA: Shit.

VICTOR: Get through 'em – somehow – and then they start doin' it all over again about A-levels. 'No pressure but these are the most important exams of your life'.

ZARA laughs a little too long.

ZARA: Don't think I'll get far as A-levels.

VICTOR: Gotta do A-levels.

ZARA: Yeah?

VICTOR: Otherwise – can't get a proper job. Else how you ever gonna get out of this dump?

ZARA: Right…that's really good advice Victor. Thanks. Name's Zara by the way.

VICTOR: Yeah – you're Ayesha's little sister?

ZARA: Only eighteen months younger than her.

VICTOR: Right.

VICTOR looks a bit uncomfortable as ZARA just grins and stares at him like an idiot.

See ya.

He turns to RICKY.

You comin'?

RICKY: Catch up. Waitin' for me little sis. Y'know what dad's like about me walking her home. She's so fucking slow.

VICTOR: Laters.

VICTOR exits.

ZARA: *(Calls out.)* We're all coming to see the match on Saturday…cheer you on!

VICTOR: *(Calls back.)* Cool.

ZARA is left standing staring after the spot VICTOR has left – doe-eyed.

SHAZ: Look at her.

KABIR: She's lost it – big time.

RICKY does a mincing walk, flutters his eyelashes and grins stupidly. He mimics ZARA.

RICKY: 'Right…that's really good advice Victor. Thanks.'

RICKY and KABIR fall about laughing.

ZARA: *(Proud.)* Vic's goin' places – especially now he's been picked for the Spurs youth team.

KABIR: Won't rub off on you Zara. You're still one of us.

ZARA: Shut up. I'll get Victor. You'll see.

RICKY: Gotta climb over a whole heap of other birds to get to him though.

And one thing's for sure. He won't like a bird who carries ammo round with her.

RICKY peers into the school playground through the wire mesh.

There she is… *(Shouts.)* Oy! Kiera! Move your fucking arse! Gotta get to training!

SCENE 3

A football match.

Kids of all different shapes, sizes, creed and colour clamber over the fence, hang off the sides, use the CCTV camera as a camera, shout and cheer and generally support the school team in a football match. The girls (especially ZARA and SHAZ) are cheering for VICTOR and RICKY and doing a little rap.

SORTED: P-pass it…k-knock it in.

ALL: OOOO!

KABIR: Unlucky!

CHORUS 1: Set it up Rick!

CHORUS 2: Switch it – SWITCH IT!

CHORUS 1: Nice pass!

CHORUS 3: Go round him.

CHORUS 4: Oh my God he is so fit!

CHORUS 5: Man on!

CHORUS 6: Fuckin' hit him, don't dance around him!

ZARA/SHAZ: 'Vic, Vic, he's off the rick,
Don't you know he's pretty slick'

ALL: OOOH!

SORTED: C'mon Ref!

CHORSU 1: Almost broke his legs.

CHORUS 2: That's ridiculous!

CHORUS 5: 'The referee's a wanker!'

ALL: 'The referee's a wanker!'

SORTED: Free kick.

CHORUS 2: Who's goin' to take it?

CHORUS 4: Let Victor take it.

ZARA: *(Mimicking.)* 'Let Victor take it!' Give it to Vic.

ALL: *(Clapping.)* OOOO!

ALL: AWWWW!

SORTED: Unlucky s-son!

CHORUS 6: Crap man!

ZARA: Never mind, 5 minutes left.

CHORUS 3: Keep at it.

CHORUS 1: Next time c'mon!

SORTED: Down the line.

CHORUS 1: First time!

CHORUS 2: Use your head!

CHORUS 6: Lay it back!

ZARA: Victor! Victor!

The spectators erupt into cheering and OTT happiness generally as VICTOR scores a goal.

SCENE 4

VICTOR and RICKY are sat on the bench. It is later in the day. Darkness is falling and it is quiet. They have their football kit bags by their feet and they are both texting on the mobiles.

VICTOR: So what's happening tonight?

RICKY: Dunno. Depends.

VICTOR: On what?

RICKY: On what you're doing.

VICTOR: Eh?

RICKY: 'Cos whatever you're doin' I'm doin' too.

Three young GIRLS out of school uniform walk past and smile at the boys.

GIRL 1: Alright Victor?

GIRL 2: Alright.

VICTOR: Yeah what's going on?

The girls hover.

GIRL 3: Great game.

GIRL 1: You were good too Ricky.

VICTOR: Cheers babe.

GIRL 2: That second goal was wicked.

GIRL 3: Yeah wicked.

RICKY nods.

The GIRLS move on, not before showering VICTOR with a few more smouldering glances.

VICTOR: Sweet kids.

RICKY: Sweet? S'not how I would describe 'em.

VICTOR: Little one's always waving at me.

RICKY: Little one'd go down on you faster than you could say 'Rooney'.

VICTOR: You're a sick boy.

RICKY: Just tellin' you how it is. You is an innocent in dis jungle of life. Tink everyone is coolio. But dem is bad.

VICTOR: *(Laughs.)* You done half chat some shit Ricky. None of the girls round here do much for me.

RICKY: What're you holdin' out for?

VICTOR: I dunno – someone special.

RICKY: Like who?

VICTOR: Like Tricia.

RICKY: Tricia Goddard?

VICTOR: Knows how to control herself…tells people how it is and can control situations…

RICKY: She's a fossil.

VICTOR: Great body though. Always had a thing for the older woman.

RICKY looks at VICTOR as if he's mad.

Mind you, Beyoncé's kinda special. Like to keep my options open.

RICKY does the Beyoncé dance (jumping up and down and wiggling his backside very fast).

RICKY: I know what you're talking about.

VICTOR stands, pulls up his T-shirt and does a quick belly dance. They dance around together like this for a while.

VICTOR: You can have Beyoncé, I'll have Shakira.

They laugh and slap palms.

Thing is, when I find the right lady, I'm gonna be true.

RICKY: No texting buff on the sly?

VICTOR: No, cuz. Gotta reward loyalty with loyalty. Otherwise it don't work.

RICKY: I guess.

VICTOR: Your dad cool with you now?

RICKY: Yeah bro. Said I play good. Give me all dis chat about my passing, as if he know…

They both laugh.

VICTOR: My dad said back in the day your old man was the best.

RICKY: A hundred fucking years ago. Thinks you're the next Aaron Lennon.

VICTOR: Always liked your dad.

RICKY: Look at this…

VICTOR leans over and reads the text on RICKY's phone.

VICTOR: Little sis?

RICKY: Tel VIC – OMG – he wikid.

VICTOR and RICKY both mimic a young girl saying:

'Oh my God! He's wicked!'

RICKY: Little sisters are supposed to worship their big bros ain't it? All Kiera does is harp on 'bout you. Makes me well vex.

VICTOR: That pretty girl – Year 11 – the one doing her GCSEs? Black girl – always hanging around here?

RICKY: Zara.

VICTOR: She's…

RICKY: Sweet…

VICTOR: Pretty…

RICKY: Her arse is mint.

VICTOR: Eyes you could drown happily in.

RICKY: Big jugs.

VICTOR: Chill cuz. You're gettin' a hard-on just sittin' thinking 'bout her.

RICKY: If I had a hard on, you'd know, poke your eye out. She fancies you.

VICTOR: She fancies *you.*

RICKY: No she doesn't.

VICTOR: She does.

RICKY: Clueless you are.

VICTOR: I ain't. She *thinks* she fancies me but actually it's you she really wants.

RICKY looks at VICTOR amazed.

RICKY: Listen Bredda. I don't mind having your cast-offs. No matta to me. But what she want is some black, not white.

VICTOR: You white?

RICKY: More black than you'll ever be.

VICTOR: Mum says you're almost Jamaican.

RICKY: Must've been in me past life 'cos I could eat your mum's curry goat from mornin' 'til night.

VICTOR: I noticed. When she knows you're comin' round, we have to slaughter an extra goat.

RICKY: Ally?!

They both laugh, do an elaborate handshake and slap palms.

Seriously tho bro. You is lucky.

VICTOR: Where's this all come from?

RICKY: Look around you man – so many kids in our class got history, countries, stories and different languages. Baxter says we got twenty-three different languages spoken in our year.

VICTOR: So?

RICKY: So, mek me feel ...dunno...I only speak English.

VICTOR: What about French?

RICKY: What? I don't speak no frog.

VICTOR: French kissing?

VICTOR cracks up.

RICKY: Fuck off. I is being serious here.

VICTOR: Don't go all heavy on me Ricky. You got history. Your dad, football, this place.

RICKY: *This place*! That's it! Grandparents came from round here. Never been anywhere else. Not even got any European blood in me.

VICTOR: What about your uncle? Where's he from? He's got a different kinda face.

RICKY: Him just retarded.

VICTOR: Seen.

RICKY: Mi yard is mi yard. Know what I mean? But sometimes, it's all so fucking dull. Ain't cool to be white nomore. Read somewhere that in about two hundred years, the average human being will be coffee coloured and six foot six.

VICTOR: Then you'll be a unique specimen. Be well cool.

RICKY: And well dead.

VICTOR leans back and looks around him.

VICTOR: Look at us. Ain't even a school day. Saturday. We sittin' outside this dump. Why?

RICKY: Dunno man.

VICTOR: Let's go and check out the action.

RICKY: I'm not going down the rec. That place is full of losers.

VICTOR: Not the rec. Fancy a bit of bowling.

RICKY: Yeah alright. You got any dosh?

VICTOR: Nah.

RICKY reaches into his pocket and fetches out some coins. VICTOR examines the amount.

One pound twenty ain't gonna get us more than a bag of chips.

RICKY picks up his kit bag and gets up.

Where we going?

RICKY: Gotta service your big sis. Get paid for it.

VICTOR shakes his head and laughs.

Wot? I'm keepin' your family happy…

VICTOR stays put.

Bet we could sting your big sis for some dosh. I know she got a soft spot for me. Way she smile dat smile at me.

VICTOR: Dream on.

RICKY: I tell her she lose weight, then she'll cough up.

They laugh as they exit.

SCENE 5

SHAZ, KABIR, SORTED and ZARA are on litter duty. They are picking up the rubbish strewn around the bench with sticks and are putting them into a rubbish bag. They do so with immense reluctance and ZARA is wearing a par of gloves so she doesn't have to touch any of the rubbish directly. Only SORTED is doing the job with any energy and the others are letting him do the dirty work.

KABIR: Go on Sorted – pick that thing up…you missed a bit there.

ZARA: Don't boss him around!

KABIR: He seems quite keen.

SORTED: I used to-to-to-to do this j-j-j-job.

SHAZ: What – like collecting rubbish?

SORTED: Me and my friends…all of us…l-l-living in-in the camp.

All three of the gang stare at SORTED slightly amazed.

ZARA: What camp?

SORTED: Refugee camp. For one year. After my f-family… after the s-s-soldiers…after…

SORTED trails off. The others are all silent.

Red Cross l-l-l-ook after me. Th-then I c-ccome here.

KABIR: What about the other kids? Your mates? What happened to them?

SORTED shrugs. Suddenly SORTED holds up a used Johnny with the end of his stick and dangles it under ZARA's nose.

ZARA: Eeeeweee – Sorted that's nasty man!

ZARA screams and runs away. SORTED laughs like a kid.

SHAZ: Shit! Stop it Sorted!

KABIR: Who's been shagging out here?

SHAZ: Some desperate twat.

ZARA: It's disgusting. I refuse to do this.

ZARA takes off her gloves and sits down on the bench.

They're supposed to be giving us an education, not training us in…in…picking up filthy shit like that.

KABIR: Suppose they reckon we got no hope 'cept in refuse clearance.

SHAZ: Speak for yourself.

SORTED bolts suddenly.

KABIR: That boy's so jumpy!

FLIPS: *(Off.)* He's over there, fuckin' come here.

FLIPS enters. He is a large sixteen-year-old white youth. He looks rough and nasty.

ZARA: Shit, that's all I need.

FLIPS is obviously looking for SORTED and is about to chase after him when he sees ZARA. He smiles at her. She does not return the smile. He approaches ZARA and leans one foot on the bench next to her.

FLIPS: Zara.

ZARA nods at him. KABIR tries to hide his fear.

You lot draw the short straw again? Litter duty?

ZARA: Yeah – worse luck…

FLIPS: You should be surrounded by flowers Zara, not rubbish.

SHAZ and KABIR exchange a frightened but amused look.

Where's your little boyfriend gone?

ZARA: Which one? I got so many.

FLIPS: The one that was just here a minute ago. Sorted.

ZARA: Dunno. Haven't seen 'im all day.

FLIPS: Yeah – right. Very touching the way you're always protecting him. Little cunt's been fleecing me – owes me big time.

FLIPS looks at KABIR.

KABIR: *(Frightened.)* Probably back in his hostel.

FLIPS: Won't let me in there. Social worker stands guard at the door.

ZARA looks down at FLIPS's foot next to her.

ZARA: D'you mind?

FLIPS: Oh ta.

FLIPS takes this as an invitation to sit next to her on the bench. He stretches out and puts one arm behind ZARA. She shifts uncomfortably.

FLIPS gives SHAZ and KABIR a hard stare. They back away a little and continue picking up rubbish.

This is nice – eh? Just you and me.

ZARA sniffs the air.

ZARA: Bit heavy duty on the aftershave Flips. What is it? Essence of BO?

FLIPS: Kouros actually. Gotta get rid of the smell of onions. Fuckin' hate onions. Make me sick.

ZARA looks confused.

It's me dad – you know – chef at the greasy café on the High Street. Chef my arse. Reckon he just chops onions, fries bacon all day and then smears it over his body. Fucking loser.

ZARA: You put Mohammed in hospital.

FLIPS: He went for me – had to defend myself.

ZARA: Hope you're proud of yourself.

FLIPS: That's what happens when anyone crosses me and my brother. *(He raises his fist in the air.)* We got a code of honour and he broke it.

ZARA: *(Flat.)* Code.

FLIPS: When he swore his oath of his allegiance to us – he gave his word never to fight a fellow bredren.

ZARA: And you never break your word?

FLIPS: Never. Never hit a woman. Never fight amongst ourselves.

Mind you there's a vacancy now – In the bird department.

ZARA: You opening a pet shop or something?

FLIPS: I'm a man and I need a lady.

FLIPS looks at ZARA meaningfully.

ZARA: What happened to Mohammed's girl? Thought you and her were an item now?

FLIPS: She's just a dirty slapper.

ZARA: Must be if she's willing to give you a shine.

FLIPS smiles indulgently.

FLIPS: Babe – like razor. You could rip a man's heart out with that chat.

He moves closer to ZARA. The smell of aftershave is overpowering.

I can tell by the way you look at me…you're sweet on me. Eh? I'm right – ally?

ZARA: *(Looks FLIPS straight in the eye.)* Move from me.

FLIPS is about to take offence but changes tack. Instead, he laughs.

FLIPS: I love the way you tease me.

ZARA: I ain't teasing Flips.

FLIPS: No use fighting me babe. When I put my mind to something, I always see it through – one way or the other.

ZARA: My Mum and Dad wouldn't approve.

FLIPS: Why? Is it 'cos I is white?

ZARA looks away.

I'll take you out somewhere nice.

ZARA: Nice? What? Round here?

FLIPS: I got money – I could take you up town if you fancy. Go on. You know you want to.

ZARA: Actually… I don't.

FLIPS: I won't take 'no' for an answer.

ZARA: What part of 'no' don't you understand? – And your breath stinks.

SHAZ and KABIR look worried.

FLIPS: You was *hot*. Now you is *not*.

ZARA holds her own and refuses to look afraid.

I understand. Playing hard to get – eh? Treat 'em mean and all that. I can wait. Makes the chase more excitin' – know what I mean?

No worries.

FLIPS gets up and stands over ZARA. He drops the charm.

Do me a favour will ya? *(Menacing.)* Tell that little shit – Sorted that when I catch up with him, either he has the money or he's dead. Get it?

ZARA says nothing.

Got it?

ZARA: Got it.

FLIPS: Good.

FLIPS gets up and walks away. He turns and blows a kiss at ZARA. She looks sick.

SHAZ: You shouldn't talk to him like that Zara.

ZARA: I ain't scared of 'im.

KABIR: You should be.

SCENE 6

We are now behind the school fence so that we are in the playground. (The fence is behind the kids.) There are groups of kids playing, hanging out, doing various playground activities. It should resemble something of a war zone with lots of different power/gender games taking place. Some kids are rapping/dancing, beat boxing/spitting whilst the younger ones are simply playing ball games. In the foreground, VICTOR and RICKY are stretching and doing some exercises. A couple of smaller kids are copying them.

ZARA: Eh Ricky.

VICTOR: Why don't you just ask her out?

RICKY: Who?

VICTOR: As if…

RICKY: Nah man.

VICTOR: What's the worst that can happen? She says 'no'?

RICKY: Gotta concentrate on my game. Woman just bring you down.

VICTOR: Jesus Ricky.

RICKY: What?

VICTOR: Never knew you were such a coward.

RICKY: Fuck off.

VICTOR: If you don't ask her out, I'll have to do it for you.

We cut across to ZARA who is with SHAZ.

ZARA checks her text messages on her phone.

ZARA: Look.

SHAZ: Flips?

ZARA: Won't leave me alone. Always hanging around. Saw him standing on the other side of the street this mornin'. Blowin' me kisses.

SHAZ: That's a bit full on.

ZARA: Sexual harassment – that's what it is.

SHAZ: Could try reportin' him to Student Services.

ZARA: Like that's gonna work.

SHAZ: True. Best thing is to send your sister round. Apparently Flips' old man's a real wimp.

ZARA: What you on? I'm not gettin' Ayesha involved! She'd mash him up and then she'd end up in Juvey.

SHAZ: Might have to.

Seriously though best avoid him though.

ZARA: Sod's law innit? The one guy I want to sit up and take notice barely knows I'm alive.

ZARA looks across at VICTOR.

SHAZ: You should ask him out. No point hanging around waitin' for him to ask you. Boys are crap like that.

ZARA: I thought about it but – I dunno.

SHAZ: You got nuthin' to lose.

ZARA: Apart from my dignity.

SHAZ pulls a face.

What if he laughs in my face? What if he says 'No'?

SHAZ: Then you put it down to experience and move on.

ZARA: I don't wanna move on. I want Victor.

SORTED dashes through the playground, in fear of his life. He pushes past SHAZ and ZARA, knocks over a few kids who all shout at him.

He falls down and turns to look back in fear. FLIPS pounds across the playground in hot pursuit.

FLIPS: Come here you little shit!

SORTED clambers up onto the fence and vaults over the top like an expert army commando. FLIPS tries to follow but is pulled down by RICKY and VICTOR.

VICTOR: Leave the kid alone!

FLIPS: Take your filthy hands off me!

RICKY: Coolio – Flips. This no place to be tekin' out your anger.

VICTOR: Yeah chill cuz.

FLIPS stands up and squares up to RICKY.

FLIPS: He owes me.

RICKY: So what you gonna do about it?

FLIPS takes a swing to hit RICKY but VICTOR blocks him and punches FLIPS in the face. VICTOR looks a bit surprised and the playground kids cheer.

FLIPS reels from the punch and gets right back up again. He squares up to VICTOR.

FLIPS: None of your business, interfering. It's between me and Sorted. Who the fuck d'you think you are?

VICTOR stands his ground. RICKY hovers close by, circling FLIPS, protecting his friend.

VICTOR: I know who I am. But what are you? Big kid picking on a little squirt like Sorted? What's that about?

RICKY: Flips man, taking it all a bit too serious. Getting angst over nuthin'.

FLIPS: He owes me money!

VICTOR: Beating him up ain't gonna get you any dosh.

FLIPS: No one crosses me.

VICTOR and RICKY laugh at FLIPS.

RICKY: Him tink him so hard.

FLIPS: And what the fuck is it with you White Boy? Talk like one of them.

RICKY: Hush your mouth.

FLIPS: Forget where you come from? Forget who you are? Think you're some kind of yardie? D'you talk like that at home?

RICKY: I is what I is.

FLIPS laughs.

FLIPS: Fucking freak.

RICKY: User.

FLIPS looks around him and realises that everyone is watching him.

FLIPS: You can tell that little refugee vermin, that when I find him, and I *will* find him, I'm gonna stab him. I'm gonna fuck him up.

FLIPS skulks away.

RICKY: Nice one bro.

VICTOR: Someone's gotta protect you.

RICKY and VICTOR do their elaborate handshake and laugh but they are obviously shaken.

SCENE 7

We are away from the school gates now. SORTED is hiding in a small dark room. Perhaps it is just him in spotlight surrounded by darkness. He looks terrified and vulnerable. There is a knock on his door.

ZARA: Sorted? Sorted? I know you're in there.

SORTED: Please… Zara… I am sleeping.

ZARA: Ain't you comin' to school?

SORTED: Not feeling well.

ZARA: 'least unlock the door so I can see you're okay.

SORTED: No! I am not d-d-d-d-ecent.

ZARA: Sorted! It's me! Zara!

SORTED relents, gets up and opens the door. ZARA enters dressed in school uniform. SORTED is jumpy though and he locks the door again behind ZARA. She looks around the room.

Bit dark in here.

SORTED pulls back a curtain to let a chink of light in. ZARA peers at SORTED.

Don't look too good to me.

SORTED: Flips…he's looking for me.

ZARA: Some heavy shit going down at the school. Kids being searched, cameras going up…

SORTED looks silently worried.

You'll be safe in school.

SORTED: I lay low for a few days.

ZARA: How d'you swing it with your social worker? Thought you couldn't get anything past him.

SORTED: He is on holiday.

ZARA: Oh…listen. I need to ditch this. Can I hide it here for today? I'll pick it up later.

ZARA produces the knife from her bag.

SORTED: Okay.

ZARA puts the knife on the side somewhere.

ZARA: You sure you're okay? Don't like leaving you like this.

SORTED: I'll be f-fine.

ZARA looks doubtful.

ZARA: Me and Shaz can walk you in.

SORTED: No. Maybe tomorrow… I'll call you.

ZARA gives SORTED a brief hug and turns to leave. SORTED unlocks the door and lets her go. He locks the door again behind her.

SORTED stares at the knife.

We hear the sound of guns and warfare, women screaming and children crying. It's as if he is reliving the memory of the war in his hometown. The sound of guns reaches a crescendo as SORTED huddles up into a foetal position and buries his head in his chest.

SCENE 8

We are back outside the school gates again and it is the start of the day. A workman is installing a CCTV camera high up on the wire mesh fence whilst a security guard is checking students' bags before they go in to school.

We see a small dribble of kids going in. SHAZ and KABIR are furiously scribbling away doing their homework on the bench.

SHAZ: So what is the difference between the fucking suffragettes and the suffragists?

KABIR: They're spelt different.
Can't believe old Baxter's making us do a
speech.

SHAZ: I ain't doin' it in all that oldee woldee lingo.

KABIR: Feel like a right twat.
Mind you, if it weren't for them, you lot wouldn't have the vote.

SHAZ: Eh?

KABIR: Y'know – birds.

SHAZ: We don't have the vote anyway – not for two fucking years. And it make's no difference even if we did. Nuthin's gonna change round here.

KABIR: You know school's making us pay for them exercise books now?
Said budget for books had run out.

SHAZ: Fucking typical.

ZARA enters.

ZARA: Lost my English coursework on the bus.

SHAZ: Clever girl.

KABIR: Creepio'll hang you out to dry.

ZARA: Tell me about it. Give us one of them lectures about how people like us are bringing down the country.

SHAZ: 'The youth today.'

ZARA: Poor diet, drinkin' an' smokin' too much, having too much sex, teenage pregnancies…

KABIR: MTV, drugs, family breakdown.

SHAZ: No respect for our elders, our education.

ZARA: Celebrity gossip, live for today, selfish…

KABIR: Bottom of the pile.

SHAZ: Self-control. That's the answer.

ZARA: Sitting down to dinner as a family every night eating a plate of fresh vegetables.

Beat.

SHAZ: My dad was a punk rocker. You know, noisy music. Lots of shouting. Got pictures of him with a safety pin stuck through his nose.

They all laugh and then turn to look at the new CCTV camera.

SHAZ: Like fuckin' Big Bruvva.

KABIR: Hey, Zara… You got rid of your blade?

ZARA: Yeah.

RICKY and VICTOR approach together. RICKY hovers around ZARA whilst VICTOR holds back a bit.

RICKY: Any sign of Sorted over the weekend?

ZARA: Hidin' in his hostel.

SHAZ: Flips' been excluded.

VICTOR looks interested and comes closer.

VICTOR: For real?

SHAZ: Teacher's heard him mouthing on. Social worker got called in.

VICTOR: Flips got a social worker too?

SHAZ: Yeah.

RICKY: Everyone's got one in this school. It's like having a personal trainer.

RICKY and VICTOR laugh.

ZARA: Seriously though you two. Be careful.
Something might kick off.

RICKY: You worried 'bout me babes?

VICTOR: Told you she had a thing for you.

VICTOR and RICKY slap palms and walk back into school together.

SHAZ and ZARA exchange a look.

ZARA: How much more obvious can a girl be?

SHAZ: Short of getting your tits out. Might have to settle for second best.

ZARA looks distraught.

ZARA: What I feel for Victor's real – ally? True love.
The way he looks at you with that shy smile, way he walks, head down, deep in thought, way he throws back his head and laughs…and he looks so strong, like a real man…

SHAZ snaps shut her book.

SHAZ: Zara, we're going to have to blag our speeches.
Were the Suffragettes the lot who burnt their bras?

KABIR: Did they have bras in them days?

SHAZ and ZARA laugh. VICTOR comes back out again. He hovers nervously, looking at ZARA. SHAZ and KABIR take the hint and walk into school. SHAZ turns and winks at ZARA who looks a bit flustered.

VICTOR: Alright?

ZARA: Be late for class.

VICTOR: Oh…right…

ZARA: You wanted to say something?

VICTOR shuffles from one foot to the other.

VICTOR: Erm…yeah…how's it going?

ZARA: What?

VICTOR: Y'know – life – stuff…

ZARA laughs.

You erm – you – erm…like you seein' anyone at the moment?

ZARA: No.

VICTOR: Good. It's just…what d'you think of my mate Ricky?

ZARA: Oh.

VICTOR: He's sweet on you.

ZARA: Why?

VICTOR: 'Cos you're…you're…y'know…nice…

ZARA: *Nice?*

VICTOR: Pretty…clever…y'know…erm…buff.

ZARA: This Ricky speaking…or you?

VICTOR: Ricky…he was wondering if you fancied hooking up with him after school – Friday.

ZARA looks fed up and picks up her bag.

ZARA: He's old enough to ask me himself.

VICTOR: Yeah but, he ain't got the bottle.

ZARA: Thanks but no thanks…

ZARA pushes past VICTOR.

VICTOR: Wait…

ZARA: What?

VICTOR: Why don't you like him?

ZARA: I don't dislike him…it's just…I got my heart set on someone else.

VICTOR: Who?

ZARA: That's for you to work out.

ZARA takes the plunge. She leans over and gives VICTOR a big kiss on the mouth. As she steps back, VICTOR is obviously reeling. ZARA turns and walks into the school, swinging her hips as best she can. VICTOR watches her, almost as if he's just woken up.

VICTOR: *(Calls out.)* Wait up! Forget Ricky! Maybe you and me could like…y'know…Friday…after school…?

As they disappear, FLIPS emerges and stands in front of the school. He stares up angrily at the CCTV cameras.

SCENE 9

It is later. We see FLIPS still standing outside the school. He is huddled with a few youths. They look like they're up to no good.

KABIR walks past, out of uniform now. He clocks FLIPS and tries to hurry on. FLIPS spots him.

FLIPS: Oy! Wait up!

FLIPS approaches. KABIR halts but is nervy.

What's happening?

KABIR: Going home.

FLIPS: Where you been?

KABIR: Park.

FLIPS: Snogging the face off your girlfriend again? You always had a way with the birds didn't you. Even back in Year 5, you got the juice man.

KABIR smiles nervously. FLIPS turns and looks at his mates. They all laugh loudly.

Need a quick word.

FLIPS puts his arm around KABIR and pulls him to one side. He doesn't want his gang to hear what he's saying but he holds his arms rather too tightly round KABIR's neck.

Here's the rub. Jake, my bro, did me a favour right? Sorted got rid of the stuff for me and now he owes me three hundred quid and I owe Jake. Keeps askin' me for the cash and it don't look good on me. Unless Sorted pays me, I'm in the shit. And you don't wanna mess with our Jake.

KABIR: I see your problem.

FLIPS: I just want to talk to Sorted.

KABIR: He's probably hiding in his hostel…

FLIPS: If you arrange to meet him somewhere – like the park – or if he comes back to school then give me the nod.

KABIR looks uncomfortable.

KABIR: What will you do to Sorted?

FLIPS: Persuade him to cough up.

KABIR looks doubtful.

You and me Kabs – We were mates back in the day. This is our patch – Sorted and all them fucking Sudanese monkeys – they're trying to take over. We gotta stand our ground.

KABIR: I can't…

FLIPS: You'll do this thing for me 'cos otherwise…

FLIPS is menacing.

KABIR: I'll see what I can do.

FLIPS: Good. Give me a text.

FLIPS lets go of KABIR.

(Lighter.) Seen Zara?

KABIR: Erm…she was in school today – so yeah – seen her.

FLIPS: Where she hang out after school? Never see her down the rec.

KABIR: Thought you been banned from there?

FLIPS: *(Proud.)* Banned from everywhere me. No one can handle Flips.

KABIR: I've gotta get back.

FLIPS: Hold up, hold up…just wondered if you could put a good word in for me – with your mate.

KABIR: Who?

FLIPS: Zara. Who else?

FLIPS looks pleadingly at KABIR. KABIR is a bit taken aback.

Can't stop thinkin' about her and she won't give me the time of day. And I wanna do things for her y'know, like take her to the seaside and go on dodgems with her. Weird.

KABIR: Right…

FLIPS: Dream about her too. Know what I mean? Any tips?

KABIR is baffled.

You got a steady girl. Scarf business don't turn me on but that's up to you mate.

KABIR: Me and Shaz…we were mates for a while and then – it kinda just happened.

FLIPS: Kinda just happened?

KABIR: Wasn't planned.

FLIPS: That's what my parents said about me.

KABIR looks around him uncomfortably as FLIPS laughs at his own joke.

Zara…she's got to me, y'know?
Never let a bird get under me skin like that before.

KABIR: Maybe you should try…being nice?

FLIPS laughs.

Works with girls.

FLIPS: Nice is naff. Ain't cool.

KABIR shrugs and tries to sidle away.

KABIR: Better get back. Mum's birthday…

FLIPS: Talk to Zara for me?

KABIR: Okay.

FLIPS: Don't wanna look stupid so if you tell her. Then… report back to me.

KABIR: Okay.

FLIPS slaps palms with a reluctant KABIR.

FLIPS: This is between you and me. Right?

KABIR: Right.

FLIPS: Nice one mate.

KABIR scurries off.

SCENE 10

RICKY and VICTOR are on the touchline of a football pitch. We can hear the sound of football practice going on in the background. The boys are stretching.

RICKY: He's like a one-legged cripple.

VICTOR: 'Llow it.

RICKY: 'Strue. Can't believe coach picked him instead of me. Only thing Icer's any good at is lobbing gobs into the goal.

VICTOR: He scored twice in the last game.

RICKY: So?

VICTOR: Scoring counts – ally?

RICKY is pissed off.

Chill man, chill. It's only one game.
Listen Rick…that girl…Zara…

RICKY: So fit…

VICTOR: I asked her out.

RICKY looks at VICTOR.

She kissed me.

RICKY: Kissed you? What? Just like that?

VICTOR: Full on the lips.

RICKY: You give it up for her?

VICTOR: Something went – whoosh – in my head.

RICKY: In your head or your jeans?

VICTOR: Don't force it.

RICKY tries to hide his upset.

Tried to ask her out for you but it kind've backfired.

VICTOR tries to study his friend's face but RICKY is closed off.

I know you liked her and I don't wanna step on your toes if…thing is…you never asked her so…but if you think it's not on, I won't…

RICKY: It's cool bro.

VICTOR: You sure?

RICKY: Like you said. Wasn't really that into her else I would've aksed her meself. Ally.

VICTOR: That's what I thought.

RICKY: Next year you'll be off to Spurs and I'll be left here, still struggling to make the borough team.

VICTOR: Football ain't everything Rick.

RICKY stands back and stares at VICTOR as if he's mad.

RICKY: What else do you suggest I do then Bredda? Be a carpenter like my dad?

VICTOR: There're worse things to do. Can't just play footie all your life. Gotta earn a living eventually.

RICKY: What the fuck's got into you?

VICTOR: Just sayin'.

RICKY: Sound like my fucking dad!

VICTOR: All you do is moan about not making the team. You're a good footballer but you're not the best – so maybe you gotta face facts.

RICKY: What? Give it up?

VICTOR: No.

RICKY: Look forward to working in the menswear section? Or a nice little desk job in telesales…

VICTOR is quiet. RICKY is furious.

What're you saying Vic? I'm not good enough eh? I is a loser?

VICTOR: You ain't listening…

RICKY: I'm listenin' innit? I got no future here. This fucking place is a dive, that dump of a school. Like a war zone. How we supposed to get a decent education when we're surrounded by fucking psycho kids everywhere. Those teachers look like they're half dead and the good ones never stay. I've got even bigger fucking problems at home. Your family got the whole world laid out on a silver plate. Nice house, nice lickle back yard with flowers and ting. Mum, dad, sisters all wrap you up in cotton wool and tell you how great you are all the time. Me, what have I got? What have I got?

VICTOR: You're always blaming everyone else.

RICKY: Fuck off.

Pause. A whistle blows somewhere and VICTOR gets up to go.

VICTOR: My folks work hard to get their nice lickle back yard with flowers and ting. Mam work as a cleaner when I was a pickney – tek me to all the houses with her. Watch her being treated like shit by them white people she work for. Hardly ever see my dad when I was little – always away on jobs. I don't take nuthin' for granted and nuthin' was handed to them on a plate. Got it?

RICKY looks away.

RICKY: Listen Bredda…

VICTOR: Don't Bredda me. You got no respect. Just 'cos you learn the lingo, don't mean you're one of us.

VICTOR sucks his teeth and walks away. RICKY looks lost.

SCENE 11

We are back outside the school gates again. It is the end of the school day and kids are pouring out. KABIR is standing to one side on his own. He is texting someone on his phone as SORTED emerges from the school with ZARA.

VICTOR stops and grins at them. ZARA rolls her eyes and walks towards VICTOR.

FLIPS suddenly appears outside the school gates carrying a baseball bat. SORTED turns and tries to run but there are other friends of FLIPS who bar his way. SORTED panicks and runs.

SORTED: Help! Help!

FLIPS: Come here you little shit.

> *A very angry FLIPS follows close by brandishing a heavy baseball bat. He swings it with violence and tries to bring it down on SORTED.*
>
> Come here you little shit. I'm gonna get you. I'm gonna fucking bust your tiny brain.

SORTED: No-n-n-no – N-o!

> *The kids outside the school scream and run in all different directions, trying to avoid the swinging baseball bat.*
>
> *SORTED dashes and ducks and slips away from the slower FLIPS but FLIPS catches up with him. He is just about to swing his bat when ZARA and SHAZ stand in front of SORTED. FLIPS stops mid-swing.*

SHAZ: Think what you're doin'.

FLIPS: Get out of the way.

ZARA: No!

FLIPS: I said…

SHAZ: Think what you're doin'. You're gonna kill him.

FLIPS: It's what he deserves.

ZARA: Please… Flips man. Calm down.

FLIPS: He's been fleecin' me. Three hundred quid he owes me.

RICKY enters.

SORTED: I do-don't owe you nothing! I pay you! We are quits.

FLIPS: Don't lie.

SORTED pleads to the others.

SORTED: He is the one lying! He is lying!

FLIPS: I ain't lying! I need that cash.

FLIPS grabs hold of SHAZ and tries to pull her away. Then he grabs SHAZ's head scarf and pulls it off viciously. SHAZ falls to the floor.

FLIPS looks at RICKY.

Get him for me.

RICKY: What?

FLIPS: I don't hit girls. Get the little shit out from behind her skirts.

SORTED is crying now.

Yeah, say your prayers you little Sudanese shit. I warned you.

KABIR: Stop it Flips. You're scarin' us.

FLIPS: Get him for me or else, you'll be next.

RICKY: Don't do this man.

FLIPS looks at RICKY, full of rage as RICKY steps forward and stands in front of ZARA.

ZARA: Ricky! What you doin'?

FLIPS: Get the fuck outa my way White Boy. You're on the wrong side.

RICKY: You ain't your fucking brother and you don't scare no one.

FLIPS raises his baseball bat and brings it down with force but in a split-second, VICTOR dives forward to protect his friend and gets the full force of the bat on his head. VICTOR collapses, blood pouring from his head. RICKY grabs his friend.

Everyone freezes, in shock.

What've you done?

FLIPS: He asked for it.

RICKY: Vic? Vic?

VICTOR is unconscious. RICKY cradles his friend and looks shocked.

(Screams.) Someone! Call an ambulance…NOW!

KABIR gets out his phone and dials.

Bredda? You okay? He ain't speaking.

FLIPS: I wasn't going for him…

SORTED steps forward and while FLIPS is standing there, unguarded, baseball bat limply hanging at his side, he pulls out ZARA's knife.

ZARA: *(Screams.)* No! Sorted! No!

SORTED plunges the knife deep into FLIPS's chest. SORTED steps back coolly and watches as FLIPS staggers back and collapses on the floor.

SHAZ: Ohmygod – ohmygod…

As the kids all stand around in shock. We hear the sound of sirens screaming as they approach the school. RICKY cradles VICTOR and weeps as he rocks him.

RICKY: Come on Bredda, wake up, wake up…stop messin' around…

SORTED drops the knife and runs.

SCENE 12

It is later in the day now, almost dusk. Groups of school kids bring in flowers and lay them in front of the school fence. Everyone is huddled up and looking ashen-faced. Some kids are weeping whilst others look deep in shock and are just staring. The flowers pile up. A TV camera crew arrives on the scene and films the pupils. No one says a word.

As the light fades, VICTOR's *football shirt is lovingly laid out and candles are lit.*

In the darkness, surrounded by flowers, the pupils sing a song.

SCENE 13

It is night time. RICKY is outside the school on his own. He is looking at the flowers and reading the messages. Wordlessly, ZARA joins him. She lights a few candles and tidies the flowers. RICKY watches her for a while and crouches down and touches the spot where VICTOR fell. He looks traumatised and sits down.

ZARA sits on the floor next to RICKY and leans against him. They sit in mutual misery for a while.

ZARA: Like wading through a nightmare.

RICKY: Make it go away.

ZARA: I wish…

RICKY: Wind it back…

ZARA: Ricky…everyone's crying. Kids from other schools, people who didn't even know Victor…turning up all day…

RICKY: Unreal.

ZARA: Flips is dead too. It's my fault… Sorted used my knife…

ZARA starts to weep.

RICKY: What did you expect?

ZARA: Not in a million years…didn't think…

RICKY: That's the problem innit? Don't think you lot.

ZARA: This wasn't supposed to happen.

ZARA cries. RICKY puts his arm around her and tries to comfort her.

RICKY: Why'd Victor do that? Why did he step in the line of fire like that? I never asked him to do that. I had it under control.

ZARA: Thought Flips was bluffing.

RICKY: Over three hundred measly quid? How did we let this happen? How'd it get so outa control?

ZARA: It wasn't nuthin' to do with Victor.

RICKY: Vic's mum…she's…keeps asking me what his last words were…how can I tell her? No words…no words…

ZARA: They can't find Sorted.

RICKY: If I ever catch the little shit – I swear.

ZARA: What?

RICKY: I'll fucking kill him.

ZARA: And what good's that gonna do?

RICKY: Someone's gotta pay for this.

ZARA: Flips' gang's out looking for Sorted.

RICKY: I hope they find him.

RICKY tries hard not to cry.

Vic was my Bredda. From back in the day…

ZARA: He was the best.

RICKY: Never hurt a fly. Always there for us. Had everything to go for.
Why dis happen to him?
Why not me?

ZARA: Rick. Don't.

RICKY: Can't do it on my own.

ZARA: Gotta carry on.

RICKY: How?

ZARA: It's what Vic would've wanted.

Beat.

We've gotta find Sorted before they do. Two kids have died.

RICKY: Don't give a fuck about Sorted.

ZARA: Think about what he's goin' through? Must be desperate. Doesn't have anyone.

RICKY looks at ZARA.

RICKY: You know where he is?

ZARA: No. Been lookin' though. Feds came round my place – askin' questions.

RICKY: Been here too. Too fucking late. Dem always too late. Shoulda been here to sort Flips out.

Beat.

He said when he kissed you something inside him went 'whoosh'.

ZARA: Did he?

RICKY: Thought you were well fit.

ZARA hangs her head.

ZARA: Scared Ricky…really scared.

RICKY: Yeah. Keep tryin' to think – what would Vic say we should do? Him always chat sense. Him know how to deal with dis thing. Him know.

ZARA: I gotta get back. Mum doesn't want me hangin' around here.

RICKY: Yeh.

ZARA: Don't stay here too long.

ZARA exits.

RICKY waits until ZARA has gone and then sits in the candlelight and weeps like a child. He curls up into a foetal position and stays like this for a while until he hears a noise behind him. He turns but can't see anything in the darkness. RICKY quickly wipes away his tears and stands up, fists clenched.

RICKY: Who's there?
Is anyone there?

SORTED emerges from the shadows. He is dishevelled and shabby. He looks devastated. He hangs back from RICKY, afraid.

You!
Look what you done.

SORTED tries to stifle his sobs.

Everyone's out looking for you –
Police…searching …as if we'd wanna hide you.

SORTED falls silent.

Why you come here? First place they come lookin' for you.

SORTED: St-st-st-starving.

RICKY looks at SORTED disgusted.

P-p-p-please.

RICKY fishes out a Twix bar from his bag and chucks it resentfully at SORTED. SORTED devours it greedily. RICKY watches SORTED carefully.

RICKY: Flips died – you know that don't you? Got him right in the heart.

SORTED stops gobbling and clutches his stomach.

And Vic's dead. Skull. Should've been you – you fucking animal.

RICKY runs at SORTED and grabs him. SORTED struggles to free himself but RICKY has him in a head lock.

I should break your neck right now and no one'd care.

SORTED: Lemme go! P-p-p-please. I am sorry. I am s-s-s-sorry.

RICKY: I tell you to keep away from Flips. I warn you him bad news. Why don't you listen to me?

RICKY throws SORTED away from him. SORTED pants and gasps for breath. RICKY is distraught.

If you listen to me, none of this happen.

SORTED: Victor was a G-g-good man.

SORTED stands up straight and stares at all the flowers.

RICKY: See how many people love him? Not like Flips. Not a word here in his honour.

SORTED: I wish I could change my life for Victor's.

RICKY: So do I. Only real bredda I ever have. Only one who really care. Only really belong anywhere when I with him.

SORTED: W-w-will you – help me?

RICKY: What?

SORTED: The P-p-p-police will torture me.

RICKY: I don't want nuthin' more to do with your lot…

SORTED: My m-m-mother wanted me to be a t-eacher. And my father, he said, if-if – if I worked hard – I could be a l-lawyer. Then, then war. Guns everywhere. T-t-trucks in the n-n-n-ight with men and g-g-guns… I hide. I watch.

RICKY: Who ask you to come into my world? Why didn't you just stay in that shit hole you come from? Why bring all your problem here? Your pain? Your misery? I ask you? I invite you? You fuckers, coming into my country with your shitty lives and your torture stories. Like animals. Change us all into animals like you. Now I don't even feel like I belong here. Like I'm the fucking odd one out.

SORTED: Why you saying all this?

RICKY: Because you mess up. And you mess us up. If it wasn't for fucked up little kids like you, we wouldn't have to deal with no shit. We could live and breathe free.

SORTED: So you can be free but we have to s-s-s-suffer.

RICKY: Why you bring your sufferrin' here? Spread like disease.

SORTED: You are lucky n-not to know what is like to live in f-ear.

RICKY: Now we all know.

SORTED: I wish we could have been friends Ri-R-Ricky. I am v-v-very sorry what ha-happened to Victor.

RICKY: I hate you. I hate what you done to me and my friends. Those kids stand outside the school – watch you with that blade – poking Flips – you not even look angry – just like it something you do every day. Little kids see that! I see it! Never gonna forget that shit. Nightmares for the rest of our lives because of you.

SORTED: I have nowhere to go. I am finished.

RICKY: And I have to stay here. Try and live.

SORTED: I should be playing in the fields near my house. Getting water from the well for my mother, chasing the chickens to catch one for her. Feeling the sun on my back. Not here. I can't go back home. I come here. I think, maybe I get a better life. B-b-but no one is here for me. Everybody busy and I can't forget. My mother – my s-sisters. I hide and I watch. They r-r-rape them and then they c-c-c-cut them up. Slice them with l-l-long knives. I have nowhere to go. I am finished. Why I live?

RICKY: Is it my fault your kin murdering each other? So you come here and mek me feel shame of what I am. Is it the white boy's fault? I try and fit, I try and bend to mek myself part of you all, to welcome you, to be your friend and dis how you repay me…open your suitcase and pull out a knife?

SORTED: I was afraid of Flips. He pretended to be my friend. Then he changed. I punished him. I liked Victor.

RICKY: He was my bredda. And now he sleeping in de mortuary. For what? Paying the price for being a good man in dis bad world – 'cos you play at gansgta.

SORTED: I am not bad. I am not bad. My country kill my family. Your country kill my hope.

SORTED cries like a child.

RICKY: Don't…don't…

RICKY finds himself holding SORTED trying to comfort him. Sirens sound in the distance.

SORTED: The Police…they will torture me. They will p-ut me inside a cage forever.

Torch search lights start flashing around the two boys. RICKY shields his eyes. SORTED looks panicked. He turns to RICKY.

H-h-hide me!

RICKY: Where?

We hear the sound of police sirens approaching from a distance. SORTED dashes towards the school fence and tries to climb it but he slips. He tries again. The search lights focus on him as the sirens get louder. SORTED is trapped hanging on to the wire mesh of the school fence sirens blaring, dogs barking all around him. He looks terrified.

SCENE 14

It is morning now and there are even more flowers, teddies, footballs, bits of paper with messages, etc, piled up outside the school. The kids are still hovering, unable to believe what has happened. They are holding hands, embracing etc. Different kids step forward and speak.

CHORUS 1: Out of all the people in da world, you didn't deserve it.

CHORUS 2: RIP Vic. Sleep wid dem angels.

CHORUS 3: U woz the best…

CHORUS 4: U had a heart of gold.

CHORUS 5: Miss you Vic. You woz da best.

CHORUS 6: What a waste. Sad, sad, sad…

CHORUS 1: Massive shame. God bless u Vic.

CHORUS 2: Why all dis violence? U tried to stoppit.

CHORUS 3: You woz smart, you woz clever, u woz always smilin' an' u woz always larfin'. Miss u so much.

CHORUS 4: Missed but never forgotten.

CHORUS 5: Spurs have lost the next Berbetov.

CHORUS 6: You woz too good for this world. The 'special One' has called you up. You'll never lose again.

SHAZ: It's just wrong wha' happened. So sorry.

KABIR: Wanna pay my respects to a boy who woz a true soldier.

ZARA: I thought you woz invincible.

RICKY: RIP Vic. May u b watching da game tonite from heaven fella.

End.

SANCTUARY

Sanctuary was first performed on 29 July 2002 at Loft Theatre, London in the Lyttelton Transformation project, National Theatre, with the following cast:

MARGARET CATCHPOLE, Barbara Jefford
SEBASTIAN CRUZ, Eddie Nestor
MICHAEL RUZINDANA, Leo Wringer
KABIR SHEIKH, Nitin Ganatra
AYESHA WILLIAMS, Sarah Solemani
JENNY CATCHPOLE, Susannah Wise

Production credits:
Director, Hettie Macdonald
Designer, John Bausor
Lighting Designer, Pete Bull
Sound Designer, Rich Walsh
Company Voice Work, Patsy Rodenburg & Kate Godfrey

Characters

KABIR SHEIKH
Asian man, gardener and general handyman in the church grounds

MICHAEL RUZINDANA
African man

SEBASTIAN CRUZ
middle-aged Afro-Caribbean man

JENNY CATCHPOLE
priest in her thirties

AYESHA WILLIAMS
fifteen-year-old mixed-race girl

MARGARET CATCHPOLE
elderly woman, Jenny's grandmother

Act One

SCENE 1

We are outdoors in the corner of a graveyard – a small Eden-like, neat patch of luscious green packed with shrubbery, ornate flowering plants (orchids) and small tubs of herbs etc. There is a wall to one side and a large tree, which overhangs the wall into the road outside. There is a shed to the other side and an old bench under the tree. The shed is covered in rambling roses and clematis, all in bloom. In the background we can see row upon row of gravestones, which stretch into the distance. A few bits of rubbish litter the otherwise beautiful garden.

It is a bright day. MICHAEL enters and sits on the bench beneath the tree, fashioning a piece of wood into a spoon. He works diligently whilst listening to the cricket commentary on the radio. MICHAEL is casually but smartly dressed. He looks completely engrossed in his work. SEBASTIAN wanders in and sits next to MICHAEL. He is shabbily dressed and dishevelled looking.

At first, he simply sits there in silence. Then he takes interest in what MICHAEL is doing.

SEBASTIAN: What're you working on?

MICHAEL: *(African accent.)* It is going to be a spoon.

SEBASTIAN: Ahhh…

SEBASTIAN watches him attentively.

You're good with your hands.

MICHAEL: My father was a carpenter.

SEBASTIAN: Family trade?

MICHAEL: Not really. He was good. He made all the furniture in our village. I just do it to pass the time.

SEBASTIAN looks around.

SEBASTIAN: I like it here.

MICHAEL: Yes.

SEBASTIAN: You like it here?

MICHAEL: Yes.

SEBASTIAN: Lots of dead people. Makes you feel lucky.

MICHAEL: Eh?

SEBASTIAN: That we're alive, man! However bad things are out there, at least we're not fucking six feet under. Know what I mean?

MICHAEL: *(Polite.)* I certainly know what you mean.

SEBASTIAN: Too right. Especially when you look at all those gravestones. Young people – half my age. Cut off in the prime of their lives.

MICHAEL continues with his work.

It's the baby ones that always get me. Tiny little coffins.

MICHAEL: Yes, that is sad.

SEBASTIAN: Sad? It's fucking tragic.

MICHAEL: Yes. Tragic. That is what I meant.

SEBASTIAN: Still, like I said. Makes me feel lucky to be drawing breath. The Good Lord up there saw it fit to spare my life.

SEBASTIAN looks heavenward.

(Shouts.) Thank you God. Not that I'm any fucking good to anyone.

The two men sit in silence.

What's your name again?

MICHAEL: Michael.

SEBASTIAN: Pleased to meet you, Michael. Put it there brother –

MICHAEL gingerly slaps palms with SEBASTIAN.

The name's Seb.

MICHAEL smiles a greeting. SEBASTIAN gets up and staggers around. He looks at the plants.

Very pretty.

We hear voices. A woman vicar wearing a dog collar, JENNY, and an Asian man, KABIR, enter. KABIR is pushing a wheelbarrow full of fresh rolls of turf.

KABIR: They are having the petition in their hands?

JENNY: Yes. I delivered it myself.

KABIR: They will be seeing sense.

JENNY: Yes, I'm sure they will.

KABIR: It is still being beyond all reasoning. They converted St Mary's into luxury apartments.

JENNY: Can't imagine the yuppies moving in round here. I'm going to speak to the bishop this afternoon. He's on our side. Oh – and don't forget, that journalist's coming in on Friday.

KABIR: Eh?

JENNY: You know, from *The Post.* Said she'd be here for most of the afternoon. *(Preoccupied.)* Hello Michael. Seb.

SEBASTIAN grunts.

MICHAEL: It is a beautiful morning.

KABIR: Hey, Mikey – what's the score?

MICHAEL: Pakistan are still batting. 223 for three wickets.

KABIR: Good. Have you seen Mumtaz this morning?

MICHAEL: No.

JENNY: She's probably hiding in her nest somewhere.

KABIR: She is always coming to greet me in the mornings – quackety – quack – but only silence today.

JENNY: She'll turn up. She usually does.

MICHAEL continues with his work.

Anyway, this journalist's going to be interviewing people – maybe even you.

KABIR: I will be telling her. This place, it is being a community asset – yes?

JENNY: Very good.

KABIR: People are coming here to pray, to mourn, to grieve and to be with their loved ones. I will be introducing her to people to speak with. Mikey?

MICHAEL: Please Kabir – leave me out of it.

JENNY: Your testament would be useful.

KABIR: You must be helping us, Mikey.

A mobile phone rings.

JENNY: This is important. The coverage would be good for us. The more people read about this place, the better our case.

JENNY answers the phone.

Jenny Catchpole? Edith…of course…he's gone into that nursing home…I took him there myself last week. Coming here? Shit.

JENNY moves aside to have a more private conversation.

SEBASTIAN undoes his flies to have a pee. KABIR spots him.

KABIR: Oy, oy, oy…don't you dare be pissing on my plants. And in front of a lady! *(He points at JENNY.)* Shame on you! Put it away.

SEBASTIAN hesitates and then puts it away.

JENNY comes off the phone.

SEBASTIAN: Sorry man. I wasn't thinking.

SEBASTIAN looks a bit shame-faced and staggers off. The others watch him go.

KABIR: Jenny – did you see what he was doing? People are thinking this is being a public toilet! The whole place always smelling of piss.

MICHAEL: *(To JENNY.)* He's a bit of a mess.

JENNY: But the kids love him and his classes at the church hall are very popular.

KABIR: I would not be trusting him with the charge of my children. In his last lesson he was having them all wandering around the graveyard taking photographs of baby graves. Isn't that being a little bit odd?

JENNY: He's an artist. Probably just being creative.

KABIR: Artist – my foot.

JENNY: What's the new turf for?

KABIR: The area by the pond. Especially for your baby photographers and my ducks.

JENNY: Wonderful. I thought that patch was looking a bit rough.

KABIR: Too many people stepping around there. Churning it up into mud – especially you ladies, with your thin pin-like heels.

JENNY: Don't blame me. I don't wear shoes like that.

KABIR: And then of course your Sylvester and Sarita – they shit all over it. Huge turds.

KABIR holds out his hands, exaggerating the size.

You wouldn't have thought they would have so much of the crap inside them.

JENNY: I don't know what you've got against those swans.

KABIR: They do not like me. In fact of matter, Sylvester attacked me yesterday.

JENNY: *(Teasing.)* I think you'll find that in a Court of Law, they would define it as self-defence. You were brandishing your spade at him.

KABIR: He was hissing at me, stretching his giraffe neck at me and spitting.

JENNY: You provoked him.

KABIR: Even your swans are racist.

JENNY laughs and then looks at the rolls of turf.

JENNY: I won't ask you how much that turf cost you.

KABIR: It was free… Present from the Parks Department.

JENNY: *(Suspicious.)* Not Bobby?

KABIR: He had some left over, so he is giving it to me.

JENNY looks uneasy.

Don't worry, Jenny. It is all above board, strictly legitimate. Only a few rolls. No one will be missing it.

JENNY looks down at the turf.

Very excellent turf. Good quality. So green. The pond will be looking very beautiful.

JENNY: You mustn't take gifts from Bobby.

KABIR: He is reformed character now. He has stopped drinking, you know and his probation officer even has signed off now. Says he is ready to enter the world as a human being. Bobby is very happy. A new man. Always smiling. See how generous he has been to us.

KABIR points at the turf.

JENNY: Bobby's gifts always come with a price.

KABIR: You are too suspicious. You must do as your God says and learn to forgive, turn the other cheek.

JENNY: Yes, but I only have two cheeks.

KABIR: Then you must keep turning.

KABIR turns his face from side to side. JENNY watches him impassively.

Don't you agree, Mikey?

MICHAEL: No. If you are struck on the cheek once, you must strike back twice.

KABIR: *(Wags his finger at MICHAEL.)* That is not being very Christian of you, Mikey.

MICHAEL: It was a new commandment I invented back home – to stop innocents from being victimised.

KABIR: But we must always be forgiving – no?

MICHAEL: Some things are unforgivable.

KABIR looks at MICHAEL and then at JENNY.

JENNY: It's all relative.

A mobile phone rings. JENNY pulls it out of her pocket and answers it.

Jenny Catchpole? *(She looks at her watch.)* I'll be right there. *(She clicks off her phone.)* I'd better get on. Another bride and groom to talk through the service.

JENNY exits. KABIR gathers his work tools for the day.

KABIR: What are you making today, Mikey?

MICHAEL: A spoon.

KABIR: Another one? How many spoons are you needing?

MICHAEL: This one is for Jenny.

KABIR walks over to MICHAEL and looks at it.

KABIR: To be stirring all her lentil soups?

MICHAEL: She cooked us a very nice meal last week – not a lentil in sight. Don't be mean Kabir. I don't want to talk to this journalist.

KABIR: We are needing the publicity for this church. This is my home, my resting place. I am not wanting to lose it.

MICHAEL: But journalists…they always try and dig up the past and I find it so – difficult.

KABIR: Don't be talking about the past. Tell them about how important this place is being to you in the present and for the future. You are coming here every day – this is being as much your home as mine.

A school girl, AYESHA, enters. She sits on the bench.

KABIR stops and stares at AYESHA.

You have been cutting your hair short.

AYESHA: Don't you like it?

KABIR: I was preferring your hair long.

AYESHA: I know.

KABIR: A woman's virtue is being in her hair.

KABIR walks up close and inspects AYESHA's hair. He looks disappointed.

Too short. You are not even asking my opinion before you are having the chop.

AYESHA: It's my hair. I have to look after it.

KABIR: Yes, but I have to be looking at you.

AYESHA: If it's that offensive, don't fucking look then.

KABIR: Hey. Language.

MICHAEL: Morning, Ayesha.

AYESHA: What's up, Mikey?

MICHAEL and AYESHA slap palms.

KABIR sits down next to AYESHA. MICHAEL picks up some rubbish that is littered around. He finds some rubbish by the side of the shed.

KABIR: Why are you being here now? You should be at school.

AYESHA looks down at her flowers.

AYESHA: Come to lay some flowers on Dad's grave.

KABIR: Oh – I'm sorry – I am forgetting. It's today? It's been five years.

AYESHA: Yep. By the way, thanks for tidying up his grave.

KABIR: It was looking a bit tattified.

AYESHA: *(Laughs.)* You mean tatty.

KABIR: How is your mother?

AYESHA: Alright. Bill's still a pig though. Wish she'd chuck the fucker out.

KABIR tuts again. MICHAEL inspects something on the ground near the shed. He looks concerned.

KABIR: You are a nice girl. Why must you be swearing so much? It is very foul to hear such words from your lips.

AYESHA: Sorry. But you should see him, Kabir. He sits around in the lounge all evening, hogging the box. Always watching football, we don't get a look in.

KABIR: You must be trying to show your stepfather some respect.

AYESHA: He's not my stepdad. They're not married and with any luck, Mum'll get bored of him, just like all the others.

KABIR: *(Firm.)* You must do well in your exams.

AYESHA: I'm not a brain box.

KABIR: You are a clever girl. You must be making your father proud.

KABIR looks heavenward.

AYESHA: Yeah, yeah.

KABIR: You must be believing in yourself otherwise nothing can be happening. You must be passing these exams.

AYESHA: Fucking hate exams.

KABIR: No, no, that is not being the right attitude. If you are doing well, you will be having a wonderful start in life. Work in an office, wear smart clothes, go out to restaurants for dinner, be having lots of friends and nice holidays…

AYESHA: *(Laughs.)* Me? Work in an office? Fuck off.

KABIR: Ayesha! Stop your foul words.

AYESHA: *(Sighs.)* Sorry.

KABIR gets up and walks back towards his shed. He washes his hands beneath the tap.

KABIR: And study hard.

AYESHA: Alright!

AYESHA picks up her bag and gets up to leave.

MICHAEL: Hey, Kabir, take a look at this…

KABIR: *(To AYESHA.)* And no going chasing after the boys – huh? That can come later.

AYESHA: I'm not chasing anyone.

KABIR: You are a pretty girl. The boys – they will come running.

AYESHA: *(Embarrassed.)* Please… Gotta go.

AYESHA exits.

MICHAEL: Kabir…

KABIR: What?

KABIR walks over to MICHAEL.

MICHAEL: Look, someone has built a bonfire here.

KABIR sifts through the ashes. He pokes around picking up a few feathers. MICHAEL looks anxious.

MICHAEL picks up a feather and shows it to KABIR. KABIR claps his hand to his forehead and looks distraught.

MICHAEL finds more feathers and some bones. He shows them to KABIR.

KABIR: I am recognising these feathers!

MICHAEL: These are Mumtaz's.

KABIR: I am thinking you are right. Someone ate my duck!

MICHAEL: And look…

MICHAEL notices something pinned up on the shed.

Her feet. Chopped off and hung up.

KABIR looks sick. He sits on the bench clutching a few feathers, rocking back and forth weeping over the feathers.

KABIR: Mumtaz.

MICHAEL carefully unpins the duck's feet and puts them in his handkerchief.

Ohhh…

MICHAEL: A very sick joke.

KABIR: Whoever it was – He's no better than an animal. It's too upsetting.

MICHAEL: It was probably children, teenagers…they broke in, thought it was a laugh…

KABIR: And her feet…

KABIR holds his head in his hands and looks very upset.

She was my companion. I was nursing her from a duckling when she was having a broken wing. When I was here, she was always waddling around by my side.

Beat as KABIR takes the duck's feet from MICHAEL, unwraps the handkerchief and stares at them.

Her poor little feet.

MICHAEL comforts KABIR.

MICHAEL: I'm sorry my friend.

KABIR is worked up.

KABIR: They are not knowing who they are messing with. I will be catching them. I will be skinning them alive and be roasting them over a fire. See how they are liking it.

MICHAEL continues to comfort KABIR.

SCENE 2

It is late afternoon. The sun is low. JENNY leans back on the bench. Her mobile phone is ringing and ringing. She pulls out the phone and switches it off. The sounds of the traffic beyond the wall continue. We hear a banging coming from beyond the wall: a workman sporadically hammering etc. An elderly woman, MARGARET, walks in and approaches JENNY. JENNY virtually ignores her.

The elderly woman stops nearby and looks around.

MARGARET: *(Plummy accent.)* Feel as if I'm in the bloody tropics.

JENNY doesn't react.

A shout goes up from the wall. JENNY and MARGARET look up. KABIR is perched high up on the wall, fixing some barbed wire in place.

JENNY: *(Calls up.)* Kabir – oh do be careful.

KABIR: *(Calls down.)* It's all right – almost finished.

JENNY stands and watches as KABIR is working on the barbed wire. He disappears from view again.

JENNY: What's he doing? He could have hurt himself.

MARGARET: He's a heathen, Jenny. You'd have to convert him. *(Simpers.)* Oh Kabir – do be careful!

JENNY: You have a one-track mind. Sad at your age.

JENNY eases off her boots and lays back on the bench. She groans. MARGARET peers down at her feet.

MARGARET: Disgusting.

JENNY: They're killing me. Been throbbing all day.

MARGARET: Unsightly slabs of meat.

JENNY continues to ignore MARGARET and rubs her feet.

MARGARET carefully lifts her dress to show off her feet.

I once had a very dashing beau – before your grandfather. Anyway, this beau once said I had the feet of a goddess. Then he touched his forehead to them and kissed my toes one by one.

MARGARET hands over a letter.

This just arrived by courier.

JENNY takes the letter and looks at it with trepidation. MARGARET peers up at the wall.

Where's Gungha Din got to now?

JENNY: *(Sharp.)* Don't call him that.

MARGARET: And where's his sidekick – Man Friday? This is his spot, isn't it? He's usually ferreting around here. Working on his 'wood'. Whole place is teeming with foreigners and now there's that peculiar Negro hanging around here.

JENNY: Do you ever think before you open that mouth of yours?!

MARGARET: Now don't get yourself all worked up…and put your shoes back on darling. You look like a hippy. Aren't you going to open the letter?

JENNY: Later.

MARGARET: Maybe it's from that awful bishop with halitosis? A proposal of marriage!

JENNY: *(Stressed.)* Do shut up.

MARGARET: I had such hopes for you. An Ambassador for the British Government, posted somewhere like Rio or Mexico City…

JENNY: Gran, I'm thirty-four. You can't keep…

MARGARET: I shall go on at you until I die. You've wasted your life marrying yourself to a dying institution. I wanted some great-grandchildren.

JENNY: Go and nag Charlie then.

MARGARET: Your brother's a dead loss. Even I know when to call it a day.

JENNY: At least he's still young.

MARGARET: Yes, but he's probably killed off all his sperm. Drowned them in neat vodka.

JENNY: I'm not interested…

MARGARET: Look at Cherie Blair. She's older than you. God knows how but her husband still finds her attractive enough to give her a good rogering. Have you noticed how the woman's got a mouth like a letterbox? How does the PM kiss her?

JENNY: Gran!

MARGARET: There's still some hope left for you. When you dress up and put on a bit of make-up – you're actually almost attractive. You could easily find yourself a husband.

JENNY: I don't want a husband.

MARGARET: There are lots of men your age – second time around – divorced, children living with wife. You'd make a tolerable step-mum – give them moral guidance – that sort of thing. You could even just about have children yourself. But you'd have to get cracking pretty sharpish.

JENNY: I am very happy as I am.

MARGARET: Of course you are dear. Positively brimming over with the joys of life.

SEBASTIAN wanders through. He is carrying a large tripod and camera. He places it carefully to one side. He virtually ignores JENNY and MARGARET.

JENNY: Are you taking some photos here?

SEBASTIAN: Twenty-four hours in the life of the garden. I've got a timer mechanism. It's set to take two pictures an hour.

SEBASTIAN looks around where to aim the camera. He decides to aim it at the bench.

MARGARET: What's this for?

SEBASTIAN: Just a little project for the kids.

JENNY: Very inventive, Seb. Is this your own equipment?

SEBASTIAN: Yup.

KABIR enters. He is carrying some tools.

KABIR: Mrs Catchpole – ah – you are looking ravishing today…

KABIR approaches MARGARET, bends down and kisses her hand. She giggles like a schoolgirl. JENNY glares at her Gran's two-facedness.

JENNY: That was very dangerous what you were doing up there, Kabir. You should have called me or Seb. We could've given you a hand.

KABIR: I was only making a hole in the barbed wire. We were having an intruder last night. Must have been jumping over the wall. He ate Mumtaz.

JENNY: What?

KABIR: Her feathers were being scattered all around shed and they were pinning her feet up on the shed.

JENNY: That's horrible… Who would do such a thing? Depraved…bastards!

MARGARET: It's no surprise though, is it? Probably those ragamuffin kids again – the ones that got in last week…

SEBASTIAN: Don't blame it on the kids.

KABIR watches SEBASTIAN suspiciously. JENNY looks upset.

JENNY: Poor Mumtaz.

KABIR: Sebastian – what are you doing?

SEBASTIAN: Twenty-four hours in the life of the garden.

KABIR: It will be getting nicked.

SEBASTIAN: I'll check it regularly.

KABIR: It will be getting in my way.

SEBASTIAN: It's only for twenty-four hours.

JENNY: Hold on, if they came over the barbed wire – why are you making the hole bigger?

KABIR: Tempting the thieving vandals in. Tonight, I will be staying here and keeping watch for them.

JENNY: You should be careful.

KABIR: We must be protecting these grounds. People are depending on us.

JENNY: I don't want you taking the law into your own hands. We're in enough trouble as it is.

KABIR: Aren't you caring about this place?

JENNY: Of course I do. It's you I'm worried about. You're not a security guard.

KABIR: They killed my duck! And I will defend this place to the end.

JENNY looks at KABIR with admiration.

Anyway, we must be keeping these grounds looking good for the journalist. Making a good impression.

JENNY: Exactly. I'll join you tonight. A midnight vigil – might be quite exciting.

MARGARET: You can't. We've got dinner at the Hendersons.

JENNY: Shit.

KABIR: I will be fine. Always we have such problems with criminals and trespassers.

MARGARET: It's a wicked world.

KABIR: When first I started my work here, it was being the Gulf War. Someone was scrawling all over the wall there – 'Bomb Iqaq'.

MARGARET: Iqaq?

JENNY: They couldn't spell.

MARGARET: The English language – murdered by illiterates and foreigners.

JENNY: Gran!

KABIR: Margaret, you are being a very naughty lady. Too many years you have been spending as a diplomatic's wife.

MARGARET: Diplomat. Anyway, Gus was a military doctor. There is a difference.

KABIR: It is still being the same, same. Looking down your nostrils at everyone. Being of a patronising nature is in your blood. You are being taught from early age to be superior – no?

JENNY: Too right.

MARGARET: Here I sit accused and guilty.

JENNY: Gran – it's nothing to be proud of.

KABIR: And it is in your religion.

JENNY has heard all of this before. She looks at her watch.

You people stampeding all over the world, killing. Bible in one hand and sword in the other. No? The foundations of your religion are being based on the blood of conquered religions, countries converted to Christianity. Missionaries in Africa, church building all over the world…

MARGARET: Hey listen, darling, I'm no Christian. I'm simply a bigot.

KABIR: At least you are being honest, Mrs Catchpole.

JENNY: Don't encourage her.

KABIR: 'And ye shall make no league
with the inhabitants of this land;
ye shall throw down their altars…
They shall be as thorns in your sides,
and their gods shall be a snare unto you.'

Judges.

JENNY laughs and applauds KABIR. He takes a bow.

JENNY: You're so good at taking things completely out of context.

SEBASTIAN smiles to himself. He checks that the camera is working by taking a few photographs.

You forget the Bible talks to us about tolerance and the humanity of all living beings, love thy neighbour, peace and understanding and…

KABIR: Jesus was taking those ideas from India. Very famous ancient texts written in Sanskrit.

JENNY: You really shouldn't believe everything you read in the papers.

KABIR: Hard evidence, Jenny.

JENNY: Still haven't convinced me though.

KABIR: They talk about how a young boy from Nazareth visited the old sages in the foothills of the Himalayas. He called himself Jesus and he was staying in India between the ages of thirteen and thirty.

MARGARET: That explains what he got up to.

KABIR: He was learning yoga and the arts of herbal medicines, meditation, rising above oneself. He was finding out about the concepts of 'love thy neighbour, turn the other cheek, peace and tolerance' and all those things you are claiming to be yours.

JENNY: Ever heard of the universality of all faiths?

KABIR: Universality is being a wishy-washy description. Very convenient.

JENNY: Like your story.

KABIR: It is not a story. It is being a fact. Jesus was nicking all his ideas from the Hindus. He got it a bit wrong when it was coming to being the Messiah. The Hindus are saying we are all the sons of God – Jesus was taking it too literally and claimed *he* was *the* son of God. Then he was travelling back to his homeland to be spreading the word about his new faith – the Romans were getting annoyed with him and were crucifying him but he was not dying because of the yoga he was learning, he rose above his pain and fell into a spiritual trance.

MARGARET: Then what happened?

KABIR: He woke up, in a tomb, got up and Mary Magdalen thought he was the gardener.

JENNY: *(Laughs.)* A gardener!

KABIR: It was giving him an idea and so he was going back to India where he was working for the rest of his life with plants. He was dying when he was about sixty-five. Some have said they are knowing where his grave is.

MARGARET: *(Fascinated.)* Where?

JENNY: In Kabir's home town, of course.

KABIR: Well – yes. In Kashmir.

JENNY: In the foothills of the Himalayas where he'd be closer to God.

KABIR: He is being buried as a Jew because the Hindus are a very exclusive club. You cannot be converting to Hinduism.

JENNY cracks up laughing.

It is true!

MARGARET: So, walking on water was nothing next to walking on hot coals.

KABIR: He was learning it from all those mad Hindu sages.

KABIR gives JENNY a meaningful look and then wanders off.

SEBASTIAN stands back.

SEBASTIAN: All set.

He exits.

MARGARET: Not very communicative, is he?

JENNY: Unlike some people round here, he thinks before he speaks.

JENNY opens the letter and reads it quickly. MARGARET watches as JENNY looks crestfallen.

MARGARET: Bad news I take it?

JENNY: I can't believe it.

MARGARET: What?

JENNY: This can't be right.

JENNY re-reads the letter.

MARGARET: What?

JENNY: They turned down our appeal.

MARGARET: I'm sorry, dear. Perhaps the petition might make a difference.

JENNY: Too late now. How am I going to tell Kabir?

JENNY looks distraught.

MARGARET: It's time you came clean. You haven't exactly been totally honest with him have you?

JENNY: Meaning?

MARGARET: Meaning, you knew this was likely to happen.

JENNY: I was hoping… I thought there might be an outside chance…

MARGARET: It's never wise to give a man false hope.

SCENE 3

It is night time. KABIR is arranging some lanterns around the bench for his midnight vigil. Once they have been set up, he gathers a shawl around his head and body, picks up his machete and sits on the bench and waits. He looks up at the tree and the wall from time to time. All he can hear is the sound of traffic and the flash of headlights.

We hear the sound of a woman's weeping, soft but anguished, coming from the shed. The woman's voice calls out his name in anguish.

WOMAN: *(Voice off.)* Kabir! Kabir!

KABIR does not flinch. Instead, he turns SEBASTIAN's tripod and camera around so it is facing the tree.

He hears the sound of a car approaching, car door slamming and footsteps. KABIR raises his machete.

MICHAEL: *(Off.)* Kabir?

KABIR: *(Calls back.)* Ah! Mikey.

KABIR throws down his machete and goes off stage. We hear the gate being unlocked. MICHAEL and KABIR enter. MICHAEL is carrying some books under his arm.

What are you doing here so late?

MICHAEL: I could ask the same of you my friend.

KABIR ushers MICHAEL to the bench.

KABIR: I am glad you are coming. Sit, sit.

KABIR looks around surreptitiously as if afraid he will be overheard.

I am doing stake out.

MICHAEL: For what?

KABIR: I am waiting for the criminal who has defiled the grave yard. Would you like some masala chai?

MICHAEL: Oh yes please…

KABIR: Good.

KABIR scurries off to his shed and disappears for a second.

He re-emerges a few seconds later carrying a thermos flask and two mugs. He gets busy pouring the tea. Then he pours a generous amount of whiskey into it.

MICHAEL: Thank you. So you think the intruder will return?

KABIR: He will come back. I just hope the end for Mumtaz was quick and that she did not suffer.

MICHAEL looks at all the lanterns KABIR has set up.

These are bad times.

MICHAEL: *(Puts his hands together in prayer.)* The Lord almighty, grant us a quiet night and a perfect end. Be sober, be watchful. Your adversary the Devil prowls around like a roaring lion, seeking to devour. Resist him, firm in Your faith. Amen.

KABIR produces a packet of cards from his pocket and automatically starts to deal. MICHAEL picks up his cards. This is obviously a ritual they have. They start to play. MICHAEL jumps as SEBASTIAN's camera flashes. He looks up at the camera – frightened.

KABIR: Don't worry – Sebastian's camera – he is doing some project – rubbish. I turned the camera away. He will be getting some very nice photos of the tree.

MICHAEL: Hey, Kabir… *(He giggles.)* Do you think he really was a photo-journalist? His hands are so shaky – how does he hold the camera still?

KABIR: He is being a liar. You ever been seeing any of his photos? All talking, talking and no evidence.

MICHAEL and KABIR share the joke.

MICHAEL: Jenny told me he used to be a famous photographer – travelled the world – apparently.

KABIR: Jenny will be believing any story she is hearing. Too trusting. They come here, they are pulling her strings, she is feeling sorry for them…

There is a rustle of leaves and the sound of someone approaching. They both freeze. KABIR gets up slowly and as the figure enters he ambushes the intruder, there is a struggle as KABIR wrestles him to the ground. MICHAEL stands by, worried.

(Shouting.) Think you can be coming in here killing my duck…? Eh?

MICHAEL: Kabir – be careful…don't hurt him.

SEBASTIAN: Help! Help!

MICHAEL shines a torch on the intruder's face.

KABIR: SEBASTIAN!

KABIR looks annoyed. MICHAEL helps SEBASTIAN to his feet and then brushes him down.

SEBASTIAN: That's quite a welcome.

MICHAEL: Are you okay?

SEBASTIAN looks a bit winded but nods. We see he is carrying a camera. He checks it to make sure it's okay.

KABIR: *(Ungracious.)* Sorry – I thought you were being an intruder.

SEBASTIAN: The gate was unlocked.

KABIR: Why are you being here anyway? The graveyard is closed now.

SEBASTIAN: This a private party?

KABIR: Yes.

MICHAEL: No. Please, sit down.

SEBASTIAN plonks himself down on the bench next to them.

KABIR looks accusingly at MICHAEL.

SEBASTIAN: Hey, you got any booze stashed in that shed of yours?

KABIR: No.

SEBASTIAN eyes KABIR and MICHAEL's drinks.

MICHAEL: It is masala chai – Kabir's special concoction. Want some?

SEBASTIAN: Yeah – since you're offering.

KABIR pours a drink from his flask and hands it over ungraciously to SEBASTIAN. He takes a sip. MICHAEL watches carefully for a reaction.

Not bad.

MICHAEL is pleased. Another sip.

Very nice in fact.

MICHAEL slaps SEBASTIAN affectionately on the back.

Taste even better if it was spiked. Still. Cheers.

SEBASTIAN gets up and looks at his camera.

Who shifted this?

KABIR and MICHAEL are silent. SEBASTIAN rearranges the camera so that it is pointing the right way.

MICHAEL: How are your classes going?

SEBASTIAN: Okay. They're good kids.

KABIR: They are ruffians. Always leaving the hall in a terrible mess.

SEBASTIAN: They're just young. Not properly house-trained.

MICHAEL: Jenny says you are a good teacher.

SEBASTIAN: *(Pleased.)* Does she?

MICHAEL: Yes. I saw the little photograph exhibition in the church hall last week. It was good.

SEBASTIAN: *(Delighted.)* Thank you. We worked hard on that.

SEBASTIAN spies a plant.

Red chillies and what's this?

KABIR: Coriander and over there methi. It is reminding me of home. Ten years since I was being there.

MICHAEL: Are you missing Nadia?

KABIR: You are knowing how it is, Mikey.

MICHAEL: Of course.

SEBASTIAN: Who's Nadia?

KABIR: My daughter.

SEBASTIAN: You got a daughter?

KABIR: Back in India.

SEBASTIAN: She ever visit you here?

KABIR: I have deliberately kept away from her. She doesn't know even that I am alive.

SEBASTIAN: Absentee father.

KABIR: She is safe, she is nearly sixteen, she will marry one day – I am sending my brother money regularly.

MICHAEL: You should write to her. It would give her hope.

KABIR: What good would it be doing?

SEBASTIAN: That's fucking heavy shit – that is. You got a kid who doesn't even know you're alive?

KABIR: I have nothing to be offering her.

SEBASTIAN: My kids don't want to know me. Think I'm a loser. Slam the phone down on me…call me an animal.

They want to come and see the world through my eyes… but they don't care…don't want to even know.
I need a drink.

MICHAEL produces his books.

MICHAEL: *(To KABIR.)* I got these for you – from the library.

KABIR: Books? For me?

MICHAEL: Mainly photographs.

KABIR looks excited as he takes the first book and crouches by the lantern to flick through it. SEBASTIAN gets up and takes a look over KABIR's shoulder.

KABIR: A shikara! *(He laughs.)* And the houseboats. My grandfather worked as a cook on one of those boats.

SEBASTIAN: Beautiful.

KABIR: This is wonderful. Thank you, Mikey.

MICHAEL: I saw them and I thought my old friend would like to see his birthplace.

KABIR continues to flick through the book excitedly.

SEBASTIAN: The light's amazing. Looks like paradise.

KABIR: That is why everyone is fighting over it.

KABIR looks at MICHAEL and SEBASTIAN full of hope.

Sometimes I am dreaming of returning to my village in a shikara, covered in lotus blossoms. In a jewelled trunk, I have beautiful expensive embroidered shawls and silken garments for my family. I see them all standing there waiting for me, cheering.

MICHAEL: It could happen.

As KABIR speaks we see the shadow of a woman's figure, standing in the doorway of the shed.

KABIR: I am walking through the village and everyone is there – my Nadia – a little girl again – my older brother – *(Laughs.)* he is still scolding me for leaving them for such a long time. I have been away ten years but they are all the same, they have not aged. My mother rushes up to me and kisses my face and my uncle is eyeing the jewelled trunk greedily. And there, I can see her outline, my wife – Nusrat – she is standing, half hidden in the shadow of our doorway, anxious. Have I changed? Has England made me different?

KABIR stretches out his arms longingly. MICHAEL and SEBASTIAN watch. The woman's shadow disappears.

I want to stroke her face but I am not being able to see her. Her veil is drawn around her head – or is it the shadow of the door?

MICHAEL: It is a nice dream to have but we cannot turn the clocks back, my friend.

KABIR is silent. SEBASTIAN looks baffled.

SEBASTIAN: You…lost your wife?

KABIR: She was taken from me.

SEBASTIAN: Sorry man.

KABIR tries to cheer himself up.

KABIR: But, no more looking backwards. I am having plans. I am wanting to start a new family.

MICHAEL: *(Surprised.)* Are you?

KABIR: Oh yes.

SEBASTIAN: Who's the lucky lady?

KABIR touches his nose.

KABIR: Everything will be revealed in the ripeness of time.

SEBASTIAN turns to MICHAEL.

SEBASTIAN: Where are you from then?

MICHAEL: Africa.

SEBASTIAN: Is a continent. You can't be more specific?

MICHAEL: Rwanda. You heard of it?

SEBASTIAN: Yeah – I've heard of it.

MICHAEL: That's my country.

SEBASTIAN: I'm sorry.

KABIR: Mikey here was a man of the cloth.

MICHAEL: A travelling pastor. Now I have no church and no country.

SEBASTIAN: What about this church?

MICHAEL: I cannot pray here.

He taps his forehead.

SEBASTIAN: Don't you think you'll ever go back home?

MICHAEL: No.

SEBASTIAN: Really?

MICHAEL: I cannot forget what I saw. And my little boy…

MICHAEL is emotional and upset. KABIR pats his friend's hand affectionately.

KABIR: Losing a child – I cannot be imagining how terrible that must be.

MICHAEL: Because of me. I should have saved him.
I should have died there with my family.

KABIR: Life is indeed being a mystery. But you must live and be counting your blessings. You are surviving for a reason. And his remains are being at peace here.

SEBASTIAN: You buried him here?

MICHAEL: No – just some of his things. I could not give him a proper grave – so I…

KABIR: We were doing it together – a few of his personal effects in a small box.

The three men sit in silence.

(Looks up at the wall.) No sign of the bastard duck murderer.

MICHAEL: I don't think he will be coming.

KABIR: Why?

MICHAEL: I dropped in because I saw the light from your lamps.

KABIR: *(Irritated.)* Oh. You see? Another example of my excellent stupidity. Sit and wait for the intruder with all the lights on. Surely, I am being the biggest genius you have been meeting for a long time?

MICHAEL and KABIR laugh.

MICHAEL: I think you are a genius.

They laugh more.

KABIR: Detective Inspector Kabir.

MICHAEL: DIK for short.

They both crease up. SEBASTIAN joins them in their laughter.

I saw your lights and I thought to myself, 'That Kabir is having a party.'

KABIR: Yes, yes, party in the graveyard with all my friends the five thousand dead. So you were thinking – 'I must be joining him.'

MICHAEL: It was just an excuse for you not to go home, eh?

KABIR: It is a warm night.

MICHAEL: It is not a place I would like to be in after midnight…

KABIR: Are you scared of the dead?

MICHAEL: No.

SEBASTIAN: I am.

KABIR: They are gone – rotting flesh and bones turned back to the earth. The graves are for the living to visit. That is all.

SEBASTIAN: Hope you're right.

KABIR: Yes. Although, once I saw Satan –

MICHAEL: You saw the Devil? Here?

KABIR: I only was seeing him the one time many years ago. And he was gone very quickly.

SEBASTIAN: You wind-up merchant.

MICHAEL: What did he say?

KABIR: He didn't speak.

SEBASTIAN: Did you tell Jenny? She wouldn't be very happy if she knew the Devil was lurking around her backyard.

SEBASTIAN puts on a rasping scary voice.

I am the evil one. Come join me in a diabolical union and together we will lead the world into corruption and devastation.

KABIR: You are taking the piss from me.

MICHAEL: I believe you!

SEBASTIAN: Come off it.

KABIR: I am telling you, he was there. I saw him sitting on Alan Harwood's grave. But before I was seeing him, I was having the smell of lots of burning matches.
I looked around and he was just…there…smiling at me.

KABIR points to a nearby grave. MICHAEL and SEBASTIAN look at it in fear.

His legs were swinging and he had a huge cloak – it wasn't exactly flapping in the wind – it was doing this magic floating around him, like waves. It made my stomach feel dizzy.

SEBASTIAN: It'd scare the shit out of me.

MICHAEL: I would be terrified.

KABIR: I was at the time. Very tremendous pounding in my heart. He has…this…most beautiful smile – like he is so delighted to be seeing you. An old friend he loves dearly. And you are feeling his compassion reaching out in that smile through the breath in his mouth. And you know, he can be drawing you in with just a small intake of his breath.

MICHAEL crosses himself.

Satan's smile – most alluring and sweet. My father was once telling me that if you see the Devil smile at you – you must be very careful.

MICHAEL: Why?

KABIR: He is wanting you as his disciple. He has been picking you out as a special candidate for his affections.

MICHAEL: And you say he never spoke to you?

KABIR: No. But I was knowing he was waiting for me. And then he was gone. Not vanished in a puff of clouds but just gone.

MICHAEL: What did you do then?

KABIR: I called to Allah for mercy and I cried.

KABIR falls to his knees and raises his hands in prayer.

We praise Allah. Peace and blessing be upon him. We bear witness that there is no God but Him. Grant to me the love of You; grant that I may do the deeds that win Your love; make Your love dearer to me than self, family or wealth.

SEBASTIAN: Did he ever come back?

KABIR: No. But sometimes I can feel him. There are certain people who he is attracted to – like a fly is to shit. I thought he was close by today – patiently marking time – on the look-out.

MICHAEL: For you?

KABIR: Oh yes.

SEBASTIAN: You were smoking some wicked shit that evening? Eh? I'm right, aren't I? A little trippy skunk maybe?

MICHAEL: He probably grows it himself.

KABIR: I am telling the truth.

MICHAEL and SEBASTIAN giggle together.

SEBASTIAN: What would Satan want with a gardener anyway?

KABIR: I have committed my sins. I have to be answering for myself.

MICHAEL: Don't talk rubbish, Kabir.

KABIR: It is true. Why do think I am here? Because I am in hiding and the only person until now who is knowing my business is the Devil. You cannot be hiding from Satan.

SEBASTIAN: What did you do?

KABIR: That is between me and the Devil. But one day, he will be catching up with me – no matter how far I am trying to run.

SEBASTIAN and MICHAEL stare at KABIR in amazed silence.

MICHAEL: If you want to really do a stake out, you need to be alert. Keep a watch out, quieten down and lay a trap for him.

KABIR: Ah yes…you are giving good advice.

MICHAEL gets up and switches all the lamps off. The three sit in the dark.

MICHAEL: There is an art to capturing and cornering your enemy. You must use the cloak of the night to cover you and work on their fear.

KABIR: But I am not seeing anything.

SEBASTIAN: Hey – switch the lights back on. It's freaking me out.

MICHAEL: Shhhh… Wait, your eyes will accustom themselves.

KABIR: I can see you now.

MICHAEL: You must keep your ears pinned back.

KABIR: I…

MICHAEL: Shhh…wait…

The three are silent for some moments. Then suddenly MICHAEL switches on a lamp and points it straight at KABIR's face. He screams at the top of his voice.

Whatareyoudoinghereyoumotherfucker? I'm going to chop you to pieces and leave you to rot with the dead!

MICHAEL grabs KABIR by the scruff of the neck and shakes him hard. At this point, the camera suddenly flashes, taking a picture of MICHAEL. MICHAEL stops abruptly and switches on the lights. KABIR is in a state.

I am sorry…oh my God are you okay?…I was just playing around…trying to show you…

KABIR takes some time to get his breath back. MICHAEL helps him up and looks suspiciously over at SEBASTIAN.

KABIR: Where did you learn to do be doing that?

MICHAEL: I am sorry.

KABIR: No, that was being fantastic!

SEBASTIAN: Good party trick man. You convinced me.

MICHAEL continues to look at the camera and SEBASTIAN uneasily.

SCENE 4

It is early morning. MARGARET enters, looking for KABIR.

MARGARET: Yoo, hooo… Kabir…Kabir?

As she goes around the back of the garden, a big figure looms up behind her. MARGARET screams to high heaven.

SEBASTIAN: Hey, hey, lady…please…it's me…don't panic.

MARGARET stops screaming and looks closely at SEBASTIAN.

SEBASTIAN: Sorry.

MARGARET: What are you doing here?

SEBASTIAN nurses his head.

SEBASTIAN: Don't shout, lady.

MARGARET: …Well really…you could have given me a heart attack. Do you know how old I am? Were you sleeping here?

SEBASTIAN: Must've crashed out.

MARGARET: More like collapsed. Young man, this isn't a doss house you know.

SEBASTIAN continues to nurse his head.

You should straighten yourself up and buy yourself a decent shirt.

SEBASTIAN sits down and rolls himself a cigarette.

You remind me of a houseboy we used to have in our place in Kenya. Jonathan.

SEBASTIAN: Do I?

MARGARET: Very surly, terrible manners but as bright as a button. I heard he went on to become an office clerk – probably running the country by now.

SEBASTIAN remains quiet.

Where are your parents from?

SEBASTIAN: Trinidad. Been there?

MARGARET: Oh yes. Beautiful.

SEBASTIAN: Too many black people though – eh?

MARGARET: I never understood why it's so difficult to have a simple conversation with you people. You always take offence and turn aggressive.

SEBASTIAN: It's too early in the morning for this.

SEBASTIAN staggers over to the tap and scrubs his face with water.

MARGARET: Have you got a woman?

SEBASTIAN: You offering?

MARGARET: *(Giggling.)* If you cleaned your act up – perhaps I might consider it.

SEBASTIAN: Ever slept with a black man?

MARGARET: Yes, Jonathan. Gus – my husband probably knew about it but he didn't care. Too busy screwing every local coloured woman he could get his paws on. God knows how many poor women he impregnated. Jenny tells me you used to be a famous photographer.

SEBASTIAN: A long time ago. Anywhere there was a story, I was there. Bhopal, Cambodia, Nicaragua…

MARGARET: The evil drink – eh?

SEBASTIAN: Got sick of hiding behind the camera lens. Still life misery.

AYESHA enters. She is carrying a tatty folder under her arm. She hesitates when she sees MARGARET.

MARGARET: Hello Ayesha.

AYESHA: *(Wary.)* Hi. *(To SEBASTIAN.)* What's up, Seb.

They slap palms. AYESHA sits on the bench. She looks upset. MARGARET spots the banana tree.

MARGARET: Good God, he's actually installed a banana tree here. Where is Gungha Din anyway?

AYESHA: Kabir?

MARGARET: I need to talk to him.

AYESHA: Apparently he's terracing the slope next to the pond.

MARGARET: Terracing? What's he going to do now? Irrigate the graveyard and stick some paddy fields there?

AYESHA: No, it's for the fountain he's planning to have installed later.

MARGARET: Fountain.

AYESHA: Yeah – he's cutting into the slope to make a terrace and then he's going to put a fountain at the top of the slope. Last of all he'll make a little pathway for the water to flow down through the terraces and into the pond.

MARGARET: That'll confuse the ducks.

AYESHA: He thinks if he makes everything beautiful, the Church Council will change their minds.

MARGARET: So he still doesn't know.

AYESHA: Know what?

SEBASTIAN: *(To AYESHA.)* Do you know where Michael buried his son's things?

AYESHA: Eh?

SEBASTIAN: He's buried something here – is it in the grave yard or here in the garden?

AYESHA: I don't know.

SEBASTIAN looks disappointed. He exits.

He's mental.

MARGARET: Should be certified if you ask me. I've been meaning to ask you, Ayesha, where exactly are you from?

AYESHA: Just down the road – Stanley Road. You know it?

MARGARET: No, I mean originally?

AYESHA: I was born in Battersea.

MARGARET: *(Seeing as she's getting nowhere.)* And before that?

AYESHA: Before my birth?

MARGARET: Your parents dear – where are they from?

AYESHA: Dad was English and Mum's from Turkey – a little town outside Istanbul. Actually, Dad wasn't really English. His dad was Scottish – that's my grandfather and my grandmother's half Irish and a quarter Norwegian and a quarter something else…

MARGARET: Quite a mix and match in your family then.

AYESHA: Yeah, s'ppose.

MARGARET: So – what are your life plans?

AYESHA: Eh?

MARGARET: Surely, you must know what you want to do in the future?

AYESHA: I'd like to travel. I'm going to be an air hostess.

MARGARET: But they're just glorified waiters.

AYESHA: Get to travel the world though. I could see me some volcanoes, a few mountain ranges – stand on top of the world… Got to hang out in Turkey for a bit – then make my way to India and the Taj Mahal…monument to love and all that stuff.

MARGARET: Don't you want to go somewhere civilized like the States or Australia, New Zealand – what about Europe?

AYESHA: Seen it all on telly. Not much different from here, is it? Apart from the open spaces. And the Americans are mad, aren't they? They carry guns and kids shoot each other in the playground. No thanks.

MARGARET: So you're after adventure of the soul.

AYESHA: Yeah.

MARGARET: *(To AYESHA.)* You ever been to Turkey?

AYESHA: A few times. Got lots of cousins and aunts out there. I'd like to go and live there one day.

MARGARET: *(Astonished.)* Would you?

AYESHA: Yeah – why?

MARGARET: Well, it's just that you seem so westernised. I mean, they'd cover you up from head to toe and you'd never be able to earn a living – always have to walk three steps behind your husband and when he tired of you he can just say 'talak, talak, talak…' and you're divorced.

AYESHA: It's not as bad as that…

MARGARET: Terrible reputation the Turks have – my husband was posted to Istanbul for a couple of years.
I, of course, was there with him. Human rights violations, not to mention what they've done to the Kurds. Mind you they were always trouble makers.

AYESHA: Who?

MARGARET: The Kurds. Nomadic farmers and goatherds. Always too proud and too nationalistic for their own good. You seen my granddaughter?

AYESHA: Erm…no.

MARGARET: Discovered God after a terrible shock – love on the rebound – fiancé jilted her at the altar and ran away with her best friend.

AYESHA: Oh…

MARGARET: Tell me – d'you think there's something going on between Jen and the gardener? You know – any hanky panky.

AYESHA: 'Course not!

MARGARET: You *are* young, aren't you, dear?

AYESHA: You got a life plan?

MARGARET: My life plan never changed. Don't want to die on my own – have them find my body rotting, full of maggots three weeks later.

Beat.

AYESHA: How old are you?

MARGARET: You should never ask a lady's age. Very bad manners.

AYESHA rolls up her shirt, baring her midriff and tucks up her skirt into her knickers baring her legs. She lays down on the bench and places her file over her face to shade the sun.

I'll let you get on then.

MARGARET exits. KABIR enters pushing a wheelbarrow. He spots AYESHA and shakes his head and tuts.

KABIR: You should be studying. Not lying around half naked.

AYESHA hurriedly gets to her feet, making herself more presentable.

AYESHA: Can't revise at home…and the sun's so warm and relaxing… Margaret was looking for you. Weird old bird, isn't she? D'you think she's alright upstairs?

KABIR: What is being the matter?

AYESHA: Nothing.

KABIR: Don't be doing that 'nothing' business with me young lady.

AYESHA: What?

KABIR: I am knowing you too long. You are looking like a lost puppy.

AYESHA: Don't talk bollocks.

KABIR: Something is happening at home?

AYESHA is quiet.

I know something is being wrong. You are coming to talk to me specifically. It is being the morning. You should be at school.

AYESHA: I've got a free period.

KABIR: You would rather be here than twittering with your girlie gang? Tell me. He has been beating you?

AYESHA: No!

KABIR: What then?

AYESHA: Nothing.

KABIR sits down next to AYESHA. He pulls her head affectionately onto his shoulder. She leans there for a moment.

I hate him.

Beat.

He did something awful.

KABIR: What?

AYESHA: He chopped the tree down.

KABIR: Your dad's magnolia tree?

AYESHA: I come back from school and the fucker had got these tree surgeons round. They chopped it down. He said it was blocking out the sun. Never even asked me.

KABIR: *Ban Chod.*

AYESHA: I remember Dad planting it.

KABIR pats AYESHA's hand affectionately. But we can see he is furious.

KABIR: Anyone who can be taking a life from a tree is not to be trusted.

AYESHA: He knew it was my dad's tree. That's why he did it.

KABIR: How can your mother be letting this happen?

AYESHA: She was upset. But she won't say anything to him.

KABIR: He is being a very bad man.

AYESHA: He's a shit. I need to get through these exams and then I can go.

KABIR: Where?

AYESHA: Away, anywhere.

KABIR: You are still being a baby.

AYESHA: I'm nearly sixteen.

KABIR: Are you believing in fate, Ayesha?

AYESHA: Fate.

KABIR: You are in my garden for a reason.

AYESHA looks uneasy.

I am remembering the day you were burying your father. You, a little girl – only ten. It was breaking my heart seeing you.

AYESHA: I loved my dad.

KABIR: I know. And that is why, I think you and I have become so close.

AYESHA: We're mates.

KABIR: I have been coming to a decision.

Beat.

I will adopt you.

AYESHA: What?

KABIR: We will be going to the authorities together and be making it official.

AYESHA: Erm…

KABIR: We will be taking out an injunction against this Bill. Jenny will be helping us.

AYESHA tries to take this information in.

I have been thinking about it for some time. Now is the time for being active.

AYESHA: You're so weird.

KABIR: I want to be helping you. You are being on the brink of your life, you are needing the protection of a father. I can be that father.

AYESHA: No offence, Kabir, but… You're serious, aren't you?

KABIR: My bedsit is being too small, so we will have to be looking for a bigger house.

AYESHA: Kabir…

KABIR: Maybe the authorities will be helping us.

AYESHA: I can look after myself.

KABIR: I will be guarding you from the world.

AYESHA: I don't want a fucking guard.

KABIR: Language, Ayesha.

AYESHA: …it's very sweet of you but the last thing I want right now is to tie myself down with yet another family. And anyway, how d'you think the authorities will look at us – eh?

KABIR: What are you meaning?

AYESHA: You're a single bloke.

KABIR doesn't get it.

KABIR: So?

AYESHA: It doesn't look good does it? And I ain't gonna shop my mum to the SS. She'll get it in the neck.

KABIR: She is not being capable of looking after you as a mother should be caring for her child.

AYESHA: *(Angry now.)* She's still my mum.

KABIR: I can be looking after you. Please Ayesha…

AYESHA: No – man.

KABIR: I can be your father.

AYESHA: No. Thanks for the offer but – no.

KABIR: I am offering you a chance to be changing your life, not to be living in fear.

AYESHA: Do I look like I'm living in fear? I'm angry, not scared.

KABIR: You should be taking the offer with gladness.

AYESHA: I don't need your charity.

KABIR: For five years I have been watching you grow and all the time, your mother has different boyfriends – it is not being good. It is not being right.

AYESHA: What the fuck do you know about my mum?

KABIR: What you are telling me.

AYESHA: You don't know her though.

KABIR: You are needing better guidance, a shoulder to be leaning on, someone who is listening to you. I am standing here, wanting to take the responsibility.

AYESHA: I'm not some little fucking stray.

KABIR: Please. Give me the chance to be proving what a good father I could be.

AYESHA: No. NO.

She exits. KABIR looks upset and confused. He sits down on the bench for a few moments and tries to gather himself. SEBASTIAN enters. KABIR ignores him.

SEBASTIAN: We need to talk.

KABIR: What would I be wanting to be talking to you about?

SEBASTIAN: It's about Michael… What's he got buried here?

KABIR: How is that being your business?

SEBASTIAN: D'you know where it is?

KABIR: Why should I be telling you?

SEBASTIAN: Just do me a favour – eh? Tell me where that thing's buried and I'll dig it up.

KABIR: You are being ridiculous.

SEBASTIAN: Tell me!

KABIR: Are you being drunk again?

SEBASTIAN: Did you see what was in the box? Did you see the contents with your own eyes?

KABIR: No…but I am not needing to. They were his sons' belongings.

SEBASTIAN: Are you sure?

KABIR holds his hands up as if in surrender.

KABIR: You are being very mad, Sebastian.

SEBASTIAN: Listen to me, man!

KABIR gets up and gets back to work.

KABIR: My head is being full. I cannot be listening to your ravings.

SEBASTIAN: Michael's a bad man. You gotta help me – I need to find that box.

KABIR: You are being a complete mess. You are being drunk all of the time – look at you! Crazy idiot.

SEBASTIAN: I'm not crazy – I can explain…

JENNY enters. She is talking on her mobile phone.

JENNY: I thought that perhaps maybe I could come and see you this evening? I see…

SEBASTIAN falls silent. KABIR tends to his plants – clipping, watering, etc. JENNY looks at him anxiously.

Okay. Fine. Thanks…for listening. I'd better go. Bye.

JENNY clicks off her phone. SEBASTIAN goes off to one side and starts dismantling his tripod and camera.

KABIR: Hot line to God? Or was it Jesus Christ?

JENNY ignores him and paces. KABIR watches her.

You are making me nervous.

JENNY: What?

KABIR: All this marching up and down…

JENNY: Sorry.

She sits on the bench and watches KABIR. She fiddles and can't sit still.

Kabir. This church and the graveyard…

KABIR: We should be hearing about the appeal any day now – yes?

JENNY: Yes… You've put a lot of work into this place.

KABIR: So have you.

JENNY: Kabir, there's something I need to tell you…

MARGARET enters with MICHAEL.

JENNY looks annoyed. She's missed her chance.

MICHAEL: They bury the bananas in the ground to help them ferment. Only takes a few days because of the heat.

MARGARET: That's how they make banana beer?

MICHAEL: Of course, that was the first hint they had in Goma that the volcano was about to erupt because the bananas only took one day to ferment. The ground below was bubbling.

MARGARET: Fascinating.

MARGARET spots KABIR.

Ah there you are…

She looks carefully at JENNY and KABIR.

MICHAEL sits down on the bench. He is clutching a Bible. SEBASTIAN is still fiddling with his camera.

KABIR: You were looking for me?

MARGARET looks around the garden with approval.

MARGARET: Such a peaceful corner of the graveyard. It really is looking quite lovely.

KABIR: Ah…but I have bigger plans. You know that little patch of green in the west part of the graveyard. I am thinking of making a little pergola there, with a small gathering of trees. Then people can be sitting and resting there. I will not be starting work until we are knowing for sure but…

MARGARET: Kabir – I thought we were being booted out.

JENNY: *(Warning.)* Gran…

KABIR: We are still waiting for the conclusion of the appeal.

MARGARET: You mean Jen hasn't told you yet?

JENNY: No – I haven't, Gran.

KABIR: Told me what?

MARGARET: You didn't know?

KABIR: Didn't know what?

JENNY: Gran. I specifically said…

MARGARET: I'm sorry…I thought you knew…me and my big mouth.

KABIR: What are you talking about, Mrs Catchpole?

MARGARET: It's nothing.

KABIR: What is going on?

JENNY: Nothing…

MARGARET: It's not for me to say – Jenny should tell you.

KABIR: You must be telling me now. I am demanding you to tell me.

MARGARET: Really – it's best if it comes from Jen.

JENNY: Oh thanks, Gran.

KABIR: TELL ME!

JENNY: I was going to get around to telling you in my own time but, since my hand has been forced… They are definitely closing the church and going ahead with the sale.

KABIR: No.

JENNY: I had heard talk before…I didn't think it would come to this but they're selling it…to a health club…going to convert it into a new fitness studio.

KABIR: No.

JENNY: I'm afraid it's true.

KABIR: And the gardens?

MARGARET: A swimming pool.

KABIR: The graves?

JENNY: Will be fenced off.

KABIR: But the petition?

JENNY: They ignored it.

KABIR: All gone? Everything finished? How long have you known?

JENNY: I only found out yesterday.

KABIR: Yesterday?

KABIR thinks for a moment longer and then exits.

JENNY: *(Calls out.)* Kabir! Please…

MICHAEL: I'd better see if he's alright.

MICHAEL follows KABIR.

JENNY glowers at her grandmother and then storms out in the opposite direction.

MARGARET: *(Smiles.)* Oh dear, I think I'm in the dog house.

She exits slowly. SEBASTIAN is left on his own on the stage. He notices a Bible that MICHAEL has left behind. He picks it up and opens it. Reading the inscription on the inside cover he looks delighted.

SEBASTIAN: Yes!

SCENE 5

It is late afternoon. MICHAEL paces anxiously. He looks at his watch from time to time. KABIR staggers in, swaying. He is swigging whiskey from a bottle and looks quite drunk.

MICHAEL: I have been looking for you everywhere.
I waited for you here for hours. Where have you been?

KABIR deliberately pisses all over his precious orchids.

(Horrified.) Kabir!

KABIR: Go away, Mikey.

MICHAEL: Your orchids!

KABIR: Fuck 'em. They are closing this place down. All my work.

MICHAEL: You can rebuild this place somewhere else.

KABIR: I have made this my garden of paradise, a place for the people who have loved ones buried here. Somewhere they can walk and think and be on their own. It's going to be flooded. It's going be a swimming pool.

MICHAEL: I am sorry.

KABIR: Why was I bothering?

KABIR starts to kick his plants and flowers.

MICHAEL: Don't do that…

KABIR: What is being the point of these plants?

He continues to kick the plants.

MICHAEL: Please, stop it, Kabir.

KABIR picks up a tub of flowers and hurls it across the garden.

What are you doing? Stop it…they are your plants…

KABIR: Better I destroy them than they are drowned.

MICHAEL tries to stop KABIR. KABIR almost fights MICHAEL off.

Leave me alone!

KABIR gets into a wild rage, uprooting things and throwing things around. MICHAEL tries to stop him.

MICHAEL: Kabir, don't do this…they can be saved…you can replant them somewhere else…

KABIR: *(Shouts.)* Replant? Where? Where am I going to be now? Nowhere!

MICHAEL tries to stop him again but KABIR is strong and flings him off.

This is being my punishment.

MICHAEL: Sit down and take rest…you have drunk too much.

KABIR: Jenny was not even telling me.

MICHAEL: She was afraid – I think she was trying to find a good moment.

KABIR: My life is being finished. What am I doing this all for? I have been rebuilding for what? I was thinking I could live out the rest of my days here.

MICHAEL: These things happen my friend. We are merely guests in this country and we have to get used to being moved around a little.

KABIR: It is Satan. He is playing with me. He is pushing me like he was doing before.

MICHAEL: There is no devil here.

KABIR: I am the Devil.

MICHAEL: Now you are being ridiculous.

KABIR: You are seeing terrible things, Mikey but you are not doing them. Not like me.

MICHAEL: What are you talking about?

KABIR: I am an evil man saturated in my wife's blood.

KABIR slumps and sits down on the ground. He is broken hearted.

My Nusrat…

We hear the distant sound of men shouting, gunshots and screaming. KABIR points. He looks terrified.

The Indian soldiers, they have come to loot our village. Houses are on fire! They say we are hiding the separatists but we are innocent.

The gunshots get closer. KABIR relives the moment. He is in a panic. He scurries around looking for a hiding place.

They are coming…Nusrat…give me the baby…they are coming here…hide…we must be hiding. Quick…out here…they have guns…they will be shooting us…

KABIR hides behind a small shrub. He is clutching an imaginary child in his arms. The gunshots and shouting stop. There is total silence. KABIR watches with horror. We hear the same screaming we heard before. Nusrat's voice calls out KABIR's name, but he remains where he is.

They are raping her. Four soldiers…they take it in turns and I am watching. I am watching, covering my child's eyes and ears with my hands, squeezing her so tight to me – afraid she will call out. I am watching with these eyes of mine and I am not saving her. I can feel he is sitting behind me.

MICHAEL: Who?

KABIR: Satan. He is watching and smiling. I can be hearing him. He is saying, 'Stay where you are.' And I am being stuck to the spot.

They are strangling her and I can be seeing the life squeezed and squeezed from her face, they are pressing harder and harder on her soft throat…and then the soldiers are leaving. As if they have finished their day's work and they must go home for dinner.

KABIR remains where he is for some moments. MICHAEL helps KABIR up.

MICHAEL: You did not kill her. You saved your daughter.

KABIR: I should have been saving my wife, I should have been giving my life for her. I can never be returning to my birth place, never facing my daughter because of the shame. What sort of a terrible man am I being?

MICHAEL: You did what you had to do to survive, to save your child. You are not evil.

KABIR: I am lost.

MICHAEL: If you think you have done wrong, you must hear what happened to me. Then we will be truly like brothers. Yes?

KABIR: You are not understanding. You have seen terrible things but you have not been sinning.

MICHAEL glances over at KABIR's shed.

MICHAEL: Listen to what happened to me. At the beginning of the killings, I was living in the Kibungo area of Rwanda with my wife and our son.

KABIR: You are being a wronged man – a noble man. I am being the worst kind of coward.

MICHAEL: I understand your guilt my friend but don't let it eat you up. I have done much worse. We hid some friends in our chicken house at the bottom of our garden. A Tutsi family who had run from their land. A man, woman and their two small daughters. They were afraid. Every day the *Interahamwe* militia were prowling the village looking for Tutsis. So we hid them.

KABIR: You see? Even in the terrible conditions of your land you still…

MICHAEL: Listen. Each day I went into the local town to fetch our food, the militia at the roadblock would stop and search me on the way back…

KABIR: Search you?

MICHAEL: To see I was not carrying any extra food. They knew there were only three of us in our family. They wanted to see if I was feeding anyone else. This went on for ten days. Each day, I would be more and more afraid. Do you know what a roadblock is?

KABIR shakes his head. MICHAEL gets up and paces. He arranges some bricks and stones in front of KABIR. KABIR watches him.

It is a pile of stones in the middle of the road – manned by drunk, mad *interahamwe* militia men. In order to travel down the road, you have to argue your way through them.

KABIR stares at the stones. MICHAEL beckons him forwards. KABIR stands. MICHAEL picks up KABIR's machete and squares up to KABIR aggressively. MICHAEL transforms himself into a militia man, spitting out questions.

Who are you? Where are you going? Where is your card motherfucker? Your identity card. If you are an *Inyenzi* you will die. All cockroaches will die. Do you understand? Give it to me. Show me your card – where is it? NOW.

KABIR looks afraid as MICHAEL viciously pushes KABIR around using the blunt end of the machete.

We know you *Inyenzi* have dug pits under your floors to bury our corpses. We will stamp the filth of the Tutsi cockroaches out of our country once and for all. Vermin! Rats! Snakes! We will kill you all!

How much money have you got? You can't get by unless you pay us. Any beer?

KABIR backs away. MICHAEL reverts back to himself.

Each time I went by, there would be a pile of bodies just off the road – Tutsis who had met their end at that roadblock. I often saw the killings and it was a truly terrifying sight – men covered in dried banana leaves – like traditional dancers –

MICHAEL dances – it is a traditional Rwandan dance. He sings and swings the machete around, bringing it down jubilantly on imaginary bodies. We hear the sound of men shouting and screaming coming from the shed. KABIR looks terrified.

On the tenth day, as I was returning home with food – they began to shout at me and kick me.

KABIR: Even though you were a Pastor?

MICHAEL: It meant nothing to them. They knew I was hiding a family – someone must have informed them.
I thought I had met my end. They marched me back home and demanded I tell them where the Tutsi family was. Otherwise, they would kill me and my wife and children.

KABIR: What did you do?

MICHAEL: What could I do? I showed them to the chicken house. We hear the terrifying sound of children screaming as they are butchered. Broken eggs and blood everywhere. The screams of the family die out and it is silent.

KABIR: They were all killed?

MICHAEL nods.

Those militia men butchered that family? In cold blood?

MICHAEL: They said it had to be done. To rid our country of vermin. 'Go to work,' they said.

KABIR: Work?

MICHAEL looks down at the machete in his hand.

MICHAEL: As if they were farmers cultivating the land. They gave me the machete and told me to do it.

KABIR: No!

MICHAEL: They said if I didn't, they would castrate me in front of my family and they would all stand around and watch me bleed to death. I did as I was told to protect my wife and child.

KABIR: You murdered children?

MICHAEL: I killed to survive.

KABIR: How could you do it?

MICHAEL: I had no choice.

KABIR: You had a choice. To die bravely and with honour without blood on your hands.

MICHAEL: It is very easy to say such noble things when you are not faced with the situation that I was.

KABIR: No…no…you were a man of the cloth…how could you be taking a life? How could you be dealing with your conscience?

MICHAEL: I was a husband and father first. I knew that my refusal would not only lead to my death but then to the rape and mutilation of my wife followed by the hacking to death of my child.

KABIR: But that family…you hacked them to death!

MICHAEL: God is my witness – I did it to save my family.

KABIR: You shouldn't have told me.

MICHAEL: But I told you because – I wanted to ease your mind. You were torturing yourself. You are my friend.

KABIR: That family were your friends.

MICHAEL: What would you have done in my place?

KABIR is silent.

You cannot answer me, my friend, because you hid and I killed. Both of us did it to save our lives.

KABIR walks away devastated. MICHAEL calls out after him.

I am not evil. Do not think badly of me.

KABIR: What does it matter what I am thinking?

MICHAEL: It matters to me.

KABIR: What you are telling me, Mikey – I cannot be comprehending.

MICHAEL: I haven't told you what happened next.

KABIR: No more…

MICHAEL: Do you know what those militia men did after I had…I had…

KABIR: Butchered that family?

MICHAEL: They called me a traitor – said they had to teach me a lesson. They killed my wife. They spared me and Charles but he saw his own mother being…killed. They forced me to kill and then they still punished me – no mercy – no compassion…my wife…

MICHAEL weeps. KABIR hesitates and then returns to where MICHAEL is seated. He puts his arm around him.

Interval.

Act Two

SCENE 1

KABIR is trying to tidy up the garden. He looks tired and upset. He is not making much headway and is slow.

JENNY enters. She stares around the garden in horror.

JENNY: God, what a mess – what happened?

KABIR ignores her. Instead, he continues tidying up.

Kabir – you okay?

Please, don't be angry. Come on, Kabir, we've been friends for too long.

KABIR: If we were being such good friends you should have been telling me the news to my face. You were being a coward – not telling me.

JENNY: I didn't know how to… I know how much this place means to you.

KABIR surveys the mess around him.

KABIR: Everything is spoilt.

He picks up the banana tree and tries to straighten it.

Nothing is the same. I don't think I can be starting all over again – from the beginning.

JENNY: We still have a couple of months, it's not as if they're throwing us out onto the streets. I don't know where they're sending me yet but as soon as I do – I can make sure you have a job…

KABIR: *(Angry.)* This is not just my job. I don't do this because I am simply working. This is my life.

JENNY: I know… I know…

KABIR: You don't know. You and I are living in very different worlds.

JENNY: Kabir – please.

KABIR: No. Don't be pretending. To you – I am like a servant.

JENNY: How can you say that?

KABIR: You have never been suffering. How can you be giving comfort to people when you have never been in any bad situation? You are living in a cocoon where everyone is being 'nice' and giving charity to all those poor little starving black babies in the 'third' world.

JENNY: Stop it.

KABIR: And I am being another black bastard you are using.

JENNY: How dare you?

KABIR: You are collecting money in your church to ease your own little conscience when it is your Church that caused the fuck ups in those countries in the first place!

JENNY: Don't take it out on me. You don't have the monopoly on loss.

KABIR: Jenny, you are not knowing what it is like to live without hope – to know the things I am knowing. Every way I am turning, I am seeing more and more suffering. However far I run, I cannot be hiding anymore.

JENNY: There's nothing to hide from. You must stop blaming yourself. What happened to your family, to Nusrat is enough to drive anyone mad. But it wasn't your fault.

KABIR: It was his fault.

KABIR points heavenward.

Too many people suffering everywhere. Too many wars and too much cruelty. How are we supposed to live? To be knowing what is good and bad when all we are being shown is evil.

JENNY: But for every evil there is good. The world is an ugly place but…

KABIR: What are you knowing about the ugliness of the world? You sit here in your safe little world of Jesus Christ – preaching to the brainwashed. What would you be doing if you were being faced with danger? How would you be reacting if your whole town was being looted and burnt to the ground by soldiers?

JENNY: I don't know.

KABIR: Your God is being rubbish. He is, as Ayesha would say, a 'fucker'. I should have been listening to my head and taking revenge.

JENNY: No. Revenge doesn't work. It never has. It simply keeps the hatred alive.

KABIR: So when will I ever be having any peace, Jenny? When will I be free?

JENNY: When you learn to forgive yourself.

KABIR: I cannot forget.

JENNY: No – but you can live and move on, Kabir. This is just a patch of earth.

KABIR: Then I am choosing the wrong patch of earth. It is being a place for the dead.

JENNY: Maybe you're right. Maybe we should all get out of here.

JENNY looks at KABIR sadly.

KABIR: If I am staying here. I will be living in hell forever afraid of being lured into the Devil's nest.

JENNY: We're all one step away from the Devil's nest.

KABIR: Some of us are being closer than others though.

MICHAEL: Ah…Jenny…Kabir.

MICHAEL looks over at the bench and then beneath it.

JENNY: What are you looking for?

MICHAEL: My Bible. I thought I left it here… Have you seen it?

JENNY: No…

KABIR shakes his head.

Was it very precious?

MICHAEL: It is from home. I cannot remember where I last had it. I always carry it around with me.

JENNY: I'll ask around for you.

MICHAEL: No…it's fine…it was a battered old thing.

MICHAEL continues to look worried.

JENNY: Did it have your name in it?

MICHAEL: Erm…no I don't think so. Actually, it belonged to an old friend…it doesn't matter…perhaps it will turn up.

MICHAEL exits hurriedly.

KABIR: I was being a peaceful man. I offered prayers to Allah five times a day and I was working hard for my family. The soldiers and the separatists were all using us in their battle for our land. We were being innocent.

I am wanting to be seeing my daughter. She is almost a woman now and all I have are photographs. It is not being the same thing.

I am thinking I should be going home. My brother is living in Delhi now. He has a new job as a school head teacher. He was always the clever one…maybe the school is needing a gardener.

The two sit in silence for a while.

JENNY: You have been my rock, Kabir. The one point of sanity in my life.

KABIR: And you have been helping me in so many ways.

JENNY: When I lose this church, I'll lose you. Maybe that's why I couldn't bring myself to tell you. I find the thought of not seeing you every day almost as unbearable as leaving this place.

KABIR: *(Smiles.)* I am just being the gardener, Jenny. A heathen, a non-believer, a foreigner.

KABIR takes JENNY's hand and kisses it. They laugh. MICHAEL enters. He looks worried.

SCENE 2

The sun is setting. A party is going on. Loud reggae music is playing and SEBASTIAN is dancing, can of beer in one hand. MICHAEL is choosing tapes for the ghetto blaster. AYESHA is stringing some fairy lights up. AYESHA drapes them across some grave stones.

KABIR: Isn't that being disrespectful?

AYESHA: They're hardly gonna complain.

KABIR looks uncomfortable.

Take a chill pill, Kabir.

SEBASTIAN: Yeah, ease up man. Loosen your collar…enjoy…

KABIR: She should be revising.

AYESHA: Give me a break.

KABIR: Maths tomorrow. You must be having a clear head.

AYESHA: I'll just stay for a bit.

SEBASTIAN: Ignore him. Stay for as long as you like.

KABIR: You are being a bad influence.

SEBASTIAN: Believe me, I'm the least of your worries.

AYESHA: I was thinking Kabir, after this place has closed – you should advertise your services locally. Lots of people need gardeners.

KABIR: I am thinking maybe…

AYESHA: The toffs up the hill have got huge gardens. You could mint it.

KABIR plugs the lights in. AYESHA claps her hands in delight.

It's like Christmas.

KABIR: Now all we are needing is a turkey.

MARGARET enters. She is clutching a bottle of vodka and some tomato juice.

MARGARET: Looks lovely dears.

She looks around at the plants etc. all in dissaray.

This place is a bit of a mess though.

MARGARET waves the bottle at KABIR.

My contribution. Thought we could have some Bloody Marys.

AYESHA grabs the bottle and looks at it.

AYESHA: Excellent.

KABIR grabs the bottle from her.

KABIR: You are not drinking any of this.

AYESHA: Come on…just one.

KABIR: No.

AYESHA: Fascist.

KABIR: You will be having one drink, getting sick, falling asleep and then not getting up for the examination.

AYESHA: Think I'm that green?

MARGARET: If you want to pass your exams and travel the world, tonight you'll have to stick to Virgin Marys, my dear.

AYESHA sulks. SEBASTIAN has a little dance around pulling MARGARET gently around with him. She laughs and does a little twirl. The others watch. JENNY enters carrying a tray of glasses and a couple of bottles of wine.

JENNY: Can't imagine why we're doing this. Don't exactly feel in the celebrating mood.

SEBASTIAN: I think it's a great idea.

MICHAEL: The end of an era.

SEBASTIAN: Exactly.

JENNY arranges the glasses on the table.

JENNY: Can't concentrate on my sermon. Keep getting these visions in my head of sweaty men pumping iron in the pulpit.

MARGARET: Sounds rather like a sexual fantasy to me.

JENNY: Gran!

MARGARET: At least the place'll be packed, Jen. Probably have more people in it than it's had in a century. The new temple to the human body.

KABIR gets to work uncorking the wine and handing out glasses. SEBASTIAN cracks open a can of beer and gives one to AYESHA. He's unsteady on his feet.

SEBASTIAN: Get that down you girl.

KABIR: *(Warning.)* AYESHA!

AYESHA: It's only beer.

AYESHA takes a swig under KABIR's watchful eye.

JENNY: Five thousand graves. Nobody's thought about what will happen to them.

MARGARET: Stop worrying about the graves.

JENNY: But I do worry. Who's going to look after them? Once Kabir's gone, the graveyard will become overgrown.

SEBASTIAN: Forgotten bones.

JENNY: Come on then, Sebastian. One last photo. You got your camera on you?

SEBASTIAN: Sure.

MICHAEL looks at his watch

MICHAEL: I cannot stay too long…

JENNY: One last photo of everyone. For my album.

JENNY herds everyone into a group. They all do her bidding except MICHAEL who stands aside.

KABIR: Mikey – please.

Everyone calls MICHAEL over. He joins them reluctantly. SEBASTIAN sways as he tries to focus.

Smile!

False smiles all round.

Look at the mad man – he cannot even be standing straight.

MARGARET: I think we should at least drink a toast.

SEBASTIAN: A good idea.

SEBASTIAN makes sure everyone has a glass.

KABIR: Go on, Jenny.

JENNY: Me?

SEBASTIAN: *(Heckles.)* Remember it's a toast not a prayer.

JENNY: Thank you for reminding me, Sebastian.

They all laugh and stand to attention with their glasses and look at JENNY expectantly.

Well…erm…to all of you, thank you for standing so close over the past few weeks. It's been…difficult. But all good things must come to an end and we must leave our lovely Garden of Eden, I'm afraid.

JENNY looks at KABIR. They smile sadly at each other.

Anyway. Raise your glasses – to a brighter and happier future.

ALL: The future.

AYESHA downs her drink in one.

KABIR: Another one.

SEBASTIAN refills everyone's glasses.

This has been my home for nearly ten years now. I have been making good friends when I was losing everything. I am wanting to thank you all and to be saying don't be becoming a stranger. And good luck to Ayesha in her exams. Bottoms up!

ALL: Cheers.

SEBASTIAN: Anyone else?

SEBASTIAN looks around at everyone. MICHAEL makes a toast.

MICHAEL: This place has been very special. You have all been like a family to me.

MARGARET: Very strange one.

MICHAEL: You will all remain in my heart forever. Thank you.

Everyone raises their glasses and drinks.

I am sorry. But now, I must leave.

KABIR: Already?

MICHAEL: I have to pack. Tomorrow I leave – a little trip to see a friend.

KABIR: But we haven't even been starting the party yet.

MICHAEL: I'm sorry…

KABIR: You were not telling me you were going away.

MICHAEL: It was a last minute thought.

SEBASTIAN: Where are you going?

MICHAEL: The States.

MICHAEL embraces KABIR affectionately.

I will be in touch my friend.

KABIR: Don't be disappearing.

They hug for some time. When they part – SEBASTIAN produces a Bible from his pocket. He shows it to MICHAEL.

SEBASTIAN: I think this belongs to you.

MICHAEL: My Bible…ahh…thank you.

SEBASTIAN opens the Bible and reads the inscription.

SEBASTIAN: *(Reads.)* Pastor Samuel. Friend of yours was he?

MICHAEL: Pardon?

SEBASTIAN: Pastor Samuel.

MICHAEL: I knew him. Yes.

MICHAEL shakes hands with JENNY.

Goodbye, Jenny.

JENNY: Take care, Michael.

MICHAEL: Thank you for everything.

MICHAEL turns to leave but SEBASTIAN catches hold of him.

SEBASTIAN: Don't you want your Bible?

MICHAEL: Yes…thank you.

But before MICHAEL can take the Bible, SEBASTIAN holds up the Bible above his head. He transforms himself into a preacher.

SEBASTIAN: The Tutsi are foreign to the area and have stolen Rwanda from its rightful inhabitants…

AYESHA: What's he on?

SEBASTIAN: I am your pastor. Listen to me. I am giving you the word from God himself…

MICHAEL: *(Upset.)* No…no…

AYESHA: He's pissed.

SEBASTIAN: Let us finish off these Tutsi cockroaches once and for all. If we don't, they will kill us. They have prepared holes in the dirt floors of their houses to dump your Hutu corpses – yes – even your neighbours and so called friends…

KABIR: Stop it.

SEBASTIAN: Do you know who this man is?

KABIR: Sebastian…

SEBASTIAN: This wolf in sheep's clothing ordered others to kill.

KABIR: You are being ridiculous.

JENNY: Sebastian – please…

SEBASTIAN: He ordered over five thousand killings.

AYESHA: Seb man… calm down.

SEBASTIAN: I know what I'm talking about. I have a photo to prove it.

SEBASTIAN scrabbles around in his pocket and pulls out a crumpled photo. He shows it to JENNY.

The Church in Kibungo. I took it myself.

JENNY: Sebastian…it's just a photo of a Church.

SEBASTIAN: This is Kibungo where Pastor Samuel lived and worked. He was killed. Why does Michael have his Bible?

MICHAEL: He gave it to me.

SEBASTIAN: I was there – in Rwanda. I took photos of the carnage…the pastor…he was the one responsible.

KABIR takes a firm hold of SEBASTIAN and tries to pull him aside.

KABIR: You have been drinking too much again. Go. Mikey. Go.

MICHAEL turns to go but SEBASTIAN calls out.

SEBASTIAN: His name isn't Michael. It's Charles Bagilishema. I've been looking for him for eight years… I've finally nailed him.

MICHAEL: You have the wrong man.

SEBASTIAN: Tell them the truth. Tell them what you did.

MARGARET: What did he do?

MICHAEL: Don't listen to him.

SEBASTIAN: Herded them into the church…innocent people…brought the killers…handed out machetes…Kibungo…the Church…

JENNY: Sebastian, stop this nonsense right now. You're imagining things.

SEBASTIAN: It was unspeakable what his kind did…

MICHAEL: No – not me.

SEBASTIAN: My people – my ancestors – people I honoured and respected – capable of such depravity. Children in the classroom, their arithmetic still chalked up on the board, mothers with their babies hacked to pieces in their arms, pregnant women with their wombs ripped out…and no one cared. No one did anything.

KABIR: You have seen too much. It has turned your mind.

SEBASTIAN: One million people killed in hundred days. Africans killing Africans and the world stood back and watched. Why? Because our sorry black faces aren't worth shit to them.

MICHAEL: He's gone mad.

SEBASTIAN: How many people did you kill personally? Ten? Twenty? One hundred? Two hundred?

MICHAEL: I am innocent. I committed no crimes. These accusations are monstrous. I lost my own son. I hid in the bushes. I was hunted.

SEBASTIAN: Because you were running away.

MICHAEL: I am innocent.

SEBASTIAN: So, go back and prove it.

MICHAEL: They won't believe me. There is so much suspicion in my country – it only takes one person to point the finger and you are thrown into prison. People die waiting for a trial – there isn't enough room – they can't even sit down. There are children in there too accused of crimes. There is no justice in my country. No truth, no dignity, only accusations and more killings.
I am not a murderer.

KABIR: Go home, Seb, and be sobering up.

AYESHA: Please, Sebastian. Stop it.

SEBASTIAN: He's lying. I know who he is.

MICHAEL: You are the one lying. Everyone here knows me. How could I do such terrible things? I lost my son.

SEBASTIAN: Because you were running away.

MICHAEL: No!

SEBASTIAN: Admit it.

MICHAEL: No!

SEBASTIAN: I spoke to witnesses. They saw him in his truck handing out weapons and giving orders…people he left for dead, who hid in fear under the bodies of their dead mothers, fathers, sisters, brothers, children…
I went in search for him…

MICHAEL suddenly becomes angry and turns on SEBASTIAN.

MICHAEL: You don't frighten me. Trying to make a name for yourself, eh? Failed – drunk? There is no evidence.

SEBASTIAN: There are witnesses…

MICHAEL: So you keep saying but anybody can say they saw anything. They are government tools – if they don't say what the new government wants, they'll be killed. And you are a government spy.

SEBASTIAN: Admit it.

MICHAEL: Never. Never. Never. I never told anyone to kill people. I could not do such things.

SEBASTIAN: You were a pastor.

MICHAEL: I admit that – yes. And what I saw in my country made me question my belief but now I am closer to God than I have ever been in my life. Hatred is the result of sin and it will only be taken away when Jesus Christ returns.

SEBASTIAN: Don't get biblical with me.

MICHAEL: It wasn't me. You have the wrong man. I am not Charles Bagilishema. I am Michael Ruzindana –

I did not kill any people – it is all one hundred per cent lies.

SEBASTIAN: And this Bible – is it one of the mementos you kept hold of? A trophy? Wasn't Pastor Samuel one of the people you killed? Didn't he write a letter to you, begging you to save the congregation's life? And how did you answer that letter?

SEBASTIAN holds up the Bible above his head again.

Rise up, Hutu brothers. Rise up in self defence. The graves are only half full! There is a new Commandment – if you are struck on the cheek once, you must strike back twice. Now, pick up your tools and go to work.

JENNY looks at MICHAEL – suspiciously. MICHAEL turns and tries to leave.

SEBASTIAN however, tries to stop him. The two men wrestle. In the struggle, bottles of wine and glasses are knocked over.

MICHAEL is desperate as he punches and kicks. He slips out of SEBASTIAN's grasp and runs away. SEBASTIAN turns on KABIR.

You know the truth. How can you protect him?

KABIR is rooted to the spot. He looks unsure.

SEBASTIAN looks disgusted and runs out after MICHAEL.

SCENE 3

It is later. KABIR has lit a lamp by the tree and is digging. As he digs, he keeps looking around to see that no one is there. Eventually, he hits something hard. As he scrabbles around in the dirt, he pulls up an old cigar box. He sits on the bench and opens it carefully. He hesitates and then examines the contents. He pulls out papers. Some of them crumble in his hands. Some remain intact. He reads them. He pulls out an old passport and examines it. There is a rustling in the tree. KABIR hides the box, stands up and looks up.

KABIR: Who is there?

The rustling continues. KABIR picks up his machete for protection.

Come down here at once.

A small bag is thrown down and MICHAEL clambers down after it. He looks afraid.

Mikey!

MICHAEL: They are after me – they came to my house.

KABIR looks around him. He puts the machete down.

KABIR: Who?

MICHAEL: The Police! Sebastian must have gone to them.

KABIR: But surely they will be looking for you here.

MICHAEL: *(Desperate.)* I need somewhere to hide.

KABIR: You are thinking you can still be selling me all your lies? You think I am being stupid?

MICHAEL: People make mistakes. You have known me for five years. Have I not been a good friend to you? We have shared joy and laughter together.

KABIR: People make mistakes but five thousand lives…

MICHAEL: I did not do those things. But it is not safe for me in Rwanda. You mustn't let them take me – hide me – in the church.

KABIR: I can't…

MICHAEL: Then hide me somewhere else – just for tonight. Tomorrow I can get to some friends – they can conceal me, take me out of this country. Then I will bother you no more. I will change my identity, I will vanish.

KABIR looks helpless.

(Panicked.) You must hide me. You are my friend. I have trusted you. Hide me in your shed. Please.

Seeing he is getting nowhere, MICHAEL takes a pouch from his pocket.

Look, take it, it's yours.

MICHAEL holds up a diamond.

It is very precious. A diamond.

KABIR: *(Disgusted.)* I don't want it.

MICHAEL tries to force the diamond into KABIR's hand but KABIR turns away.

MICHAEL: It is worth a lot of money. A rich man gave it to me when I was fleeing persecution through Zaire.

KABIR: You were the persecutor.

MICHAEL: It will mean certain death for me if they take me back. They hate the Hutus – they plan to kill us all. They won't give me a fair trial – they took our land from us before, forced us into slavery and servitude – they will do it again. I can't go back there.

KABIR: You must be facing up to your sins.

MICHAEL: Will you help me?

KABIR: If I am truly being your friend, then I want to be hearing the truth from you.

MICHAEL: I have told you the truth.

KABIR: You haven't.

MICHAEL: I harmed no one. Why don't you trust me?

KABIR: You are still lying! I know you have killed to be saving your family.

MICHAEL: And I know *you* have stood back and allowed your wife to be killed.

KABIR looks away – hurt.

I did not want to leave without saying goodbye. I will trouble you no more.

MICHAEL turns and walks away.

KABIR: *(Calls out.)* Come back. I will be giving you shelter for the sake of our old friendship – if you are telling me the truth. Is it true what Sebastian is saying?

MICHAEL stops and hesitates.

Well?

MICHAEL: No. He has the wrong man.

KABIR produces the cigar box from its hiding place.

KABIR: I was finding your real passport – with your real name – Charles Bagilishema. It is having your photo.

MICHAEL: You dug it up?

KABIR: You were making a fool of me. I was thinking, this was in the memory of your boy. Were you even having a son?

MICHAEL: Yes.

KABIR: And was he really dying?

MICHAEL: They were after us. Hunting us like animals. We had to hide in the bush – there was no food. I tried to feed him with grass but it was no good. I could not keep him alive. He was only eight years old.

KABIR: Who were you running from?

MICHAEL: The enemy.

KABIR: Who was being the enemy?

MICHAEL: The army.

KABIR: Whose army?

MICHAEL: The Tutsis.

Beat.

KABIR: And they were hunting you because you had been killing Tutsis.

MICHAEL: So they said.

KABIR: You must be telling me the truth. If you are wanting shelter for tonight – otherwise I will be calling the police.

MICHAEL: No.

KABIR: Were you killing those people in the church?

Beat.

MICHAEL: I had no choice. Truly. The militia wanted me to help them. Every day, they came to my house, they threatened me. They had already slaughtered my wife. They kept saying that if I did not help them, they would do the same to me and Charles. I was afraid. I had to live on my wits – to save my son's life. Violence feeds on violence, like a fire. People went mad and killed and killed and killed.

KABIR: You were the pastor in your district, surely you could have stopped it?

MICHAEL: No one would listen to me. I tried to resist at first, to reason, but there was a kind of madness, chaos…and I began to think, if it wasn't my turn today, it would be my turn tomorrow. Kill, so as not to be killed – that was my motto.

KABIR remains silent.

Everyone was spying on everyone. Peasants were killed because they refused to beat the dead bodies of their Tutsi neighbours. Even my son wanted to stand at the roadblocks and help with the killing. I would not let him go but he said, 'Father, at least I can help kill the little ones.' It was like a poison that spread through my body so fast, I didn't even realise how sick I had become…

KABIR: How many people were taking refuge in that church?

MICHAEL: About three thousand. I told them to go there… that it would be safe for them. I believed they would not be harmed – that God would protect them. And then I received my orders.

KABIR: To be killing them?

MICHAEL: To kill them all. Hobble the children first. Slash their Achilles tendons so that they could not move far. Then the parents would come running to protect them… those were my orders. It took four days and nights. When the dogs heard the cries of the people. They too began to howl.

MICHAEL closes his eyes.

KABIR: How many people were you killing personally, Mikey?

MICHAEL: I don't know.

KABIR: How many?

MICHAEL: I lost count. One hundred? Maybe two hundred?

KABIR: *(Incredulous.)* You were losing count? And how many children?

MICHAEL: Only those two, in the chicken house. I never killed children after that.

KABIR: You were leaving that to the others?

MICHAEL is silent.

What were you doing with their bodies?

MICHAEL: They were thrown into mass graves.

KABIR: Were there prayers being said over the graves?

MICHAEL: *(Ashamed.)* No.

KABIR: And those people in the Church – you were ordering their killings?

MICHAEL: I was forced to do it. The leadership, they told me that if I didn't prove my Hutu solidarity – they would come after me. Don't you understand? – it was a war – and I had to take sides otherwise I would have been killed.

KABIR: Is your life really being so important?

MICHAEL: It is to me. You don't understand my country – the Tutsis were our enemy. For years they looked down on us – treated us like slaves. This was a situation waiting to happen. It was a coming together of the people against their oppressors. One hundred days of vengeance.

KABIR: And the children? The babies? Were they also being your oppressors?

MICHAEL: One day, they could grow up to be so.

KABIR: How many women were you mutilating?

MICHAEL: None.

KABIR: I was reading stories of pregnant women's wombs being ripped open to get at the unborn foetuses. Were you doing that too?

MICHAEL: No!

KABIR: But you must have seen it happening?

MICHAEL: Once or twice – but not by me.

KABIR: But you gave the orders.

MICHAEL is silent.

How are you sleeping at night? Aren't the voices of your victims calling out to you in your nightmares?

MICHAEL: I am human, with all the failings that come with it. But surely, I deserve another chance – to prove myself a worthy man.

KABIR: What about the people you are killing? What chances do they have now?

MICHAEL: They were Tutsis. They stood no chance of survival in that country at that time.

KABIR: And you think I should be helping you? Aren't you being ashamed to be breathing? To be surviving?

MICHAEL: Ashamed? Yes. But then I think, God must have singled me out for a purpose.

KABIR: What purpose?

MICHAEL: To show mercy on my soul.

Beat.

KABIR: Did you rape the women?

MICHAEL is silent.

Did you?

MICHAEL: We had to be seen to show no mercy. The Tutsi women were part of the problem – they had used their feminine wiles to dilute our Bantu blood. They had to be dealt with, punished, humiliated.

KABIR: Tortured.

MICHAEL: Their men ran away. They did not protect them. They hid or sacrificed their wives to us to do as we pleased.

KABIR: You are an animal.

MICHAEL: We were at war. And in war, gang rape is more effective than any military weapon.

KABIR struggles to maintain his calm.

KABIR: If I were being a Tutsi – you would have been killing me too, to save your own skin? Would you be raping and killing my wife and daughter?

MICHAEL does not answer. KABIR picks up the machete. He brandishes it menacingly. Suddenly, KABIR looks frightening.

(Shouts.) Now I am a Hutu and you are a Tutsi.

MICHAEL cowers and tries to protect himself with his hands. KABIR aims the machete at MICHAEL's head.

MICHAEL: *(Frightened.)* No…please Kabir.

KABIR: I am seeking vengeance for all those people you killed.

MICHAEL: *(Screams.)* Please.

KABIR: Who will be mourning your death here? No one. Who will care? No one.

KABIR raises the machete deliberately over MICHAEL. MICHAEL tries to run but KABIR chases after him with the machete. MICHAEL trips and falls. KABIR is screaming and shouting.

Vengeance is mine!

MICHAEL collapses to his knees and clings to KABIR's feet weeping and sobbing. KABIR hesitates – machete poised mid-air.

MICHAEL: Please I beg you, don't…don't… *(Babbling a prayer.)* Almighty and most merciful Father, we have erred and strayed from Thy ways like lost sheep… We have offended against thy holy laws… O Lord, have mercy on us miserable offenders.

KABIR pulls roughly away from MICHAEL leaving him kneeling on the ground praying feverishly to himself.

And grant, O merciful Father, that we may hereafter live a godly, righteous and sober life, Amen.

KABIR brings the machete down with all his force on MICHAEL's arm. MICHAEL's arm is hacked off. Blood gushes out across the floor. MICHAEL looks at his severed arm in disbelief and screams with agony.

KABIR: An eye for an eye, a tooth for a tooth.

MICHAEL crawls away begging all the time. KABIR prowls after him.

MICHAEL: No, no…Kabir…we are friends…don't do this… you said you would help me…no…no…

KABIR picks MICHAEL up by the scruff of the neck and drags him backwards towards the shed. MICHAEL is screaming all the way. As the shed door is shut behind him we hear the blood curdling screams for help coming from MICHAEL and the sound of a machete. Night descends. In the darkness, we hear the roar and crackle of a huge fire.

SCENE 4

As the dawn rises, we see the shed has disappeared. Instead there are the smouldering ashes of what has obviously been a raging fire. KABIR sits on the bench beside the shed. He looks shell-shocked and is silent. His face and hands are covered in soot. MARGARET is sat next to him. She is comforting him.

SEBASTIAN enters. He looks at the shed and then at KABIR. He looks aghast.

SEBASTIAN: What the hell happened here?

KABIR remains silent. MARGARET looks at SEBASTIAN as if the question is rather obvious.

Kabir? What happened to your shed?

MARGARET: Burnt to a cinder. Vandals I shouldn't wonder.

SEBASTIAN: Someone's got it in for this place.

JENNY enters. She is in a flap.

JENNY: I've called the fire department but I told them there's no point really – it's all burnt down now. They said that as long as there's no danger, they'll send someone along later this morning to have a look. I'm so sorry, Kabir.

MARGARET: It's very bad luck.

SEBASTIAN: Michael got away. The police couldn't find him at his house. He probably never went home.

SEBASTIAN kicks the dirt floor in frustration.

Can't believe I fucking lost him.

KABIR: He came here.

SEBASTIAN: Last night?

KABIR: Yes. He wanted me to hide him.

SEBASTIAN: *(Angry.)* You should have turned him over to the police. Why didn't you call me?

JENNY: Where did he go?

KABIR: Not far.

SEBASTIAN: Where?

KABIR: Where we cannot be finding him.

SEBASTIAN: *(Angry.)* I hope you realise what you've done man. Where did he go? Did he tell you?

KABIR remains silent and withdrawn.

JENNY: What did he say to you?

KABIR: He confessed.

JENNY: Confessed what?

KABIR: His name was Charles, not Michael.

KABIR produces the passport with MICHAEL's photo. JENNY and MARGARET examine the photo. SEBASTIAN takes the passport and scrutinises it.

MARGARET: So, Sebastian was right.

SEBASTIAN: Only, none of you would listen…and now, God knows where he's gone. *(Anguished.)* Man! I found him. After all this fucking time –

SEBASTIAN does a double take and looks at the smouldering ashes of the shed. He can just make out the charred remains of a human body.

Jesus Christ.

JENNY: What?

SEBASTIAN points at the remains. JENNY walks over and looks.

MARGARET: What is it, Jen?

JENNY groans. She covers her mouth and rushes to the corner. She wretches. MARGARET stays where she is. SEBASTIAN inspects the remains.

KABIR: That is being Mikey. He was wanting somewhere to hide.

JENNY: You hid him in the shed? Is that it? And some vandals broke in?

MARGARET: What happened here last night, Kabir?

KABIR is silent. JENNY looks horrified.

JENNY: No…this can't be true. Kabir? What have you done?

KABIR is silent.

Kabir?

KABIR: He was thinking I would be helping him to escape. That he could be forgiven just by praying.

SEBASTIAN: Is this for real? Is that Michael? I've searched for him for eight years and you…you've just murdered him?

I was going to take him back, to face his accusers. What about justice?

JENNY: Justice has been done.

SEBASTIAN: How can you say that?

JENNY: He would have been executed anyway or he would have rotted and died in jail.

SEBASTIAN: But we have no right to act as judge and executioner. What about the survivors? The families of his victims?

JENNY: This isn't about them, it's about you. Thought you'd get a bestselling book out of it did you?

SEBASTIAN: People deserve to know the truth.

JENNY: You would have basked in some of the glory though wouldn't you? Made a tidy sum.

SEBASTIAN: He was a criminal, he had to be held to account.

MARGARET: He's been punished. What more do you want?

SEBASTIAN: As long as he was alive he would have suffered but now…he's been released.

KABIR: He was suffering.

SEBASTIAN: What gives you the fucking right? How could you do this?

KABIR: He was evil.

SEBASTIAN: So what does that make you? Jesus. Jesus Christ. You burnt him alive?

KABIR: He is dead. That is all you are needing to know.

SEBASTIAN: I haven't been able to sleep properly for eight years. Every time I close my eyes I see those people, their faces, those kids in their classroom…
I could have taken him back to face the families whose lives he devastated.

KABIR: He was being my friend. Only I could be punishing him.

SEBASTIAN: He confessed?

KABIR: Everything.

Beat.

MARGARET gets up.

MARGARET: *(Urgent.)* We've got to get rid of it – before the fire department arrive.

MARGARET fetches a couple of spades and hands one to JENNY. Without a word, MARGARET starts digging a shallow grave beneath the tree. SEBASTIAN and JENNY watch her confused.

JENNY: Gran? What are you doing?

SEBASTIAN: We should go to the police.

JENNY: We can't cover this up.

MARGARET: Yes we can. All of us protected Michael. You took him under your wing.

JENNY: I didn't know…how was I supposed to…?

MARGARET stops.

MARGARET: Look at him, Jen.

JENNY: I can't be seen to condone this.

MARGARET: So, we just stand back and wash our hands? We're all culpable.

JENNY: No.

MARGARET: For once in your life, Jen, will you please listen to me? Look at him.

JENNY looks over at KABIR.

You want to ruin another man's life?

JENNY is torn.

I can't do this on my own.

JENNY picks up the other spade and helps MARGARET in her digging.

SEBASTIAN is upset.

SEBASTIAN: How are you going to get away with this?

KABIR: He was defending his actions. He was saying that he ordered people to kill and rape. He was killing children. He could not even be remembering how many.

SEBASTIAN: I wanted to hear him admit what he did. To my face. He said all this to you?

KABIR: Yes.

SEBASTIAN reluctantly takes the other spade and starts to dig. Between the two of them, they manage to dig a small pit. KABIR picks up MICHAEL's charred body and throws it down into the pit. SEBASTIAN goes back and forth collecting more bits and pieces of bones and finally the skull. As he puts it into the pit, KABIR smashes the skull with the machete and then collapses weeping. SEBASTIAN covers the grave up again with soil. He hesitates.

SEBASTIAN: Shouldn't you say a few words? A prayer, or something?

JENNY: If you want to say a prayer – be my guest.

SEBASTIAN hovers for a moment looking down at the shallow grave. KABIR produces the cigar box. He opens it and pulls out an old crumpled letter. He stands by the grave and reads.

KABIR: Pastor Samuel's letter. Our dear leader, Pastor Charles Bagilishema. How are you! We hope you will be able to come to our assistance. We wish to inform you that we have heard that tomorrow we will be killed with our families. We therefore ask you to speak up for us especially to the mayor. We trust that, with God's help who has placed you at the head of this congregation, which faces destruction, your mediation will be accepted with gratitude, just as the Jews were saved by Esther. We give respect to you.

JENNY supports KABIR and exits. SEBASTIAN stands by the grave, a while longer and then exits.

SCENE 5

It is a bright sunny day. MARGARET is seated on the bench. She is dressed and ready to go out somewhere. AYESHA enters. She looks delighted and is on a high.

AYESHA: Ask me a question.

MARGARET: I beg your pardon?

AYESHA: Ask me a question. 'Was King Charles I a misunderstood monarch?'

MARGARET: What?

AYESHA: Go on, ask me…

MARGARET: Oh alright…was Charles I a misunderstood monarch?

AYESHA: I don't know – fuck off!

AYESHA giggles maniacally.

MARGARET: Well really!

AYESHA: No more fucking exams, no more lessons…that's the last time I ever have to walk into that miserable grey building with its arsehole teachers and their wanky lectures…

She pulls off her tie and throws it to the ground and stamps on it.

Last bloody time I have to write anything, ever about kings or queens or bloody useless, fucking novels. I'm free!

AYESHA dances around and laughs and skips.

MARGARET: I take it you've finished your exams. How did you do?

AYESHA: Who gives a fuck?

MARGARET: You know, you really are going to have to improve your language skills if you want to become an air hostess. Telling passengers to eat their 'fucking' breakfast isn't going to go down too well.

AYESHA comes up and hugs MARGARET and gives her a big kiss. MARGARET reels.

Steady on.

AYESHA: *(Emotional.)* I've been institutionalized all these years. It's like breaking free from prison. I've got the key in my hand and I've opened the door. Step out into the light and breathe the fresh air. My life begins today.

MARGARET: That's when the problems really start.

AYESHA: It's a fucking amazing feeling.

(Emotional.) Next week I'll be sixteen. I'm a grown up woman. It's my life and I'm going to live it.

AYESHA dances around the garden and bends down and looks at one of the few remaining flowers.

Hello, little flower, ain't you beautiful? Ain't you exquisite? Shining with the radiance of the fucking sunlight, oh and little banana tree, how small your leaves seem but one day you'll be able to poke your head up higher than that wall. Then they'll really notice you.

MARGARET: Kabir has gone.

AYESHA: Gone? What d'you mean?

MARGARET: He left this morning – moved in to his new place.

AYESHA: He never told me. Is he coming back?

MARGARET: I don't think so, dear.

AYESHA: Mean bastard. He could have rung me.

MARGARET: He probably couldn't face it.

AYESHA: He's really gone?

MARGARET nods.

He never even said ‘goodbye’.

MARGARET: Jen got him a job in her new parish. Only difference is there’s no garden, just a car park around the back of the church hall.

AYESHA: What’s he going to do in a car park?

MARGARET: Hand out tickets I suppose.

AYESHA: Sounds like hell.

MARGARET: It’s time to move on. Taxi should be arriving any moment to whisk me and Jen off to Dover. Apparently the vicarage where we’ll be living has one of those electric stair lifts for me. Can’t wait to use it.

AYESHA: You’ll be up and down there like a bleedin’ yo-yo.

MARGARET: Like Bette Davis.

AYESHA: Who?

MARGARET: Before your time, dear. Thought Jen might see sense and leave the church but no – she’s addicted to it. It’s like a very bad habit.

JENNY: *(Calls offstage.)* Gran! Taxi’s here.

MARGARET: That’s me. Good luck. Oh erm – Kabir left this for you. Apparently he found it in the shed – after it had burnt down.

MARGARET hands AYESHA the diamond.

AYESHA: Thanks. What is it?

MARGARET: A girl’s best friend.

AYESHA looks confused. She holds it up to the light.

It’s very valuable. Take my advice, run along to a jewellers and get it valued. Should be enough for you to see the world.

AYESHA looks in disbelief at the diamond.

AYESHA: You sure about that?

MARGARET: Certain.

AYESHA bends down and kisses MARGARET.

Bye, bye…

MARGARET waves and exits. AYESHA is left standing on her own. She looks at the diamond, chucks it in the air and catches it again. She smiles and exits.

End.

SUGAR MUMMIES

Sugar Mummies was first performed on 5 August 2006 at Royal Court Jerwood Theatre Downstairs. *Sugar Mummies* continued at the Octagon Theatre, Bolton 12 September 2006 and the Birmingham Repertory Theatre 20 September 2006, with the following cast:

REEFIE, Victor Romero Evans
ANGEL, Lorna Gayle
SLY, Javone Prince
NAOMI, Vinette Robinson
ANDRE, Marcel McCalla
ANTONIO, Jason Frederick
MAGGIE, Lynda Bellingham
KITTY, Heather Craney
YOLANDA, Adjoa Andoh

Production credits:
Director, Indhu Rubasingham
Design, Lez Brotherston
Lighting, Rick Fisher
Sound, Paul Groothuis
Video, Mesmer

Characters

ANGEL
48-year-old Jamaican woman,
masseuse and hair braider on the beach

REEFIE
50-year-old Rastafarian, experienced gigolo,
Yolanda's lover

KITTY
38-year-old white school teacher

SLY
streetwise gigolo, 22 years old

ANDRE
grill chef at the hotel, 24 years old, Angel's son

ANTONIO
17-year-old hotel staff who puts out sunbeds

NAOMI
mixed-race woman, in her late twenties

YOLANDA
American woman in her early fifties

MAGGIE
white woman in her fifties

Act One

SCENE 1

We hear the sound of the waves lapping gently in a calm bay. The sun rises on a tropical beach in Jamaica with white sands and palm trees – the perfect beach.

A white woman, KITTY (thirty-eight), is lying flat out on a sunbed sunbathing.

REEFIE enters. He is a Rasta man in his early fifties, good looking, slim built and lithe. He is busy building a boat in the background, going to and fro, fetching wood etc. He carries a machete with him.

ANGEL, a middle-aged Jamaican woman, enters carrying a large heavy bag. She turns and waves at REEFIE.

ANGEL unlocks a small beach hut and rakes the sand out front. She puts up a sign: 'ALOE VERA MASSAGES AND HAIR BRAIDING'.

She stands and looks out to sea. She looks tired. REEFIE approaches her with a flask and pours her a hot drink from it. She takes it wordlessly and drinks.

REEFIE: Look tired.

ANGEL: Early start.

REEFIE: Long journey from de mountains.

ANGEL: Yeah mon.

REEFIE: Tiny doin' okay?

ANGEL: Fifteen an' him want to pack in school. Him wan earn him living like him big brother.

REEFIE: Him earn better livin' wid some school behind him.

ANGEL: Me tell him. Andre tell him. Cyan tell de buoy nuttin'.

A plane flies overhead.

ANGEL: Boat comin' on?

REEFIE: Comin' on good.

ANGEL: *(Laughs.)* Den what? You sail off into de sunset?

REEFIE: *(Teases.)* You come wid me. We be like Adam and Eve in Paradise.

ANGEL: Adam and Eve dem fall from grace.

REEFIE: We can change de story.

ANGEL: *(Laughs.)* What about all your women? Dey come after me and try drown me.

REEFIE: Me jus' wan' me a nice island girl.

ANGEL pushes REEFIE playfully. They laugh.

ANGEL: You hear about my man?

REEFIE: Me hear.

ANGEL: Him a walking duppy. Him die soon.

REEFIE looks at ANGEL with sympathy. She looks sad. ANGEL hands back her cup to REEFIE. He pads away through the sand back to his boat. ANGEL sits and waits for custom.

NAOMI enters. She is a mixed-race woman in her late twenties, in a swimsuit. She stands for a moment and stares out to sea in wonder.

We hear the distant call of hawkers calling out their wares.

'Coconut, pineapple, mangoes, bananas
Cigarettes, Marlboro light, cigarettes.
Coconut, pineapple, mangoes, bananas.'

NAOMI pulls out a camera and takes a picture of the sea.

SLY walks by.

SLY: Pssst.

NAOMI ignores him.

Pssst. Hey. Pretty lady.

SLY beckons NAOMI to him.

NAOMI looks away. SLY looks around surreptitiously and approaches NAOMI.

What's your name?

NAOMI: *(Resigned.)* Naomi.

SLY crouches next to NAOMI.

SLY: Sly.

He puts out his hand. NAOMI shakes hands. SLY holds on to her hand a little too long.

Wanna go jet-ski?

NAOMI: No…thank you.

SLY: Parasailing?

NAOMI: No…

SLY: How 'bout a glass bottom boat? I tek you out to the coral reef. We can go snorkel?

NAOMI: No…maybe another time.

SLY: You interested in a lickle weed? Ready-made, Bob Marley cones…only five dollars. Look.

SLY reaches into his pocket.

NAOMI: No…

SLY: Ten dollar bags. Island weed. De best.

NAOMI looks away.

What else I can offer you?

NAOMI: Nothing – really.

SLY: You're a pretty lady. Maybe we can walk together on de beach?

ANDRE appears in the background, dressed in a white apron, wearing a chef's hat. SLY clocks ANDRE.

ANDRE: Cho Sly. Don't hassle de tourists.

SLY: No problem man.

SLY stands up and looks down at NAOMI.

Naomi. Nice meetin' you.

He touches fists with NAOMI.

One love.

SLY saunters off. NAOMI turns and smiles at ANDRE who doesn't smile back. Instead, he gets busy cleaning surfaces in his grill/bar. He puts out a large black board with the names of all the cocktails and another one with the menu.

He waves at ANGEL who waves back before disappearing into her hut.

ANTONIO, a very young Jamaican man (seventeen) with 'STAFF' emblazoned on his T-shirt, appears behind her, carrying a sunbed and a towel.

ANTONIO: Miss. You want a sunbed? Towel?

NAOMI: Oh hi. Yes please.

ANTONIO expertly snaps open the sunbed, brushes off the sand and lays it down for NAOMI, near the sunbathing KITTY.

Thank you…

ANTONIO: Yeah mon.

NAOMI sits down gingerly.

ANTONIO places the towel on the back of the sunbed for her. He looks at NAOMI with interest.

This your first time or you hab family here?

NAOMI: Erm…my first time…

ANTONIO: My name is Antonio. Welcome to Jamaica. Respect. Anyt'ing you want. I be here.

ANTONIO touches fists with NAOMI.

NAOMI: Thank you.

ANTONIO: Me pleasure.

NAOMI settles down on the sunbed and continues to savour the sea.

MAGGIE, a woman in her fifties, walks down to the beach and stands looking out to sea. Her grey hair has been braided back into cane row. She smiles at NAOMI. ANTONIO is by her side immediately with a sunbed. He snaps open the sunbed. MAGGIE sits down.

MAGGIE: Thank you.

ANTONIO: Me pleasure. Welcome to Jamaica.

As ANTONIO exits, MAGGIE watches after him with interest.

MAGGIE: Sleep well?

NAOMI: Not at first. Those cicadas are so noisy!

MAGGIE: Nothing you can do about them.

NAOMI: And my room was boiling.

MAGGIE: What's wrong with the air con?

NAOMI: Gives me a headache.

MAGGIE: You just lay there sweltering?

NAOMI laughs apologetically.

NAOMI: Dropped off at some point though, then woke up early. Went for a walk along the beach.

MAGGIE: Beautiful isn't it?

NAOMI: Breathtaking. Think I'll take a quick dip.

MAGGIE: Go for it.

NAOMI exits towards the sea.

MAGGIE settles down on her sunbed, gets on with the business of taking out magazines from her bag etc. KITTY sits up on her sunbed and starts applying some sun cream to her body. For a while the two women ignore each other.

MAGGIE: Hi.

KITTY: Oh – hi.

MAGGIE: Don't you love it here?

KITTY: My third visit!

MAGGIE: My first time. Usually travel on my own. Bit expensive here. Not like the Dominican Republic. Everything's dirt cheap out there. Still, the Jamaicans are more laid back. I like that. And I love the accent.

Beat.

KITTY: First thing I did when I arrived yesterday was to go for a massage.

KITTY points in ANGEL's direction

Try her out. She's great.

MAGGIE looks across at ANGEL.

MAGGIE: Might just do that. Thanks for the tip. By the way, name's Maggie.

KITTY: Kitty.

MAGGIE: From London. You?

KITTY: Manchester.

MAGGIE: My brother lives there.

KITTY: Really? Where?

MAGGIE: East Didsbury.

KITTY: That's where I live!

MAGGIE: Rathen Road.

KITTY: Round the corner from me!

MAGGIE: Small world.

KITTY: How funny.

They both soak up the sun for a bit.

KITTY: When did you arrive?

MAGGIE: Yesterday afternoon. Went straight along to Rik's Café.

KITTY gets excited at this information.

KITTY: Rik's café?

MAGGIE: Yeah.

KITTY: Best sunsets there.

MAGGIE: Great views all round.

KITTY: *(Laughs.)* Oh yes.

Beat.

Watch all those men diving off the cliff?

MAGGIE: They're amazing.

KITTY: Hmmm…

MAGGIE: Climbing up those rock faces like crabs then doing all these somersaults in the air before plunging into the depths.

KITTY: Incredibly agile.

MAGGIE: Beautiful bodies.

KITTY: Beautiful bodies.

MAGGIE: Flat stomachs, muscles all over…

KITTY: Watch them and you kind of… How did you hear about this place?

MAGGIE: Word of mouth – Lonely Planet…

KITTY: Men here certainly know how to treat a lady. They love us!

MAGGIE: Least they pretend to.

KITTY: They're so sweet.

MAGGIE: And really black.

KITTY: Blue black.

MAGGIE: Nice smiles – white, white teeth against black skin.

KITTY: Tall and strong.

MAGGIE: Big, luscious, kissable lips.

KITTY: Real men.

MAGGIE: Much bigger than white men. The Big Bamboo.

KITTY: Jamaican Steel.

They both laugh.

And it's not over in two minutes. They can keep going all night.

MAGGIE: And they've got the rhythm – so they can move – so athletic.

KITTY: Such supple bodies.

MAGGIE: 'Once you've had black, you never go back.'

They both laugh happily.

KITTY: Pretty much get the pick of the bunch. They don't look at your wrinkles – just at your face. They like eyes. They're so romantic.

MAGGIE: Know how to talk the talk.

KITTY: Wouldn't do this back home.

MAGGIE: It's not illegal to have a good time.

KITTY: I know…but still.

MAGGIE: You're on holiday! Enjoy yourself!

KITTY: I have every intention of enjoying myself.

MAGGIE: Good.

KITTY lays back down on her sunbed and continues with her sunbathing.

NAOMI re-enters. She is wet from the sea. MAGGIE passes her towel to her and NAOMI towels herself dry.

YOLANDA, a fifty-year-old American woman, walks out in a flashy swimsuit, looks out to sea and sighs deeply.

YOLANDA: I think I just came.

NAOMI exchanges an amused look with MAGGIE. YOLANDA turns and looks at ANDRE.

There's my man – Andre!

ANDRE: *(Smiles.)* Yolanda.

YOLANDA: You're grilling me lobster for lunch, you hear?

ANDRE: No problem.

YOLANDA: Hey, where's Antonio? *(Calls out.)* Antonio! Sweetcakes!

ANTONIO bustles out.

ANTONIO: Yolanda, you back!

YOLANDA: Yep.

ANTONIO: Good to see you. Respect.

YOLANDA: Hey, you grown taller since last time we met?

ANTONIO laughs. YOLANDA and ANTONIO touch fists.

ANTONIO: Sunbed? Towels?

YOLANDA: Yep.

ANTONIO bustles off. YOLANDA picks up some confetti from the sand.

Looks like someone got themselves married again.

NAOMI: Bride was dressed in a very skimpy white bikini.

YOLANDA: Should be grateful she was wearing something. They got themselves a nudist colony down there *(She points.)* in Bloody Bay. Locals call it 'the zoo'.

NAOMI: That nudist stuff, really doesn't turn me on. All those bits…

MAGGIE: Oh I don't know – it can be quite liberating.

YOLANDA: European folk sure do like baring their flesh.

MAGGIE looks away slightly annoyed.

You folk from England?

NAOMI: Yeah. London.

YOLANDA: I could tell from the accent.

MAGGIE: And you're from the States?

YOLANDA: Sure am.

MAGGIE: *(Sarcastic.)* I could tell from the accent.

ANTONIO returns with a sunbed. He pulls it out, dusts the sand off and lays it down for YOLANDA. YOLANDA sits down.

ANTONIO: Yolanda, lookin' good.

YOLANDA: Thank you sweetcakes. Hey, hey, take those shades off, Tony-o…

ANTONIO takes off his shades.

See those eyes girls? Ever see such beautiful eyes?

NAOMI glances at ANTONIO's eyes. He flutters his eyelashes.

NAOMI: Curly eyelashes!

MAGGIE: Not fair.

YOLANDA: Tony-o, honey cakes – you make an old woman very happy.

ANTONIO: Yolanda is forever young. Ever get tired of your boy, you be tellin' me.

YOLANDA: Don't get fresh with me.

ANTONIO: Me cyan help it. Yolanda mek Antonio sweat.

YOLANDA shrieks with laughter. ANTONIO and YOLANDA slap palms. NAOMI watches on and smiles. ANTONIO bustles off again. MAGGIE watches him go.

MAGGIE: Such a sweet kid.

YOLANDA: Ain't he just?

ANDRE appears by YOLANDA's side with a cocktail.

Dirty banana?

ANDRE: Yeah mon. Your usual.

YOLANDA: Just put it on my tab. Oh, and here…

YOLANDA fishes around in her purse and hands over a small tip.

ANDRE: Tanks.

ANDRE turns to NAOMI and MAGGIE

How about you Ladies? Can I get you a drink?

NAOMI: No, I'm fine. Thanks.

MAGGIE: Maybe later.

SLY walks by again. He stops when he sees YOLANDA.

SLY: Hey! My Size!

YOLANDA: Sly…according to you – all women are your size.

SLY: You is lookin' finger lickin' good. Like rice and peas and dumplin'.

YOLANDA: Why you always talk about food when you see me?

SLY: Me like de girl with de big batty. More to hold on to…

He grinds his hips suggestively.

YOLANDA: Don't you be trying to sweet talk me.

SLY: Yolanda…

YOLANDA: Old enough to be your mother. Look, there's a pretty girl next to me. Talk to her instead.

SLY: Me no wan' the kitten, me wan' the cat.

YOLANDA: Miiaowww!

They laugh.

NAOMI: *(To SLY.)* Oh, so now I'm not good enough for you? You men, so fickle.

SLY: Me no mean no disrespec' Naomi, *(Looks at MAGGIE.)* lady… So many pretty ladies, it turn me head.

NAOMI: *(Happy.)* Yeah, right…

SLY: *(To YOLANDA.)* How long you here for?

YOLANDA: Two weeks.

SLY: Hook up with de Lion yet?

YOLANDA: I'm waitin' on him.

SLY: If me see 'im, me tell 'im you here.

YOLANDA: No… I just want thinkin' time this morning.

SLY: Yolanda gettin' a lickle tired of the Lion?

YOLANDA: Yolanda's just fine.

SLY: You have your rest, me always here if you wan' some real sweet loving.

YOLANDA: Yeah, yeah…

SLY walks off again – on the lookout.

MAGGIE lays back on her sunbed. NAOMI can't help watching YOLANDA. She is fascinated by her.

NAOMI: So, you obviously come here a lot.

YOLANDA: Sure do. It's my sixteenth visit. You lookin' for anything in particular?

NAOMI: Needed a break.

YOLANDA: Uh-huh. Lot of women folk come here looking for a break.

NAOMI laughs.

NAOMI: I noticed.

YOLANDA: *(Knowing.)* Uh-huh.

NAOMI: I'm not here for…but gotta admit. Blokes here are gorgeous.

YOLANDA whoops and slaps palms with NAOMI. Then she makes a big deal of untying her sarong, adjusting her straps, sipping her drink, etc.

YOLANDA: Time to pay my respects to the Caribbean.

YOLANDA goes for a swim.

NAOMI: I was actually born here.

MAGGIE: That's why I had to bring you back.

NAOMI: Thanks Maggie.

MAGGIE: I just want you to have some fun. You deserve a change of scene. Actually, you deserve a good shag. Spoilt for choice. Look at these handsome men round here? Imagine having one of those rocking between your legs all night?

NAOMI: I guess it'd be one way of getting back to my roots.

MAGGIE loves this and laughs uproariously. NAOMI watches her amused.

It's good to see you so relaxed Aunty Mags.

MAGGIE: For Christ's sake don't call me Aunty…

NAOMI: *(Laughs.)* Whoops. Don't wanna cramp your style do I?

MAGGIE: Too right.

NAOMI: Hungry. Think I'll order some breakfast.

MAGGIE: I'll join you in a bit.

NAOMI exits. SLY walks past yet again. He clocks ANTONIO before sitting at some distance. ANTONIO clocks SLY's look and steps forward.

ANTONIO: Anyting you want, me be here.

MAGGIE: Really?

ANTONIO: Really.

MAGGIE: In that case…

MAGGIE fishes out her suntan lotion from her bag. She hands it to ANTONIO and lays on her front and undoes her bikini top. ANTONIO stands, a little surprised, clutching the suntan lotion.

What are you waiting for?

ANTONIO kneels by her sunbed and starts to rub the sun tan lotion into MAGGIE's back. He looks a bit nervous. SLY watches from a distance and smirks.

Nice strong hands.

ANTONIO: Tanks.

ANTONIO finishes rubbing suntan lotion into MAGGIE's back. MAGGIE rolls back over and does up her bikini. She rubs oil into her legs. ANTONIO stands by watching awkwardly. MAGGIE smiles at him.

MAGGIE: Thank you.

ANTONIO is uncertain what to do next. MAGGIE plugs in her walkman and lays back down. ANTONIO exits, passing SLY who makes a big show to ANTONIO of walking over to KITTY.

SLY: Pssst…Kitty Kat. Remember me?

KITTY: Oh…it's you…

SLY: I see you back dere – yesterday on de beach? You have a good massage?

SLY crouches by KITTY's sunbed. MAGGIE is still lying down but has one eye on the couple.

KITTY: Fantastic.

SLY: Angel's the best masseuse on de beach. She have de touch.

KITTY: All my aches and pains gone.

SLY: Me also have de touch.

KITTY: Oh…please…

SLY: I see you on de beach, prettiest ting I ever see. Ooohhh…

KITTY: *(Loving it.)* Stop it.

SLY: Me tink, if me can get a 'oman like dat…

KITTY: I'm not falling for your tricks.

SLY: What trick? Me trick you? No man!

KITTY: I know what you Jamaican boys are like.

SLY: Me see you for you. Me don't see you for what you got… Me cyan fake it. Me have to be real and you are real nice.

KITTY laughs.

You give Sly good vibes.

KITTY: Is that your name?

SLY: Yeah man. Respect.

He touches fists with KITTY. She hesitates and then touches fists with him.

You here on your own?

KITTY: Yes.

SLY: You need someone to look out for you.

KITTY: I know my way around.

SLY: But you so pretty you need someone to chase de dogs away.

KITTY: Thanks but – no.

SLY: You from Englan'?

KITTY: Yes.

SLY: What work you do?

KITTY: I'm a teacher.

SLY: Then maybe Kitty can teach Sly some tings? Yeah?

They laugh.

Right now, me lookin' for a new 'oman. Yeah man. Me need to be loved. Been on me own too long now.

KITTY: Really?

SLY: And you need to hook up with a good man.

KITTY: Really?

SLY: You laughing at me. So pretty when you laugh. Me like to see you happy. Me want to see your smile from morning 'til nighttime.

KITTY: Look, this isn't going to work with me. I'm not looking for…a man.

SLY: But when a man come lookin' for you, maybe you should give 'im a chance.

KITTY: You're far too smooth.

SLY: I cyan help meself. You mek me feel like melted chocolate in a hot muffin. When me see you being massaged back dere, I tink to meself, from the tip of her head to de tip of her toes, dat 'oman is pure sweetness.

KITTY melts.

Come, I tek you for a walk.

KITTY hesitates. She is very tempted. She decides to play it cool.

KITTY: Actually, I'm quite happy here. Still a bit jet-lagged… tired.

SLY: I check you later then.

KITTY settles down. SLY walks away, looking around, constantly on the make.

MAGGIE sits up and grins at KITTY.

MAGGIE: You don't want to let that one go. He's hot.

KITTY: Gonna take it slowly. Window-shop for a bit…you know?

KITTY gets up.

Go and cool down. Nice meeting you.

MAGGIE: See you around.

KITTY smiles and heads towards the sea.

ANTONIO approaches MAGGIE. He tries desperately to be flirtatious.

ANTONIO: You want anything? A drink? Some breakfast?

MAGGIE: I'm going to join my friend – thanks.

ANTONIO: What your room number?

Beat.

Maybe I could come visit you after work?

MAGGIE: What for?

ANTONIO: *(Grins.)* Me want to get to know you – better. You a real nice lady.

MAGGIE stares at ANTONIO for a beat and then laughs out loud. ANTONIO looks hurt.

MAGGIE: That's a good one.

MAGGIE can't stop laughing.

No offence, but… How old are you?

ANTONIO: Eighteen.

MAGGIE: You're a kid.

ANTONIO: Me old enough.

MAGGIE: Old enough for what?

ANTONIO is lost for words. MAGGIE laughs at him. ANTONIO looks humiliated.

SCENE 2

It is early evening. REEFIE and YOLANDA are sitting on the beach together. They look happy and relaxed. REEFIE puts his arms around YOLANDA.

REEFIE: Me arms ached for you. It's good to have you back Yolanda.

YOLANDA: It's always good to be back.

REEFIE: You looking good enough to eat.

YOLANDA: There you go again. What is it with you boys out here? One look at me, and you think of food.

REEFIE: Night food.

YOLANDA: Don't be dirty.

REEFIE: One look at you, and we all tink of some loving, some rolling… Reefie love every inch of you. Him miss you. Him dream of you. Him tink on you every day.

They kiss.

YOLANDA: You say the sweetest things.

REEFIE: It for real. You is an empress of womankind. Men should worship on their knees to you.

YOLANDA: Line them up. The more men on their knees to me, the happier I am.

REEFIE grabs YOLANDA's ample breast. YOLANDA screeches and laughs. They kiss again.

REEFIE: We go for a lickle lovin' beneat' de palm trees?

YOLANDA: Didn't you get enough lovin' this afternoon?

REEFIE: Got a lot of time to make up for.

YOLANDA: Later.

They kiss again. REEFIE lays his head on YOLANDA's lap. She strokes his hair.

How's the boat coming on?

REEFIE: Nearly there.

YOLANDA: How big is it?

REEFIE: Twenty feet.

YOLANDA: You ain't gettin' me on any damn boat.

REEFIE: But you love boats.

YOLANDA: Going out on a little glass bottom boat, to the reef is one thing. Least I can see the land. But the big open sea? No way.

REEFIE: Caribbean is calm man.

YOLANDA: Except for when you have those terrible hurricanes.

REEFIE: When you retire, we take a lickle island hopping trip, just we two, 'cross the Caribbean.

YOLANDA: I ain't that old.

REEFIE: You work too hard. Always stress yourself.

YOLANDA: Ain't that the truth. I have to earn a living.

REEFIE: You don't need to earn so much. Come be wid me an' I tek care of you, look after you every day. You don't have to worry your head 'bout nuthin, cos Reefie be there.

YOLANDA: *(Melts.)* Yeah – sounds good to me.

REEFIE: We set out for lickle adventure. Just we two.

YOLANDA: Leave Babylon way behind.

REEFIE: Spend our days in de sun, explorin', swimming.

YOLANDA: No worries.

They kiss again. YOLANDA looks wistfully out to sea. The sun starts to set. A warm pink glow fills the beach.

Ain't that just beautiful?

REEFIE starts to roll a joint.

Reefie, you're not even looking!

REEFIE: Me see it everyday.

YOLANDA: But it's so spectacular. Look how fast it's going down…dipping into the sea…

REEFIE: That's why me cyan leave dis place. Me need to be here. Dem busy cities you live in – make me suffocate.

YOLANDA: Tell me 'bout it.

REEFIE: Need to be surrounded by nature, wid green, wid de eart' between my toes.

YOLANDA: Yeah – I know it.

REEFIE: This where you belong.

YOLANDA smiles happily at REEFIE.

YOLANDA: Twenty foot boat. I don't think you've built it all on my money.

REEFIE lights his joint.

Not that I care.

REEFIE blows smoke into YOLANDA's face.

REEFIE: You have the red eye.

YOLANDA starts to cough.

YOLANDA: What d'you expect? You have to blow that stuff in my face?

REEFIE: No, red eye – mean Yolanda is jealous.

YOLANDA: Bullshit. You smoke too much.

REEFIE: Holy smoke.

YOLANDA: Give me a break.

REEFIE: Give me a line of communication to Jah.

YOLANDA: Makes you completely high.

REEFIE: First step to Jah.

REEFIE passes the joint to YOLANDA. She turns it down.

YOLANDA: Your spliffs blow my mind.

REEFIE: Live a lickle.

YOLANDA: I'll live my life my way, you live it yours.

The sun has set now, darkness starts to descend. YOLANDA slaps at her arms and scratches.

REEFIE: No see-'ems.

YOLANDA: Little shits. Always bite the fuck out of me.

REEFIE: They after your sweet blood. We go back.

REEFIE gets up and helps YOLANDA up.

NAOMI hurries along the beach.

YOLANDA: Hey! Naomi! Hey girl!

NAOMI stops and peers in through the darkness.

NAOMI: Oh, hi Yolanda.

YOLANDA: Reefie, this here's Naomi.

REEFIE: Fiyah, the name's Reefie.

NAOMI: Hi.

YOLANDA: Where you going chile?

NAOMI: Back to the hotel. Apparently there's some live music at Alfred's tonight. Thought I'd get a bite to eat first.

YOLANDA: We're going to Alfred's tonight as well.

REEFIE: Naomi, you walk too fast.

NAOMI: Sorry?

REEFIE: This your first time in Negril?

NAOMI: Erm…yeah…

REEFIE: You gotta learn to take it easy – chill. No problem. You in Jamaica now. What's the hurry?

NAOMI: *(Laughs.)* Oh…yeah…I guess…

REEFIE: Let me show you.

REEFIE walks along the beach, slowly.

REEFIE: See…this be Jamaican style. Let me see you do it.

YOLANDA: Awww…Reefie…c'mon – leave the girl alone.

REEFIE: I teaching her something.

NAOMI hesitates and then copies REEFIE.

Too fast. Try again. Walk the walk. 'Tink Jamaica.

NAOMI tries again.

Look out to sea Naomi…take in a breath of air…slow… slow…yeah mon…that's it.

REEFIE and NAOMI laugh.

YOLANDA: That's exactly how the waiters in my hotel restaurant walk. You yell at them to hurry up and they say 'soon come!'

There is a flash of orange on the horizon.

NAOMI: What's that?

There is another flash of orange.

REEFIE: Lightning.

NAOMI: Amazing.

YOLANDA: It's a long way off.

REEFIE: Me bredren in Cuba is having a storm.

NAOMI: That's Cuba over there?

REEFIE: Yeah mon. Not far. I could get there in my lickle boat in a day. Pay my respects to Fidel.

NAOMI: Cool. Anyway, best be getting back. See you later – yeah?

YOLANDA: You take care now.

NAOMI: Nice meetin' you Reefie.

REEFIE: One love.

NAOMI exits.

She one uptight gyal.

SCENE 3

At a live gig on the beach under the stars, with the sound of the waves behind them, loud reggae music is playing. MAGGIE is smoking a joint and dancing wildly on the beach to the music. KITTY is drinking beer and dancing too. REEFIE and YOLANDA are there too. SLY and ANTONIO stand by and watch but their attention is fixed on the two dancing white women.

REEFIE and YOLANDA dance together, like an old married couple.

Eventually, SLY and ANTONIO move in. They dance up close to the women – SLY with KITTY, ANTONIO with MAGGIE. They show up the women with their superior moves as they dance closer and closer, grinding hips, touching, holding, basically seducing the women.

KITTY and MAGGIE are delighted.

We cut away to the beach.

NAOMI sits in the dark on the beach.

ANDRE walks along the beach. He stops when he sees NAOMI sat there.

ANDRE: Hey, you okay?

NAOMI: Yeah…non-stop party here isn't it?

ANDRE: Yeah mon.

NAOMI: Painful to watch them – especially Aunty Mags.

ANDRE looks back.

ANDRE: That who you come with?

NAOMI: My mum's old friend. Terrible dancer.

They laugh.

ANDRE: She havin' a good time. You from England?

NAOMI nods.

My uncle go to live in a place call Bristol. He die there last year. I remember seeing him once when I was a boy. He come back with presents and tings. Bought me a lickle car, the size of my hand. Me love that car. He never come back again. You wan me go? Me botherin' you?

NAOMI: No…no…

ANDRE hovers.

ANDRE: Word is – you born here.

NAOMI: News travels fast.

ANDRE: And you never come back before?

NAOMI: No.

ANDRE: Why?

NAOMI: *(Shrugs.)* Don't have ties here.

ANDRE: You not curious?

NAOMI: Sure… But…didn't know anyone here. Apparently my dad's from here.

ANDRE: Who your daddy?

NAOMI: Never kept in touch.

ANDRE: Sound like a Jamaican man alright.

NAOMI: You're very lucky to live here. It's so beautiful.

ANDRE: In de ole days, used to be turtles here. Certain time of year all o' de eggs hatch on this here beach and we see lickle baby turtles struggling, crawlin' on their bellies to get to sea. Thousands of dem. Our parents tell us not to touch the babies, not to help dem get to the sea 'cos they need to learn to be strong. Very hard to watch when lickle baby turtles get stuck in de sand, cyan move.

NAOMI: Don't the turtles come here anymore?

ANDRE: Tourism, dem frighten. But dem tourist bring in de dollar so now we can all eat.

NAOMI: You're the cook at the hotel?

ANDRE: 'Beach Grill Chef', dat's what dey call me. The food here is pretty basic. I wanna be a proper chef.

NAOMI: Wow.

ANDRE: Need to get some training course but I'll get there eventually. Dis hotel here – de owner say him send me to college after me work here two year.

NAOMI: How long have you worked here then?

ANDRE: Comin' up to the end of my first year. Fish is my speciality – mainly cos my Mam is such a good fish person. Knows everything there is to know.

NAOMI: What's your favourite recipe?

ANDRE: Tiger prawns in coconut. The way I cook it is to fry the prawns separately first – then I make the onions, garlic and ginger into a paste, fry that. Then you put in the prawns, coconut milk and freshly grated coconut – salt, pepper, dash of chilli sauce and let it all simmer together for a bit. Serve it up in coconut shell and a sprinkle of hot red chilli on the top. Eat it up with a nice cold beer. Hmmmm-hmmm.

NAOMI: Delicious…

ANDRE: Fresh lobster with mango and spinach is pretty good too and stuffed jalepeno peppers…that's a speciality of the island.

NAOMI: I really hope you make it. Maybe I'll switch on the telly one day and there you'll be – a celebrity chef!

ANDRE: Me like it. 'Hi, this is Andre Marley live in Paradise, showing you how to make crab soufflé.'

NAOMI: Marley? Is that your surname?

ANDRE: No. But it sound good. And I could grow me some dreads and skank it up while I cook jam.

He sings a chorus of Bob Marley's Jammin'. NAOMI laughs.

NAOMI: You're definitely onto something there.

ANDRE: Why you never come to the island before? Truth now?

NAOMI: I don't know.

ANDRE: You like what you see so far?

NAOMI: Yeah!

ANDRE looks at NAOMI.

What?

ANDRE: Nuttin'.

NAOMI: What?

ANDRE: You differen'.

NAOMI: What, you mean weird?

ANDRE: No, like dem udder touris' gyals.

NAOMI: Yeah?

ANDRE: You look like a good person. But me tink you look like you lose someting.

He stands up.

I gotta get home.

NAOMI is disappointed.

NAOMI: Yeah. Course.

ANDRE: Nice chatting.

NAOMI: Yeah.

ANDRE: Don't sit around here on your own. You get hassled. Dem Jamaican byahs, dem never tek 'no' for an answer.

NAOMI: Don't worry. I'll be fine.

ANDRE walks away. He looks back momentarily, waves and moves on. NAOMI watches him go. Then she gets up and exits.

We cut to another part of the beach.

KITTY and SLY run in. They roll in the sand furiously kissing and hugging, giggling and tugging at each other's clothes. Eventually KITTY pushes SLY away.

KITTY: We should wait.

SLY: *(Kissing her neck.)* What for?

KITTY: Someone might come by and anyway, that ugly security guard's got his eye on us.

SLY looks back.

SLY: Come, we go to your hotel room.

KITTY: Let's just sit here for a minute. It's so romantic.

SLY holds KITTY as they look out onto the dark sea.

SLY: You the prettiest girlfriend I ever have.

KITTY: I don't believe that for a second.

SLY: You mus' believe me.

KITTY: Hey, mind if I take a picture?

SLY: Be my guest.

KITTY produces a camera which she holds up in front of her and SLY. The camera flashes.

SLY: You got a man back home?

KITTY: No…

SLY: I cyan believe it. You so sweet.

KITTY: Lived on my own so long.

SLY: You a strong woman.

KITTY: And lots of men have a problem with that.

SLY: Sly know how to give you some good lovin'.

KITTY: In your strong arms.

KITTY wraps SLY's arms tighter around her.

Hmmm…

They kiss as he rubs her breasts.

SLY: You like a flower in my hand waiting to bloom.

KITTY: You're perfect. Just what the doctor ordered.

They kiss some more.

SLY: Mi been lookin' for a 'oman like you for ever.

KITTY smiles.

Mona Lisa be jealous of your smile.

KITTY: I'm a bit old for you.

SLY: You ageless. But you have wisdom and intelligence. Me love an intelligent 'oman.

KITTY: Bet you say that to all the girls.

SLY: Me fallin' for you. You're real, you know?

They kiss again.

SCENE 4

MAGGIE is sat drinking a bottle of beer on the beach. She looks a little dishevelled and tired. It is morning. She looks out to sea. REEFIE walks past and she raises her bottle to him.

REEFIE: Mornin'.

NAOMI comes down, dressed.

NAOMI: *(Bright.)* Starting early. That your breakfast?

MAGGIE: Haven't been to bed yet.

MAGGIE offers NAOMI a swig of her beer. NAOMI declines but sits down next to MAGGIE.

NAOMI: Have a good time last night?

MAGGIE: Fantastic.

NAOMI: You okay?

MAGGIE: Fine. Enjoying yourself?

NAOMI: Yeah.

MAGGIE: How come you're all dressed up? You going somewhere?

NAOMI: Spanish Town.

MAGGIE: That's miles away.

NAOMI: Takes about two or three hours. Probably stay the night – come back tomorrow.

MAGGIE: What're you up to?

NAOMI: Bit of sight-seeing that's all.

MAGGIE looks at NAOMI suspiciously.

MAGGIE: I know you better than that Naomi. What's in Spanish Town?

Beat.

NAOMI: Public records office.

MAGGIE: Shit. Your dad?

NAOMI: I only have his first name registered on my birth certificate – no surname – I figured they might have some kind of official documentation in their central office.

MAGGIE: Why are you doing this?

NAOMI: Curiosity?

MAGGIE: This is exactly why your mother didn't want you to come back here.

NAOMI: She's not here to stop me.

MAGGIE: I wanted you to come back to your roots. I wanted you to see the beauty of the place, be surrounded by your culture, your people.

NAOMI: And you were right. Thank you. But I want to know who my dad was.

MAGGIE: You'll be opening a can of worms.

NAOMI: I should've done this a long time ago.

MAGGIE: So take things easy. One step at a time.

NAOMI: Only here for another ten days. Can't hang around.

MAGGIE: Why d'you want to go looking for trouble?

NAOMI: You think I should just put a lid on it?

MAGGIE: Don't go poking around the dustbins.

NAOMI: You didn't see what mum was like at home.

MAGGIE: She loved you.

NAOMI: She was a bitch.

MAGGIE: Please – don't start…

NAOMI: Told me I ruined her life.

MAGGIE: All mothers say that to their kids.

NAOMI: You said that to yours did you?

MAGGIE: Sometimes. Didn't mean it. Only when I got tired or…look, what's the point of beating her up now? Okay so she wasn't the world's best mum – who is for fuck's sake?

NAOMI: She was ashamed to have a brown-skinned child.

MAGGIE: She adored you.

NAOMI: She denied me any knowledge of my father.

MAGGIE: It's just a fucking name.

NAOMI: It's my fucking name. See you tomorrow.

NAOMI kisses MAGGIE briefly on the cheek and walks away. MAGGIE watches NAOMI go – worried.

MAGGIE: *(Calls out.)* Be careful for fuck's sake! Jamaica's a dangerous place!

MAGGIE remains where she is, swigging from her bottle. It's empty. She chucks it into the sea. SLY, ANTONIO and ANDRE enter together. ANTONIO clocks MAGGIE.

SLY: Another plane load flew in today.

ANTONIO: Me see 'em.

ANDRE: Dere's a hen party from Frankfurt.

SLY: Lots of white milk bottles?

ANDRE: *(Laughs.)* Yeah mon.

SLY: The whiter the better. Fill dem up.

ANTONIO: You see Earl is back?

ANDRE: Me see him.

ANTONIO: Say America no good.

SLY: Wha'appened to his milk bottle? She trow 'im out?

ANTONIO: He tell me she no good – get there and she as poor as us. Live in tiny apartment high up in de sky. Bath the same size as our sink.

ANDRE: Me hear from him sister he slap him milk bottle around too much. Neighbours complain, police come around again and again and then him get arrested and deported.

ANTONIO: Shit. He trew it all away.

SLY: Earl a wurtless fool.

ANDRE: He always was dumb. Remember at school? He always brag and lie. Him say fadder was a doctor. Boy, him born a liar.

SLY: – Hey – Andre – on de beach last night you was with a gyal.

ANDRE: I just chat with her.

SLY: Just chat?

ANDRE: She nice.

SLY: 'Nice'? Ooohhh – Andre gettin' soft.

ANTONIO laughs.

You gonna 'fall in love' again?

ANDRE: Shut your mowt'.

SLY laughs.

You always judge everyone by your own low standard Sly.

REEFIE approaches. ANTONIO and SLY both walk over to REEFIE. They treat him with respect. ANDRE is polite but distant with REEFIE.

ANTONIO: New plane load in today.

REEFIE: Yeah Mon.

ANTONIO: Reefie – you gonna fix me up?

ANDRE: Antonio –

REEFIE: Dem ladies all ask after you Andre.

ANDRE: I got me a job.

REEFIE: Show a few ladies around the island and after six month you go to cooking college no problem.

ANDRE: Sebastian say…

REEFIE: …he send you to college? *(Laughs.)* Yeah – right.

SLY: Him a chi chi man.

ANDRE: Me cyan sleep with dem mampi, ugly 'oman.

SLY: Close your eyes and imagine you is with Beyonce.

ANDRE: Me promise Mam never to do dat kinda ting again.

SLY: You do every ting your mam say?

REEFIE, ANTONIO and SLY laugh at ANDRE's expense.

Anyway, what you got dat's so precious – eh? You tink you got yourself some kinda gold tip, red hot poker?

ANDRE: Man respec' himself, den de woman trust him.

SLY: You so clever –

ANDRE: I is not for sale.

SLY looks pissed off.

ANTONIO: So – Reefie? You gonna fix me up with some 'work'?

REEFIE: Maybe.

ANTONIO: Me need the money.

REEFIE: What for?

ANTONIO: Washing machine.

SLY, ANDRE and REEFIE laugh.

For me gran. She set her heart on a washing machine. Me see a nice one in town. Five hundred US dollars it cost. All chrome and nice and shiny. Wash a whole week's washing in one go.

REEFIE: Five hundred US dollars?

ANTONIO: It tek me years to buy dat ting wid de money me earn here. Me need to earn some proper cash.

ANDRE: What use your gran hab wid a washing machine when she hab no electrics in her shack?

ANTONIO: Dey bringing the electric to her lane.

ANDRE: When?

ANTONIO: Soon.

SLY: Dem always say soon. But when it happen for real?

ANTONIO: Reefie. Only you can help me.

REEFIE: It depends on the ladies. What they want.

ANTONIO: *(Boasting.)* I had one last night, right here on the beach.

REEFIE: A touris'?

ANTONIO: *(Lies.)* Yup. She rich too. Diamond rings an' dripping with gold chains… She really like me.

ANDRE and SLY don't believe ANTONIO and wind him up.

Me have plenty 'oman before. She was sweet. Reckon I got me a nice girlfriend.

REEFIE: De higher de monkey climb, de more him parts expose.

ANTONIO: Me not bragging Reefie – me still need your… guidance.

REEFIE: She pay you?

ANTONIO: Yeah. Lot of cyash.

REEFIE: How much?

ANTONIO searches his head for a figure.

ANTONIO: *(Proud.)* Tirty dollars.

SLY laughs at ANTONIO.

REEFIE: Fool. You giving it away.

ANTONIO looks embarrassed. He thought thirty dollars was a lot of money.

You go through me and only me. None of this lone ranger shit.

ANTONIO: You taking me on?

REEFIE: You not even a proper Rasta. You is a wolf. Me see you eating meat.

ANTONIO: The milk bottles dem like Bob Marley.

REEFIE: Where's your respect?

ANTONIO: Me respec' Marley. My ma said she slep' with him once.

SLY: You're Marley's bastard?

ANTONIO: Could be. You see a lickle resemblance?

ANDRE: Him only seventeen. Him born five years after Marley passed on.

SLY and ANDRE crack up.

REEFIE: If I fix you up you get one hundred dollars a night or fifty dollars a fuck. They pay you directly. You gettin' me?

ANTONIO: A hundred dollars?

REEFIE: And you pay me forty percent.

ANTONIO: Massive cut!

REEFIE: Me not cheap.

ANTONIO: How about twenty?

REEFIE: Me say forty.

ANTONIO: Twenty-five?

REEFIE: Tirty-five.

ANTONIO: Tirty.

REEFIE: Okay.

ANTONIO goes to slap palms with REEFIE but he holds back.

One condition. You treat me gyals like ladies. Anyting me hear 'bout any beatings and me cut you off. You got me?

ANTONIO: Yeah – course man.

REEFIE: You bust dem up and they don't come back. Dey don't need to pay good money for that. Still got me some nice ladies come back every season and why? Because me treat them good. You gettin' me?

ANTONIO: Cool man.

REEFIE: We better than their white man. They ain't up to the mark, so when dey come out here and see that we black boys healthy and look good and ting, dey wan' try someting new.

ANTONIO: Cool man.

REEFIE: Me only go for de older ones – young pretty gyals – dey look nice but dey don't have no cash. Dey wan' a man for free. But de older ones – you show dem a good time and they'll be generous. Tell dem they got pretty eyes – it always works.

SLY: Yeah, I use that one.

ANTONIO and REEFIE slap palms on the deal. ANDRE watches with disapproval.

ANDRE: Reefie – how much dey pay you?

REEFIE: Cockroach no business in a fowl yard.

ANDRE: Me jus' curious, is all.

SLY: Reefie part own a glass-bottom boat now.

ANTONIO: Since when?

REEFIE: Last month. The ladies, they like to see the reefs and fish and coral and tings.

ANTONIO: Dat's why dey call you Reefie.

REEFIE: After they see the nature, they all relaxed and happy.

SLY: Den you move in for the kill.

REEFIE: Nature takes its course. You gettin' me?

ANTONIO and SLY laugh.

SLY: Listen to the pro.

REEFIE: *(Suddenly angry.)* What you call me?

SLY: As in pro-fessional. No harm meant. Me givin' you respec' man.

REEFIE: Right.

KITTY comes down onto the beach.

KITTY: Hi there.

SLY: Dere's my sweet lady. Hmmm…mmm…lookin' delicious.

SLY walks up to her, kisses her, holds her hand.

KITTY: You ready?

SLY: I go wherever you take me.

KITTY: We're only going shopping for groceries.

SLY: Me follow you to de end of de eart' sweetness.

KITTY laughs. She and SLY exit, hand in hand. ANTONIO watches jealously.

SCENE 5

NAOMI and ANDRE are on a glass-bottom boat out at sea. We can hear the sound of the sea closer now, almost as if they are underwater. They have obviously just been snorkelling. NAOMI stares down at the glass, awe-struck and childlike. ANDRE watches her as he takes off his snorkel and flippers.

NAOMI: *(Exhilarated.)* It's a different world down there. So many colours! Did you see that enormous school of fish?

ANDRE: I saw it.

NAOMI: Like they were lit up from inside.

ANDRE: Lickle fairy lights.

NAOMI: Yes!

ANDRE: There's a large bay at Rock, 'bout a mile east of Falmouth – place called Glistening Waters. At night, it glows green when de water move. Fish swimming through it look like green lanterns.

NAOMI: *(Points.)* Look! A turtle!

ANDRE looks.

ANDRE: Hawksbill.

NAOMI: It looks so sweet… Are there sharks round here?

ANDRE: Yeah mon. Nurse sharks. But you not bodder dem, dey not bodder you. Barracudas de ones to watch for.

NAOMI: So many fish.

ANDRE: Seven hundred different species dey say – always zippin' around dese waters. Parrotfish, flounder, blue chromis, goat fish…

ANDRE gazes at NAOMI.

You look like a mermaid.

NAOMI looks pleased but embarrassed.

NAOMI: And you look like a dolphin underwater.

ANDRE: It second nature. Plenty real dolphin here too. Sometime, dey come swim wid you, play games…always look like dey are smiling.

NAOMI: Can't say I've ever seen a depressed looking dolphin.

NAOMI and ANDRE laugh.

Water's so clear down there!

NAOMI points at the water.

What was that?!

ANDRE peers into the glass bottom.

ANDRE: Sea urchin. Dey like hanging round de coral walls. You step on one o' dem, their quill can pierce your skin and break off. Agonising.

NAOMI: You ever been stung by one of those?

ANDRE: No, only jellyfish. Sting bad but hot sand tek away de pain. Me bes' friend at school – Stevie – he stand on a stingray. It all buried under de sand so he not see it. It slash his leg wid its tail. Full of poison. My fren' he screaming for hours. He nervous of de water since.

NAOMI looks shocked, ANDRE laughs at her.

Caribbean may look calm and beautiful but it hide a lot of tings you have to be careful of.

NAOMI: Thanks for the warning.

ANDRE: I jus' lookin' out for you.

ANDRE reaches forward across the glass-bottom boat, kisses NAOMI tentatively. At first they are both shy and then they linger a little more. ANDRE breaks away.

Me should tek you back to land.

NAOMI looks puzzled.

It gettin' late.

ANDRE stands and starts the motor.

SCENE 6

In the light of the full moon we see MAGGIE and ANTONIO have been trying unsuccessfully to have sex. MAGGIE rolls away from underneath ANTONIO. She is pissed off and humiliated.

ANTONIO: Me sorry, dis never happen to me before…

MAGGIE: Forget it.

ANTONIO: Me always…me never hab this trouble.

MAGGIE: *(Annoyed.)* I said forget it.

ANTONIO: It a busy day…me tired…we try again later.

MAGGIE looks bored.

It the sand, it get everywhere.

MAGGIE: Yeah – right.

ANTONIO: It don't mean nuthin'. You is a beautiful 'oman. Me like you, me tink you attractive…

MAGGIE: It doesn't matter.

ANTONIO: Me wan' you but for some reason – my body… I dunno…

MAGGIE: Enough!

ANTONIO: You is pretty…me wan' roll wid you…it's jus… jus…me not know why it not work tonight.

MAGGIE: Stop it.

ANTONIO: Maybe, we can try in your bed. It more comfortable.

MAGGIE: Maybe.

ANTONIO stands up, pulling his trousers up, but MAGGIE pulls them down again.

I wanna play a little game with you.

ANTONIO: You wanna play some more?

MAGGIE: I want you naked.

ANTONIO looks dubious.

No need to be shy. There's only the moon to see us.

ANTONIO strips.

Now stand up against the tree.

ANTONIO does as he is told.

ANTONIO: What you gonna do?

MAGGIE tips a bottle of rum to ANTONIO's lips. He drinks and then she drinks. She stands back and looks at ANTONIO.

MAGGIE: You look good. Such a handsome boy.

MAGGIE fetches a length of rope from behind the trees.

ANTONIO: Where you get dat from?

MAGGIE: Borrowed it from one of the boats.

ANTONIO: What you gonna do wid it?

MAGGIE: Tie you up. If you don't mind.

ANTONIO: Is a game you say?

MAGGIE: Yeah – it'll be fun. Stand still.

MAGGIE ties ANTONIO up to a palm tree with a length of rope.

This way, Antonio, you're all mine, even when you beg for mercy.

ANTONIO: *(Giggles.)* You one mean 'oman.

MAGGIE: And you've been a bad boy, so you need to be punished.

ANTONIO: You not going to hurt me?

MAGGIE: That depends on how well you behave.

ANTONIO: Me cyan move.

MAGGIE: That's the whole point.

ANTONIO: Owww…you pulling the rope too hard.

MAGGIE: Stop complaining.

MAGGIE finishes off tying ANTONIO up and stands back and laughs. ANTONIO looks unnerved.

ANTONIO: What happen now?

MAGGIE bends forward and kisses ANTONIO full on the mouth. He kisses back.

MAGGIE: This is what I love about this place – being one with nature. The moon, the sound of the surf, sand between my toes and a nice young buck. Makes me feel so horny. It's like you've become one with the tree – tall…hardwood.

MAGGIE bursts into fits of giggles. She moves away and hides in the shadows.

ANTONIO: Maggie? MAGGIE? Where you are?

MAGGIE: *(Deep voice.)* I am the voice of your conscience.

ANTONIO: Stop it. You scarin' me now.

MAGGIE: This will teach you to take advantage of innocent tourists.

ANTONIO: Come out where me can see you.

MAGGIE: Taking our money, making us buy you drinks, food, giving you a place to sleep for the night.

ANTONIO: Me jus' love me woman. Nuttin' wrong with that.

MAGGIE emerges from the shadows again. She squeezes her body against ANTONIO's, 'manhandles' him, licks his face.

Me cyan perform like dis. All truss up.

MAGGIE: But it's the way I like it.

ANTONIO: Me cyan hold you.

MAGGIE sits on the beach looking out at the sea. ANTONIO yawns.

That it?

MAGGIE: For now.

ANTONIO: You gonna untie me? Me have to work in de mornin'.

MAGGIE: It's nearly morning already. Let's watch the dawn rise.

MAGGIE looks out to sea wistfully. ANTONIO hangs his head. He is dropping off to sleep.

Back home I get the odd shag every now and then with some loser in my local pub. None of them can perform. By the time the morning comes, can't stand the smell of them in bed. Have to boil the sheets to get rid of the stench. All my dreams slowly melted away. You listening?

ANTONIO's head jerks up.

ANTONIO: Hmmm…

MAGGIE: Don't you dare fall asleep on me. What are your dreams?

ANTONIO: Eh?

MAGGIE: What d'you want to do with your life?

ANTONIO: Work. Mek some proper cyash to tek home.

MAGGIE: On the back of some rich tourist no doubt.

ANTONIO: Me lookin' for love. Me want to work, to have a chance.

MAGGIE: And so the means justifies the ends.

ANTONIO: If me have jus' one lickle chance to prove meself… Me could love you…be your man…

MAGGIE: I hardly know you.

ANTONIO: There's no rush. But you could help me as a friend.

MAGGIE: Why should I help you?

ANTONIO: We roll together.

MAGGIE: Get real.

MAGGIE stares out. ANTONIO struggles against his bindings.

ANTONIO: Me uncomfortable now. Please…

MAGGIE: You're all the same. All you blokes. Users – the lot of you. Leeches – sucking our blood, our life, our talents until we're wizened old hags – then you move on.

ANTONIO: You is still a beautiful 'oman. You still have a 'oman's charms, a good body…

MAGGIE: *(Angry.)* No I don't.

ANTONIO: You do!

MAGGIE: Don't lie.

ANTONIO: I not a liad.

MAGGIE: Not really much of a man are you?

ANTONIO: I is a man.

MAGGIE: Can't even get it up for me.

ANTONIO: Me tired, that's all.

MAGGIE: Why d'you do all this pretending? I know you don't find me in the least bit attractive. Maybe you prefer men.

ANTONIO: *(Insulted.)* I is not a batty boy.

MAGGIE: For all I know…

ANTONIO: Hey, hey! Untie me! Untie! You facety to raas gyal!

MAGGIE: *(Taunts.)* Make me – 'batty boy'.

ANTONIO: I is not…

MAGGIE: That's fine if you prefer boys to girls…maybe you should just come to terms with it.

MAGGIE laughs at ANTONIO. He sees red.

ANTONIO: Let me go. Who'd wan' fuck an ugly bitch like you? You a raas blood claat…gorgon…bomba clawt…old duppy hag!

MAGGIE walks away.

Where you go? Come back! Untie me!

MAGGIE comes back towards ANTONIO. She is carrying the branch of a palm. She attacks ANTONIO with it, lashing out, beating him with ferocity. ANTONIO screams.

Stoppit 'oman. You hurtin' me! Why you doing this! Stoppit! Do, me a beg you! You a fuckin' mad 'oman.

MAGGIE takes some dollars out of her purse and tucks them into the rope bindings.

MAGGIE stares angrily at ANTONIO. Then she exits. ANTONIO remains tied up shouting abuse at her.

Interval.

ACT TWO

SCENE 1

REEFIE walks across the beach, carrying a machete and some more timber for his boat. He passes ANDRE and ANGEL walking together. ANDRE is carrying ANGEL's bags. They all greet each other. None of them see ANTONIO tied up to the tree behind them. REEFIE walks on.

ANDRE helps to set up, rakes the sand etc.

ANGEL: You 'ave words wid Sebastian?

ANDRE: Not words. Him speak him mind. I speak mine.

ANGEL: But you work one year for him hotel. He mus' pay you more. All o' de other cooks in hotels get pay better.

ANDRE: Me know it Mam. Me look around for a new job but without de training, me cyan get anyting better.

ANGEL is about to unpack her bag when she notices something in the palm trees behind her. She approaches ANTONIO, still tied up and fast asleep. ANDRE follows her.

ANGEL: What a ting!

ANTONIO wakes with a start.

ANTONIO: Angel…Andre…untie me – please.

ANDRE hurriedly unties ANTONIO.

ANDRE: You been like dis all night byah? Who do this to you?

ANTONIO weeps. He collapses on the floor.

ANGEL: Kiss me neck! Look at all dis money. It belong to you?

ANTONIO scrabbles around in the sand, scraping up dollar notes, shoving them in his trouser pockets, weeping like a child all the time.

ANDRE: Cho, Antonio, what kind of folk you gettin' mix up wid?

ANTONIO: Me a beg you, don't tell no one 'bout dis…

ANGEL: Your face all cut up.

ANTONIO: I is fine.

ANGEL: You no look fine to me.

ANTONIO: De gyal ramp wid me. Please. This be our secret. Me no wan' no carry go bring come 'bout 'dis.

ANGEL: Which one of dose touris' women?

ANTONIO: No one…

ANGEL: *(To ANDRE.)* Who?

ANTONIO: Smaddy.

ANDRE: Reefie introduce you to this 'oman?

ANTONIO is silent. ANDRE looks furious.

ANGEL: You mustn't get mix up with dey kind. Dey mess wid' you, abuse you. Dey no good.

ANTONIO: Me need to get me to work.

ANDRE: Antonio, dis not work.

ANGEL: You got no respect? For youself? Your people?

ANTONIO: Me a beg you. Don't chat about me to no one.

ANGEL: Swear to me, you never do dis kinda ting again.

ANDRE: Don't sell yourself.

ANGEL: Don't sell your soul.

ANTONIO: It me body, not my soul. Dat's all dey is interested in.

ANGEL: So why you cry?

ANTONIO tries to stifle his sobs. ANDRE is angry. He cuffs ANTONIO around the face a few times.

ANDRE: Why you cry like a baby? Fool! You tink dis here is a game?

ANGEL pushes ANDRE off ANTONIO.

ANGEL: De body an' soul Antonio – dey steal it. I see it 'appen wid my own man.

ANTONIO runs up the beach. ANGEL watches him go sadly.

ANDRE follows ANTONIO. ANGEL unlocks her small beach hut and rakes the sand out front. She puts up a sign: 'ALOE VERA MASSAGES AND HAIR BRAIDING'.

She stands and looks out to sea. She looks tired.

SCENE 2

In KITTY's hotel room, there are unopened bags of shopping strewn around the room. SLY is sat at the table, wearing only his boxer shorts, eating from a tray of room service food. KITTY lies back in the bed, covered only by a sheet, smoking a cigarette watching him eat. SLY eats desperately, like a half-starved man.

KITTY: Jesus, Sly, slow down! *(She laughs.)* You'll get indigestion.

SLY: Me hungry.

KITTY: I can see that.

SLY: *(Between mouthfuls.)* The chef here, he good. Best jerk chicken in any of the hotels round here. But me should take you to a proper restaurant – 'Sweet Spice'. The food there is real – home cooking.

KITTY: You eaten in all the hotels and restaurants round here?

SLY: Most o' dem.

KITTY: You've been with a lot of women.

SLY: Cyan help the call of a beautiful 'oman.

KITTY: *(Laughs.)* What are you like?

SLY: Me work in the touris' industry. What you expec'? I work as a waiter, a cleaner, a porter, even a captain of a glass-bottom boat…

KITTY: Captain Sly. Nice one.

SLY: Best job I have is as a hotel rep. Wear a nice uniform, check de guests are okay. Walk around de place, chattin', advising – best places to go, fixing up tours – dat sort of ting.

KITTY: What happened then?

SLY: New manager, not like the look of me…

KITTY: You remind me of one of my sixth formers. Look just like him. Handsome boy – Aaron – doing his 'A' levels. All the female teachers have a soft spot for him.

SLY: You roll with him?

KITTY: God no! He's a student, I'm the deputy head teacher.

SLY: But you want to.

KITTY: That would be completely unethical. How old are you by the way?

SLY: How old you tink?

KITTY: Twenty-five?

SLY: No.

KITTY: Twenty-six?

SLY: Down.

KITTY: Younger? Shit. Twenty…three?

SLY shakes his head.

Twenty-two?

SLY nods. KITTY looks horrified.

I would never go out with a twenty-two year old back home.

SLY: Let alone a black man?

KITTY: No! What makes you think that?

SLY: Way you keep going on about my skin – so black – like dark melted chocolate. Like you is doing someting naughty. *(SLY laughs cruelly.)*

KITTY: Oh just hurry up and come back to bed.

SLY: Lickle while. Sly has to have some fuel.

KITTY smiles. She stretches on her bed.

KITTY: God, I wish I could stay like this forever. You wouldn't believe how tough being a teacher is these days.

SLY: Any Jamaicans in your school?

KITTY: Loads. Second and third generation of course. Actually, I'm one of the few members of staff who has a bit of a rapport with them.

SLY: Yeah?

KITTY: I feel comfortable around black people. I like the food, the music – R 'n' B, reggae – I come out here regularly.

SLY: Kitty have a black soul.

KITTY: *(Laughs.)* I guess.

SLY: Black soul trapped in a white body.

SLY laughs, more to himself.

KITTY: You laughing at me?

SLY: No mon. Me know you different. Me feel you understand us. So, Kitty like her job?

KITTY: Couldn't do anything else.

SLY: De pay good?

KITTY: No. Could never afford to live and work in London.

SLY: But you can afford holidays here. Ever marry?

KITTY: Nearly got hitched once.

SLY: No babies?

KITTY: No.

SLY: Your belly don't ache for babies?

KITTY: Never had the time…didn't meet the right man. And way I see it – there are too many kids in the world and not enough responsible parents there to guide them.

SLY: You is right. Pickneys, dem hard work.

KITTY: I have only myself to please. That's what I love about this place. It's so laid back.

SLY: The Jamaican way.

KITTY: Back home, it's rush, rush, rush…

SLY: But you have a good life?

KITTY shrugs.

You ever go hungry?

KITTY: No.

SLY: So, it's a good life. Me always want to see the world.

KITTY: You never left this island?

SLY: In my head – yes. But for real – no. Me hear there are plenty jobs in your country.

KITTY: Plenty shit jobs yeah. But you have to have some qualifications to earn a decent wage. And even then – it's hard.

SLY: Me can go back to school. Study hard. You can be my teacher. I is a good learner.

KITTY: *(Laughs.)* Oh no…

SLY: You like me – yes?

KITTY: You know I do.

SLY: Me can learn to be an English gentleman. You can introduce me to all a your friends.

KITTY: I'm not introducing you to anyone.

SLY: We could trow parties, I teach you tings too like…how to dance, how to cook jerk chicken, how to suck a mango…

KITTY: You really want to come with me to England?

SLY: You could have me all a de time den. When you come back from work – I be dere – waiting for you.

KITTY: My house boy.

SLY: Dere to feast your tired body. You be me mistress. You look after me, I look after you.

KITTY: A prim school teacher by day and a wild uncivilised animal at night!

SLY: We fit like hand in glove. You mek mi nature rise. Way me feel when me grinding inside you – perfec'.

KITTY giggles.

You not feel how good we is together? Me make you hot, me make you wet, me make you moan for more.

KITTY squirms under the sheets in delight.

Me like to hear you moan an' cry for more. An' I can give you more. Much more den you ever dream of. You be my sugar mummy and I be your coochie daddy.

KITTY moans.

Is true what dey say about Jamaican man. We big an' we can work all night for de 'oman we love. We know how to keep 'oman happy.

KITTY: Please stop eating and come back to bed.

SLY smiles and carries on eating.

SLY: Me can order some more on room service?

KITTY: More…? You've eaten…

SLY moves on to the ice cream. It dribbles down his chin.

You eat like a savage.

SLY looks furious.

SLY: Say wa?

KITTY: You heard me.

SLY wipes his face. He is in a rage. KITTY panics. She realises she has said the wrong thing.

Go ahead, order some more food…

SLY: I is not hungry.

SLY is silently fuming and pacing.

KITTY: I'm sorry…it just slipped out… I didn't mean… please… I just got upset. I wanted you back in bed. It was just a stupid word.

KITTY reaches for her purse. She pulls out some dollars. She is desperate.

Look, I went to the bank. I've got some cash. We can have a good time tonight… Nice meal in the evening… Go to 'Jungles' after…

SLY looks at the money. He sits down on the edge of the bed, still fuming, but trying hard to remain calm. He needs this job. KITTY looks relieved. She massages his shoulders.

You said I was the sweetest girl on the beach.

Beat.

SLY: Yeah mon.

KITTY: You said you loved me.

SLY: Me care for you.

Despite his humiliation, SLY remains sitting on the edge of the bed.

SCENE 3

Back at ANGEL's hut – YOLANDA is sat on a chair, facing the sea whilst ANGEL braids her hair.

YOLANDA: Reefie's a man of means now.

ANGEL: Him hab plenty money.

YOLANDA: You know he has a house in the mountains?

ANGEL: Him build it with his own bare hands.

YOLANDA: Part owner of a glass-bottom boat.

ANGEL: Hmmm…hmmm…

YOLANDA: And now he's building a boat!

ANGEL: Plannin' his escape.

YOLANDA: What's he runnin' from?

ANGEL: Oh Reefie – him jus' always like building tings. You ever go to his house?

YOLANDA: Went there last night. So dark up there at night. You know he forced me up this ladder onto the roof? I said to him, 'I ain't going up there. No way you gettin' my fat arse up that rickety ladder.' He stood underneath me and pushed my butt up, literally shoved me up there with his head. I was afraid, that if I slipped and fell, I'd land on top of him and squish his puny body like a fly.

ANGEL laughs.

ANGEL: Reefie small but him a strong man.

YOLANDA: Must be, cos he got my ass up there. Anyway, there I am, on top of this fucking roof. I'm so giddy I start to whine. Felt like a real idiot. Oh, I forget one small but important detail. I had to close my eyes when I got to the top. I'm wailing and saying, 'What's the point Reefie, there ain't no light up here...' Anyway, he jumps up after me and makes me lay me down on the roof. My eyes are still closed. I'm thinking, is this crazy mother gonna screw me up here on the roof?

ANGEL laughs more.

Then he says, 'Open your eyes.' So I open them. I'm staring up at this sky, studded with stars. I ain't never seen so many stars. I can't speak, I can't breathe. It's so dark around me but the stars...oh my...twinkling, winking, Jesus...it was beautiful. And I lost count of how many shooting stars I saw. One...two...three... four... Hundreds of them! I cried all over again.

Can't see the stars in New York – not like that. Then, there's a breeze and the clouds part, like a misty curtain and the moon...the full moon emerges. She looks at me and she smiles. Felt like I could reach out and touch her. So close!

ANGEL: We see the stars like that every night. Tek it for granted.

YOLANDA: Lay there like that for a couple of hours, sipping rum under the midnight sky.

ANGEL: Cool.

YOLANDA: Took me forever to get down that ladder again. So drunk. 'Course, Reefie don't drink but he was so stoned, he more or less fell back into the house.

ANGEL: He know how to treat a lady – that Reefie.

YOLANDA: Uh-huh…why d'you think I keep coming back for more? But I ain't under any illusions 'bout him. Frank's a good husband…

ANGEL: He know about Reefie?

YOLANDA: No.

ANGEL: Him have another 'oman?

YOLANDA: Frank? *(She laughs.)* All I want out here is some fun. Mind you, I can't be doin' what all them other tourists do. You see them?

ANGEL: Me see dem alright.

YOLANDA: Old women walking down the beach with these young boys.

ANGEL: Dey come 'ere to screw dem sons.

YOLANDA: You said it baby. Pretending they're sex kittens. They reckons black men got bigger… *(YOLANDA points down.)*

ANGEL laughs.

ANGEL: Wish it was true.

YOLANDA: They reckon Jamaican men can keep goin' all night.

ANGEL: Too much ganja for dem to perform.

ANGEL makes a rude gesture with her finger. ANGEL and YOLANDA have a good laugh.

YOLANDA: They say, 'Black men like fucking, black men enjoy the sex act, they don't make love.'

ANGEL: And the beach byahs dem love dat chat. Dem good actor.

YOLANDA: You ever sleep with a white man – Angel?

ANGEL: Many year ago.

YOLANDA: Was he…you know…smaller?

ANGEL: Not dat I remember. But dem byahs, dem tink all dat matta is size. It the loving that count.

YOLANDA: Tell me about it. You hear these ladies on the beach mouthing on, 'He's big, he's like an animal, untamed, primitive, he'd fuck you in the sand and wouldn't think anything the matter with it…' Jesus.

ANGEL: Dem touris', dem buy de fantasy wid hard cyash and tink it real.

YOLANDA: Your boy Andre's doing good.

ANGEL: Yeah mon.

YOLANDA: You met this girl he's been hanging out with? Pretty young English gal?

ANGEL: Me hear but I not meet her.

YOLANDA: How's that man of yours?

ANGEL: Me not see 'im no more. Dat man a Ginnal.

YOLANDA: He work round here?

ANGEL: Him 'work' de beach in Mo Bay. Although, now, it jus' a matter of time.

YOLANDA: Matter of time?

ANGEL: Any day now…

YOLANDA: Shit.

ANGEL: Last time me see him, he a walking duppy. 'Tin, eyes all up in his sockets…walkin' so slowly… No 'oman look at 'im now.

ANGEL trails off.

YOLANDA: God, I'm so sorry.

ANGEL: No matter.

ANGEL looks away, upset.

Me 'ave the test. Me clear. But him…

YOLANDA is quiet.

ANGEL finishes off YOLANDA's hair-braiding and sits down next to YOLANDA for a moment. She looks out to sea. YOLANDA holds her hand and squeezes it. She reaches into her bag and pulls out some dollars which she slips ANGEL.

A little extra. Buy something nice for the kids.

ANGEL: Tanks.

NAOMI walks up the beach. She approaches ANGEL and YOLANDA. She is exhilarated.

NAOMI: Yolanda, nice hair.

YOLANDA: Angel's got damn fast fingers. Best hair-braider I ever come across.

ANGEL: *(To NAOMI.)* You should get your hair done. It look pretty on you.

YOLANDA: Oh! Angel – this is Naomi. Naomi – Angel.

ANGEL nods at NAOMI.

NAOMI: Hi – wouldn't mind a massage.

ANGEL: Tirty dollars.

NAOMI: Twenty?

ANGEL: Twenty-five.

NAOMI hesitates.

Twenty-five a good price.

ANGEL produces a mirror from her bag and shows YOLANDA off in it.

YOLANDA: Perfect. Well I'm all done. Gotta be gettin' myself ready for a night out. Thanks again Angel. Be seein' you.

YOLANDA walks away. YOLANDA produces a bench and motions at NAOMI to lie down.

NAOMI: Okay.

NAOMI lies down. ANGEL gets a large aloe vera leaf and starts to massage NAOMI.

Hmmm…that feels good. Ohhh…

ANGEL: This your first time?

NAOMI: In Jamaica?

ANGEL: No, massage.

NAOMI: Oh…no…I've had a few back home.

ANGEL: You is looking for romance?

NAOMI: No! I'm just here…you know…holiday… I'm not like the others who come here looking for a man.

ANGEL: You don't need to. You probably have to fight dem off.

NAOMI: I wish.

ANGEL: No man back home?

NAOMI: No.

ANGEL continues with the massage.

You live round here?

ANGEL: Up in the mountains.

NAOMI: Kids?

ANGEL: Six… And two grandchile.

NAOMI: You don't look old enough.

ANGEL: My fourt' chile – him work hard, here on de beach, in a one of dem restaurant.

NAOMI: What's his name?

ANGEL: Andre – him a grill chef.

NAOMI: You're Andre's mother?

ANGEL: Him bright. Me only worry…him cyan get proper training – in a catering place.

NAOMI: I thought the hotel was going to pay for his training?

ANGEL: Dat manager – Sebastian – him a tight-fisted rass. Him got Andre's arse in a vice. Him say after two years of Andre workin' dere – but me no trust him.

NAOMI: He's a nice man your son. Works very hard.

ANGEL: Yeah mon, me have high hope for 'im.

Beat.

You look mix.

NAOMI: Yeah…I am.

ANGEL: Mudder?

NAOMI: My dad. From here apparently. I was born here.

ANGEL: A Negril baby?

NAOMI: Yep.

ANGEL massages NAOMI's back. They are both in silence for a while.

I never knew my dad. Went to the public records office in Spanish Town. Maybe you know him?

ANGEL: Jamaica a big island, you tink me know everyone?

NAOMI sits up for a moment and stops the massage. She rummages around in her bag and pulls out some papers. She shows them to ANGEL who glances at them.

This him name here?

NAOMI: Yeah.

ANGEL: Very common name. Sorry. Me know fifty man o' dat name.

NAOMI: My mum was called Julie – everyone called her Jules. She came here on holiday and got pregnant with me – stayed until I was born. Maybe you remember her?

ANGEL laughs.

ANGEL: Don't be foolish chile! How many white gyal come here and have baby?

NAOMI laughs at herself.

NAOMI: I even got an address of my dad's birthplace.

ANGEL: You been there? You ask around?

NAOMI: Yep – but there're no houses there anymore. Just guest apartments. Talked to the owner – he was an American. Said he didn't know anyone by the name...

NAOMI lies back down again. ANGEL continues with the massage.

ANGEL: He probably move on.

NAOMI: Yeah. Could be anywhere.

ANGEL: Why you want to find your daddy anyway?

NAOMI: Mum died a couple of months ago. Cancer.

ANGEL: Me sorry. You tink your daddy rescue you? Mek you feel whole again? Be dere to look after him lickle baby girl?

NAOMI: No. Just...curious to meet him.

ANGEL: This where your forefathers are from. Jamaica is in your blood. You born here. Fadders come, they go, but the island still floatin' in de Caribbean Sea. Main ting is – you here now. Welcome home Naomi.

NAOMI starts to cry.

Hey…hey…I don't mean to upset you… Sorry mon.

NAOMI: Sorry, sorry…you must think I'm an idiot…

ANGEL: No, mon…no…this place…it touch you…

NAOMI: But this isn't the real Jamaica is it?

ANGEL: Real Jamaica no different from anywhere else. Everyone suffrin' – lookin' for the next dollar. Fishermen in Whitehouse Bay, mek more money dese days hauling nets full of cocaine rather than fish. Dem yout' earn more selling ganja on de beach than workin' as a grill chef. You see dem fourteen-year-old girls up in Bourbon Beach selling their bodies to old white men?

If you want to see the real Jamaica, find your roots, dat sort of ting – jus' gwan. Travel around. Go to the Blue Mountains and Port Antonio. Go to Ocho and Black River. Drink de islan' up wid your eyes. Plenty beautiful tings to see here. And good people. Not everybody after your money. Not everybody hustlin'.

ANGEL massages NAOMI's shoulders and neck.

SCENE 4

MAGGIE, YOLANDA and KITTY are sat out on sundecks sunning themselves. They are all sipping cocktails.

KITTY: This time I have really fallen on my feet. Sly is gorgeous.

YOLANDA: He go down on you?

KITTY: Not yet. But I'm working on it.

MAGGIE: They don't like doing that out here. Apparently it's taboo. How about your man?

YOLANDA: Reefie's a Rasta so he's vegetarian.

MAGGIE laughs but KITTY doesn't get it.

MAGGIE: Very good.

KITTY: Eh?

YOLANDA: According to him, he doesn't eat meat so why should he eat that?

KITTY smiles.

KITTY: It's so different out here. Women are worshipped – regardless of size. So…so…

YOLANDA: Liberating.

KITTY: Yes.

YOLANDA: See all them skinny women in their tiny bikinis walking down the beach – they don't even look at them!

KITTY: They only sell extra large condoms at the local shop. And the local women have chicken fat injections in their arses to get bigger. Can you imagine?!

MAGGIE: You know what gets me? Is how effortlessly thin the men all are.

YOLANDA: Probably a lifetime of not getting three square meals a day.

KITTY: It's not poverty. It's the way they're built – part of their nature.

YOLANDA: What you mean the way we're all good at sports, the men all have big dicks and the women make good 'mammys'?

KITTY looks uncomfortable.

KITTY: I'm sorry, I didn't mean to offend you.

YOLANDA: No worries girl. You can't help it. It's part of your nature.

Awkward silence.

So, girls, you got what you came for?

KITTY: Oh yes.

MAGGIE: I've had a few good nights.

KITTY: I've been thinking…well for some time now…of moving out here.

MAGGIE: For good?

KITTY: Jack in the job, use my savings to buy a place out here and set up home with…someone.

YOLANDA: Someone?

KITTY: Buying a nice house in the UK is virtually impossible for me. But here – I could afford to live well.

MAGGIE: What about your friends? Your family?

KITTY: They could come and visit. And besides, they all have their own lives now – families, kids… I'm…well…I fancy a change.

YOLANDA: Honey…

KITTY: I think Sly's the one for me. No more shopping around.

YOLANDA: You only just met him!

KITTY: But it feels so right.

YOLANDA: Sweet Jesus.

MAGGIE: Please, tell me you're joking – right?

KITTY: No. I'm not.

MAGGIE: These boys only want a way off the island.

KITTY: This is different.

YOLANDA: Keep taking the pills.

KITTY: I used to be like you – cynical.

MAGGIE laughs. YOLANDA nearly chokes on her drink.

MAGGIE: No offence Kitty but look at yourself in the mirror. Who are you kidding?

KITTY: I'm only thirty-eight. So what if he's nearly half my age? Age doesn't matter. I can make this work.

MAGGIE: Been all over the world and everywhere I go, it's the same story. The boys only want a passport.

KITTY: Not all of them.

YOLANDA: Need to get to know him better – can't walk away from your life on a whim.

MAGGIE: I know where you're at. It's good to be held tight in a man's arms. Chases away all those lonely nights and stops the questions.

KITTY: No.

MAGGIE: Find yourself asking the same old questions – why am I here on my own? What's wrong with me? If I'm so great – why am I so single?

KITTY: No…no…

MAGGIE: Look. I know the score. I was married. I know how it goes. Staying with a man is about settling for second best. It's an economic contract.

KITTY: Wish I'd settled down. Always too busy with my career.

MAGGIE: Yeah, but marriage is a compromise.

YOLANDA: I have a very good marriage.

MAGGIE: So why are you here?

YOLANDA looks away, irritated.

MAGGIE: Some women can cope with boredom. You have kids, you nurture them, teach them, love them, they grow up and leave you. And then your man leaves you too.

KITTY: Is that what happened to you? Your husband left you?

MAGGIE: *(Ignoring the question.)* Women are strong. We can exist quite happily on our own. But then there comes a point in a woman's life where she aches to be touched, desired… Real love? It never lasts.

KITTY: *(Angry.)* I think that's just horrible.

MAGGIE: All I'm saying is wake up before you get hurt.

KITTY: It's different between me and Sly. It's real.

YOLANDA: How can it be honey?

KITTY: Fuck off! Love conquers all.

MAGGIE bursts into laughter. KITTY walks away, upset.

YOLANDA: D'you think we were too hard on her?

MAGGIE: Truth always hurts.

YOLANDA: Yeah. Two weeks and she wants to settle down? She's heading for a fall, ain't that the truth?

MAGGIE and YOLANDA slap palms and laugh.

REEFIE enters, kisses YOLANDA briefly and squeezes next to her on the sunbed. They rub noses and do a little canoodling. MAGGIE watches on – a little envious. ANGEL walks by. She waits quietly but says nothing. REEFIE looks up.

REEFIE: Hey, Angel.

ANGEL: Can me have a word?

REEFIE: Sure ting.

ANGEL walks away. REEFIE gets the hint. He gets up and follows her. ANGEL and REEFIE stand to one side.

Everyting cool Angel?

ANGEL: That mix gyal. Naomi?

REEFIE looks none the wiser.

She staying here at the hotel. Young, pretty gyal. From Englan'.

REEFIE: Oh – yeah mon – me know her.

ANGEL: She lookin' for her daddy.

REEFIE: Me hear.

ANGEL: She twenty-eight. Her English mam call Jules and Naomi, she born here.

REEFIE doesn't flinch.

She have a name. She have your name. Me tink you should know.

ANGEL turns and leaves. REEFIE is stunned.

SCENE 5

ANDRE and NAOMI are sat by the sea together.

ANDRE: You come back soon?

NAOMI: I'm not going yet. Thought I'd extend my holiday and see the island. Roaring river…Blue Mountains… Auntie Mags has to get back.

ANDRE: When you leave?

NAOMI: Tomorrow. I'll miss you.

ANDRE is moved. He reaches out and touches NAOMI's face. She enjoys his touch but then he pulls away.

Andre. I wanted to do something for you.

ANDRE looks wary.

ANDRE: Why?

NAOMI: Why not?

ANDRE: Me not want your money.

NAOMI: What?

ANDRE: Me like you, you mek me feel good, but me not want your cash.

NAOMI: I know.

ANDRE: I see it too much round here. Friendships dey call dem. But you cyan have a friendship based on cash. It not balance.

NAOMI: But friends do help each other.

ANDRE looks very uneasy.

I know you want to go to catering school – your mum was saying…and I was talking to one of the chefs up at the Grand Lido. He said that there's a good catering school in Kingston. It's a year's diploma course – you learn all sorts of chef skills and you get a certificate at the end of it. Apparently, it's hard work, full-time and it costs.

ANDRE: Me know de school.

NAOMI: I could pay for you to go there – for a year. I could support you – as a friend.

ANDRE looks angry.

ANDRE: Why you do dis? Me look like a charity case to you?

NAOMI: No.

ANDRE: You see me in de same two shirts every day and you feel sorry for me – is dat it?

NAOMI: No.

ANDRE: So why you have to spoil our friendship?

NAOMI: You've taken this the wrong way…

ANDRE: Me not my fadder's son.

NAOMI: I never said you were.

ANDRE: You you wan' someting in return?

NAOMI: I'm offering you help. If you're too fucked up to accept it – fine.

ANDRE: I is not fucked up.

NAOMI: Then why can't you see my offer for what it is?

ANDRE: You cyan buy a lickle piece of me. I is not for sale.

NAOMI: Okay. I offered. You declined. End of story. Let's not get all worked up about it. I'm sorry if I offended you.

The two look out to sea.

ANDRE: What you do tonight?

NAOMI: Pack.

ANDRE: Me see you den.

ANDRE gets up to go. NAOMI looks at him, upset.

NAOMI: That's it?

ANDRE: What you wan' me to say?

NAOMI: Wish me luck with my trip? Goodbye? Whatever.

ANDRE: Me wish you luck. Me hope you find what you is lookin' for.

ANDRE exits. NAOMI is crestfallen.

SCENE 6

It is later. ANTONIO is sat on the beach looking out to sea. SLY enters.

SLY: So, where your girlfriend Antonio?

ANTONIO: Where yours?

SLY: Mekin' herself pretty for me. We going down to Roots Bamboo tonight. She fly back tomorrow.

ANTONIO: They have a good band down dere tonight?

SLY: So me hear.

ANTONIO: You see Reefie 'round?

SLY: No man.

ANTONIO: Him say him give me work but so far…I only get one crazy 'oman…

SLY: Jus' try a lickle patience man. Reefie see you arright.

ANDRE enters, looking upset and wound-up.

Andre – how's your gyal?

ANDRE does not reply.

She's so fine that Naomi… She hab money?

ANDRE: Me not after her money.

ANTONIO: So you is after her?

SLY: But he is superior to all of us because he wind himself round her heart first, for free, den he move in for de kill.

ANDRE: Me not gravalishus like you.

SLY: Talk nice to her, mek her feel it's for real or it ain't gonna last.

ANDRE: Why you always mek fun?

ANTONIO and SLY have a good laugh at ANDRE's expense.

SLY: It not funny Andre – it sad. You is lyin' to yourself.

ANDRE: Only liar I see is the one facin' me.

SLY stands up and faces ANDRE but REEFIE enters. He looks downcast, a little troubled. He beckons ANTONIO over. ANTONIO approaches.

REEFIE: Me have a girlfriend for you.

ANTONIO: For me? Really?

REEFIE: Sure ting. She comin' down to the bar. She want you to show her a good time.

ANTONIO: Tanks Reefie.

ANDRE: Antonio – don't…

REEFIE pushes ANDRE aside.

REEFIE: You keep outa dis. I is warning you.

ANDRE stands to one side and silently fumes. REEFIE goes back to ANTONIO.

German lady. Name of Anna.

REEFIE pulls out some money from his pocket.

She pay me arredy.

REEFIE counts out seventy dollars and hands it over to ANTONIO. ANTONIO can't believe his luck.

I tek my cut. This is yours. Seventy dollars. Check it. Me no wanna hear no accusations flying later.

ANTONIO counts the money out and kisses it.

ANTONIO: She pretty?

REEFIE gives ANTONIO a look.

No matter. Me no care. Tonight Anna is de most beautiful ting on dis island.

REEFIE: What else you gonna tell her?

ANTONIO: That she has hair de colour of gold spun in the sun.

REEFIE: She hab black hair.

SLY laughs. ANDRE looks pissed off.

ANTONIO: Oh – den – she hab hair de colour of night, wid de moon glistening and shimmering in her locks….

SLY: Yeah mon.

ANTONIO: And when de stars come out…

ANDRE: Her fangs come out.

SLY cracks up. ANTONIO ignores them both.

ANTONIO: …When de stars come out dey weep to see her eyes, twinkling, dat hide their beauty.

SLY: He rappin now…

ANTONIO and SLY slap palms. ANDRE looks unimpressed.

ANTONIO: How long I got?

REEFIE: Half-hour.

ANTONIO: Me take a shower.

SLY: And change your shirt man.

REEFIE: Some tips Antonio. Never look at your watch. You have all de time in de world.

ANTONIO: Got it.

REEFIE: Always you look in her eyes.

ANTONIO: Sure ting.

SLY: Be cool. Don't go too far wid de compliments. Den dey suspec' you fakin' it.

REEFIE: Mek her feel like she de only 'oman for you. Den, maybe she call you back.

SLY: Or tek you to Germany!

ANTONIO: Tanks Reefie. You a good man. How me know who she is?

REEFIE: She know you. She see you on de beach. She find you in de bar. An' one more ting Antonio.

ANTONIO: Yeah mon?

REEFIE: Don't let her tie you up naked to a tree and whip your arse. No need to be dat cheap.

ANTONIO looks embarrassed.

ANTONIO: Awww…Reefie…how you hear 'bout dat?

He looks accusingly across at ANDRE.

REEFIE: Everybody know.

ANTONIO hangs his head.

Me on de case. No one treat my boys like dat.

ANTONIO: Don't do nothing. She a fucked-up old lady.

REEFIE: She Naomi's friend – Maggie – right?

ANTONIO is silent.

Right?

ANTONIO nods.

SLY: We should mash her up.

ANDRE: No…

REEFIE: Jus' a lickle revenge.

SLY: Tie her to a tree and whop her arse.

REEFIE: Me slip a little someting in her drink tonight.

ANDRE: No man – don't be doin' that…

SLY: She deserve it.

REEFIE: Nuttin' heavy. A lickle laxative.

SLY: Bring on de shits.

REEFIE: And I set her up with Mad Eye for tonight.

SLY: *(Cracks up.)* Mad eye? Oh man. Him hab real personal hygiene problem.

ANTONIO touches fists with REEFIE.

ANTONIO: Tanks Reefie.

REEFIE: We look out for our own. Got it?

ANTONIO nods.

ANDRE: You don't need to do dis ting Antonio. You young. You can work and keep your self-respec'.

ANTONIO turns and looks at ANDRE.

ANDRE: Please. Tink careful.

ANTONIO: It for my gran. She old. She deserve some rest.

ANTONIO exits excitedly.

SLY: *(Calls out.)* Skank it up!

ANDRE looks at REEFIE and turns away, angry.

ANDRE: You turn little Antonio into a whore.

REEFIE: I give him what he want.

ANDRE: It not right. One day, I'm gonna get out of this place.

SLY: Yeah – right.

ANDRE: You watch me Sly.

SLY: You always had your head up in the clouds.

ANDRE: I got me ambition.

SLY: Ambition is one thing. Stupidness is another.

ANDRE: Shut your mowt'.

SLY: *(Laughs.)* You always tink you is better than us.

ANDRE: No. Me tink me can do better if me put my mind to it.

SLY: In a shack with no water. Ghetto chef cooking in the gutter.

REEFIE: Me hear about you mekin' de moves on Naomi.

ANDRE is silent.

You tink a nice gyal like dat would have anyting to do wid a wurtless grill boy? A kitchen hand?

ANDRE: You wicked Reefie. You bring everyone down to your level. Me different. Me not like you.

SLY: Blood claat.

REEFIE: You no better dan your fadder. He sell himself for a plate of food.

ANDRE: I is not like my fadder.

REEFIE: You can pretend but you have his blood.

ANDRE: But I not de one whorin' for a livin'.

SLY *(To ANDRE.)* Look in de mirror before you chat shit. You the same as the rest of us.

ANDRE: When I look in de mirror, I see me. I know who I is. What you see? Gigolos? Whores? Lyin to dese harpy 'oman – pretending you like dem. How you do it? It make my flesh crawl to see you at 'work'. Rubbing oil into dem fat, white whales, playing de obedient loverman. Always pretending.

REEFIE: Don't disrespect me or my ladies.

ANDRE: You believe all a dat shit you chat? Me know you. Me know you is nuttin' more dan a rascal. You lie to eat. You hate dem ladies. You hab no respect for nobody – not even youself.

REEFIE: Me hab plenty respec'.

ANDRE: You is false, you is a fake.

REEFIE: Stop! Your mudder my frien'.

ANDRE: You no frien' to my mudder. You de one who mek me sell dem ganja to dem touris. I is eighteen den. You not stand by me when I get arrested. You no even put up me bail. I never tell me Mam it you who set me up. If she know de trut' about you, she spit on you. She step over your dead body in de street, she kick you rass arse.

REEFIE: Enough!

ANDRE: You is a devil hiding behind your dreads. A wolf.

REEFIE: If I is a wolf, why my ladies come back for more?

ANDRE: Because they is sad and lonely and you is nuttin' more dan a renta dread and a dirty pimp.

There is a hush as SLY looks anxious.

SLY: Tink 'pon what you say Andre!

ANDRE: Him know me right.

REEFIE: And who give me my firs' job? Eh? Your good for nutten, rass claat, renk dread – daddy. Least I makin' someting of my life, what he doin'? Eh? Rottin' in some shack. Dress in rags I hear. Starvin', beggin', nobody wan' know him.

ANDRE is furious. He lunges at REEFIE. REEFIE tries to back off.

Don't mek me do it.

ANDRE: Do what old man?

REEFIE: Me not wan' hurt you.

ANDRE: You a toothless lion.

REEFIE: Don't vex me.

ANDRE: You not even a man anymore.

ANDRE punches REEFIE hard. REEFIE reels and then hits back. They start to fight viciously.

REEFIE: You say that again and I'll cut you up so bad, your mudder won't know you!

ANDRE: Think you so big?

REEFIE: Me a come wid me mashait!

REEFIE grabs his machete and brandishes it menacingly at ANDRE. ANDRE eggs him on.

ANDRE: Come, come! I show you how to fight like a man. Den when me kill you, I fuck your mudder, I fuck your woman and den after dat I fuck your dawta.

YOLANDA and ANGEL enter. They see the men fighting and wade in.

YOLANDA: No! Stop it! No!

YOLANDA tries to pull REEFIE off ANDRE – to no avail.

REEFIE: Yolanda – stay away from dis.

ANGEL: You tek your hand off me byah right now Reefie.

REEFIE: Your byah need to learn him lesson.

ANGEL: Leave him – please!

YOLANDA: *(Starts to shout.)* Stop it! I mean it! If you don't quit this I'm callin' the police. Don't think I won't!

SLY manages to hold ANDRE back.

Will the two of you grow up? I don't know what the fuck you're playing at Reefie, but this has got to stop right now.

REEFIE looks down.

ANGEL grabs ANDRE and pushes him away. ANDRE glowers at REEFIE, as ANGEL frogmarches him out.

YOLANDA, REEFIE and SLY are left together. SLY looks a bit shaken.

SCENE 7

ANDRE is pacing on the beach by ANGEL's massage hut.

ANGEL: Why you fight? Why?

ANDRE: Me have nuthin' to say to you.

ANGEL: I not recognise my own son. Wha'appen?

ANDRE: Nuthin'.

ANGEL: It not look like nuthin' to me.

ANDRE is silent.

This not like you Andre. Look at me.

ANDRE refuses to look.

Look at me!

ANDRE faces ANGEL.

ANDRE: Him call me wurtless…him tell me I not good enough for Naomi.

ANGEL: *(Realising.)* Dis about her?

ANDRE: Why you old folk cyan keep your noses outa my business? Why you all gotta make trouble?

ANGEL: What trouble I mek?

ANDRE: What it to Reefie if me mek friend with Naomi?

ANGEL looks disturbed.

ANDRE: You all a de same. You, my fadder, Reefie…

ANGEL: How you say that?

ANDRE: How you any differen'? You my mam, you tell me to have self respec'. Me listen to you. Me try to do the right thing…

ANGEL: Me know. You a good bwoy. Why you so vex wid me?

ANDRE: You speak to her.

ANGEL: Who her?

ANDRE: Naomi! You tell her me need money for school. She offer me money like me is like all o' dem others.

ANGEL realises.

ANGEL: Me only mention…

ANDRE: On purpose. She insult me.

ANGEL: She a nice girl. She like you.

ANDRE: Me no wan' her money. Me not a lickle slave boy who need education.

ANGEL: Hush yourself now. You overreacting.

ANDRE: Me meet a girl. Me like her. Me tink, if there a chance of maybe…and then you walk in dere and poison it.

ANGEL: No…

ANDRE: You prostitute me, Reefie wan' sell me too. And now Naomi, she wan' buy me. How you do this to me mam?

ANGEL sits down.

ANGEL: Me no wan' nuthin' but happiness for you.

ANDRE: So how come I not happy?

ANGEL: You need to get off dis island.

ANDRE: You wan' me to go?

ANGEL: No. But there no future for you here. Only way forward is off dis island. It cursed. For people like us – no money, no school, we cyan' afford to live.

ANDRE: That not true.

ANGEL: You tink I don't want the best for you? My son? Look at your oldes' brudder in Kingston. He work so hard. Him clever but him never have enough. Him can barely afford to send him dawtas to school. Me live in tin shack, no runnin' water, no car. When it change? It always the same. You go to school, you have a chance. You cyan work anywhere in de world.

ANDRE: I work my way through to college.

ANGEL: How?

ANDRE: Someting will happen.

ANGEL: Your fadder wait for someting to happen and it never happen. Him try for years. Him work in sugar fields in Florida, in bar, in kitchen, in hotel. Him never manage. You have a chance to escape.

ANDRE: And how dat mek me differen' from my fadder?

ANGEL: She offer help.

ANDRE: You set me up Mam.

ANGEL: No. I try and push you in the right direction. Naomi nice. She not some fat old woman. She lost. She searchin' for somebody to love. And me know you feel someting for her.

ANDRE: Me only know her two week.

ANGEL: Me no wanna lose you. You my precious chile but me no want to see you sink. Sometime, you have to grab your chances.

ANDRE: Mam, I don't get you. You full of...

ANGEL: You special Andre. You set an example for your lickle brother an' he will follow you. You have ambition and you can have everyting.

ANDRE: Me jus' wan' work Mam. Good work – not dis grilling lobster and cooking jerk chicken day an' night.

ANGEL: So go and study more! She pay for it – what of it? Me wan' sit and eat in my bwoy's restaurant one day. Me wan' to see you with your own place.

ANDRE: *(Grins.)* Yeah mon. Likkle place up dere on de cliffs. Tables with fancy light and lot of chef runnin' around de kitchen.

ANDRE is calmer now. He sits at his mother's feet.

ANGEL: Me hear life in Englan' is hard and it a cold country. But there are plenty Jamaicans there.

ANDRE: Me no wanna leave here Mam. This my home.

SCENE 8

YOLANDA is pacing while REEFIE sits with his back to her.

YOLANDA: This place – always violence bubbling away under the surface.

REEFIE: We have a violent history.

YOLANDA: That's no fucking excuse. What was that all about?

REEFIE remains silent.

My last night as well. Thanks Reefie.

YOLANDA walks a little distance away and sits down. She sits and looks out to sea. They remain in silence for a while.

REEFIE: Seem like you only jus' arrive.

YOLANDA: Looks like I'm leaving in the nick of time – just as you turn nasty.

REEFIE: Him start it.

YOLANDA: Listen to yourself.

REEFIE: Me want grow old with you.

YOLANDA: Not sure what my husband Frank would say to that.

REEFIE: Frank know about me?

Beat.

Him know?

YOLANDA: Yeah.

REEFIE: You tell him?

YOLANDA: We had words. It got heated. He found your texts on my cellphone.

REEFIE: Rass.

YOLANDA: He never let on 'til I was leaving for the airport.

REEFIE: You love him?

YOLANDA: He's the father of my kids. We've been together since we were virtually kids.

REEFIE: And me?

YOLANDA looks away.

Jus' a lickle holiday romance?

YOLANDA: Five years Reefie. I've come back to you five years on the trot. What does that say to you? I know what you do for a living.

REEFIE: You different. Me give it all up for you.

YOLANDA: Pardon me if I don't believe you.

REEFIE: Five years and you still tink me a liad? Admit you love me.

YOLANDA: 'Course I love you. I just don't trust you.

REEFIE: Then come and be with me.

YOLANDA: I can't.

REEFIE: You break my heart every time you go.

YOLANDA: I can't leave Frank. Not even for you. There are some things you just don't do.

Beat.

You spoken to Naomi yet?

REEFIE: Me not her fadder.

YOLANDA: That why you've been hanging around the hotel gazing longingly at her?

REEFIE: Me gazing longingly at you, not her.

YOLANDA: You know her mother died.

REEFIE looks upset but covers up.

If she's your daughter…as Angel says she is…

REEFIE: That woman talk too much.

YOLANDA: What are you afraid of? She ain't gonna reject you – she wants to meet you.

REEFIE: Dis is none of your business.

YOLANDA: I know it but that doesn't stop me from…

REEFIE: Enough!

YOLANDA: Explain it to me Reefie cos I sure as hell can't figure it out. I know you have kids on this island – several – from what you said and I also happen to know that they don't want nothin' to do with you cos you were never there for them.

REEFIE: Me let them free.

YOLANDA: More like they rejected you. And now here's this gorgeous long-lost child with the same blood flowing through her veins as you, travels thousands of miles to search you out and you can't even be bothered to wave your hand at her?

REEFIE: I said enough!

YOLANDA looks out to sea and sighs.

YOLANDA: You don't like to hold on to people do you?

REEFIE: Dem always slip from me hand. But me care for you Yolanda.

YOLANDA: Keep comin' back for you Reefie but we ain't going no place are we? So what's the point? This is my last visit Reefie. I ain't comin' back.

YOLANDA gets up and walks away. REEFIE sits on his own.

SCENE 9

ANDRE and NAOMI are together again. NAOMI looks at ANDRE's cut eye.

NAOMI: Nasty cut. D'you get into a lot of fights?

ANDRE: No. Me usually avoid dem. Dis one I walk into eyes open. Idiot dat I am.

NAOMI: Andre – I know you're angry with me…your mum but she only wants what's best for you. I like your mum.

ANDRE: She always stand by me.

NAOMI: And I stand by my offer to help you. After the course, you could get yourself a good job in time. You could get paid well – you'd have a future – if you did well you might even be able to travel. You have a skill and you need to develop it.

ANDRE is torn.

I don't want you to feel beholden to me in any way. The offer comes from me. I earn enough to support you for a year. I inherited a little from my mother…and I work…and I like you. I like your spirit and I want to help.

ANDRE: You like my spirit?

NAOMI: Everything I say seems to piss you off! I'm trying to… I want to…

ANDRE: Me wan' to go to catering school. Me need the training but…if me tek your money, it a deal – I pay you back. When me mek my money as a proper chef, me pay you back – however long it take – even if it tek forever.

NAOMI: Okay.

ANDRE looks at NAOMI.

ANDRE: A gentleman's word.

NAOMI: Okay.

ANDRE: On my honour.

NAOMI: Okay!

They shake hands.

It's a deal.

ANDRE: Good. Only one ting complicate it all.

NAOMI: What?

ANDRE: How me feel. Me like you more dan a friend. So where dat leave me and you?

NAOMI: I don't know – depends on where you want to take it…

ANDRE: Two week – too short a time to get to know you. But…

ANDRE moves forward and kisses NAOMI.

Me wan' get to know you better.

NAOMI: I'd like that.

They kiss again.

Just so you know – I'm different – from all these women out here.

ANDRE: And I is different from all o' dese island men.

They kiss again, more passionately. They part again, guiltily – both looking out to sea, unsure of what to do next.

NAOMI: Would you...would you like to...maybe...?

ANDRE: We can go to your hotel room?

NAOMI nods nervously. ANDRE kisses her again. They get up, hold hands and exit together.

SCENE 10

We are in KITTY's hotel room. Her bag is packed and ready. She is all dressed up to go out with SLY and is putting on the finishing touches to her face. SLY enters.

KITTY: Hi there.

SLY: You areddi?

KITTY turns and smiles at SLY.

Pretty dress.

KITTY: Thank you.

SLY: Me gonna have to be your bodyguard tonight.

KITTY and SLY embrace.

All dem guys gonna want to chat wid you.

KITTY: I'll stick like glue to you.

They kiss.

Last night.

SLY: Me gonna miss my Kitty Kat. No one to cling to at night. Me miss you already. What time your flight tomorrow?

KITTY: Not until the evening.

SLY looks at the suitcase.

SLY: You already pack?

KITTY: There's a couple of things I've planned to do in the morning. Can you stick around in the morning?

SLY: Cool mon. And you mus' give me your cellphone number.

KITTY: You going to call me? All the way in England?

SLY: You not want keep in touch?

KITTY: 'Course I do. I'll be phoning you every day.

KITTY hugs SLY again.

SLY: Sure ting. And you come back…soon?

KITTY: You mean that?

SLY: Yeah mon. I cyan wait for you.

KITTY: What if I came back soon.

SLY: Eh?

KITTY: Come, sit with me. I want to tell you something.

SLY sits with KITTY on her bed. She wraps her arms around him while she talks.

I was thinking of going to see some properties on the way out to the airport tomorrow. I want you to come with me. Have a look…give me some advice.

SLY: You wanna buy some place? Like a holiday home?

KITTY: A holiday home to start with but then…

SLY: Den what?

KITTY: A home.

SLY: You wan' live here?

KITTY: I feel like I've finally found the island of my soul.

SLY looks confused.

SLY: But you have a job.

KITTY: Don't want to work like a dog all my life. Got some savings…could move out here.

SLY: Cool mon.

KITTY: You think that would be a good idea?

SLY hesitates.

SLY: If you like it here – sure mon.

KITTY: And us…

SLY: I see you more.

KITTY: Yes but…it could be your home too.

SLY stares at KITTY.

I know it's a bit sudden Sly but, I don't want it to end. I don't want us to end. I'm not getting any younger and I figured, we're good together…we should just make a go of it.

SLY: You give up your house? Your country? Your job? For me?

KITTY: For our future. Come back in say three months time. It'll take me that long to sort out my shit back home. Will you wait for me?

SLY: Sure ting.

KITTY: You think I'm mad?

SLY: No…is just sudden….two weeks…is quick man.

KITTY: But it just happened didn't it? I've had other boyfriends but I've never felt like this…. *(She giggles.)* I want to wake up next to you every morning.

SLY: You hab money to survive out here? Without a job?

KITTY: For a while. Then I'm sure I could get a job – teaching even.

SLY: Yes. But you cyan survive on what de schools pay teachers here and I cyan look after you…

KITTY pulls out her purse and hands over some dollars to SLY.

KITTY: I can give you some money to tide you over.

SLY turns the money down.

We're so good together. I feel so happy with you…I love you…

SLY: Me love you too but…

KITTY: I can even wire you money if you need me to.

SLY: Kitty…

KITTY: I want us to have a family.

SLY looks at KITTY incredulous.

I want to have babies. I want to have your babies.

SLY stands up and paces.

I'm older than you, I know. But that's why I can see things clearer than you. Experience I guess. We're good for each other. I could help you. Put you through school or college. You could get a good job – maybe even in the hotel industry – whatever you want. I could help you.

SLY: Listen to me Kitty. Me like you, me care for you, but all o' dis too fast for me. You got to slow down gyal.

KITTY: I've thought about it.

SLY: You say you don't wan' kids.

KITTY: I lied.

SLY: Me have other tings in my life. Is complicated.

KITTY: Oh right, so I give up everything for you but you can't do the same for me. That's not fair is it?

SLY: Rass man! I ask you to give up everyting for me? I ask you?

KITTY looks at SLY's angry face and relents.

KITTY: No – okay. It's too fast. I'm sorry. You're right.

SLY: Tink about what you sayin' Kitty. We not know each other well enough.

KITTY: What more is there to know? If a thing feels right.

SLY: But it have to go two way 'oman. Me have to feel de same.

KITTY: And you don't?

Beat.

SLY: Is too soon to chat 'bout family. Too early.

SLY looks sorry for KITTY but moves towards the door. He looks back at KITTY.

Me sorry Kitty.

KITTY: Don't go!

SLY looks uncomfortable.

SLY: Me cyan give you what you want.

KITTY: Doesn't matter. So I jumped the gun a bit. Time of life. Forget it. We can go back to the way things were. No strings – that how you like it?

SLY: You leavin' tomorrow…we hab us some good times but…

KITTY: I'll be back and we can take up again. Who knows where it might lead?

SLY: Kitty. Me already have a 'oman and tree pickney. Me 'ave to work to feed dem.

KITTY looks up at SLY in fury.

KITTY: What did you say?

SLY: You hear me.

KITTY: But you're only twenty-two! How can you have three kids?

SLY: I is not twenty-two. I is tirty-five.

KITTY: But you said…

SLY: I said what I said cos that what you want to hear. You want a young man. Someone who remind you of dat nice schoolboy o' yours. I be whoever you want me to be. But it not me. It not real.

KITTY: *(Furious.)* You evil, evil bastard. You fucking liar… fucking two-faced fucking shit. You led me on.

SLY: How is dat?

KITTY: You lied.

SLY: I give you what you want. You pay me. Dat how it work. Me tink you know.

KITTY: Was this all a game for you?

SLY: No, it work. Life on dis island not a game. Me have to feed me kin.

KITTY: I thought you felt something for me?

SLY: Me feel someting for you?

KITTY: You bastard. Motherfucking pile of shit.

KITTY lunges at SLY, slapping and kicking. SLY laughs holding onto KITTY's flailing arms.

SLY: For someone who is so educated, you is remarkable stupid.

KITTY: Lowlife scum. You people can't be helped.

SLY: Is that so?

KITTY: Just like all those good-for-nothing students of mine. You think the world owes you whilst you just take, take, take…

SLY: You is not fit to be a mother. Me hope you stay barren.

KITTY kicks and screams. SLY holds on tight to KITTY's arms and avoids the kicks.

KITTY: You worthless piece of filth. I hate you! You'll live and die in poverty, never able to provide for your miserable kids. Boy, did you miss your chance. I could've lifted you from your shit life. I hope you rot on this stinking island.

SLY: Me should be so grateful?

KITTY: You'll regret this! You will. You'll look back and wish you'd treated me better – with respect!

SLY: And how am I suppose to respec' a gyal like you? You tink me a savage, a house slave. You look at me and you is jealous of my skin, but glad you is white. You tink you is superior.

KITTY: I am superior because you're nothing more than a prostitute.

SLY: And you is jus' a client. You hab to pay for each lickle second me spend wid you. Every lickle compliment costs. One cent for every step me tek wid you, every footprint in de sand. One dollar for me to say you is lookin' good;

five dollars for me to hold you tight; ten dollars when me say me care for you. You pay for every kiss, every whisper, every stroke, every fuck. How empty your life mus' be Kitty when you hab to pay smaddy to say a lickle sweetness to you.

KITTY: Let go of me. I'll scream. I'll bring the manager in and have you whipped. Have you thrown in jail you fucking black bastard. NIGGER!

SLY: Kitty. Mek me tell you. Tek a long hard look at yourself and tink straight. What man would want a desperate, ugly, bitch like you?

SLY pushes KITTY aside roughly and throws her on the bed. KITTY looks frightened as he raises his hand to hit her. He decides against it and instead, he opens her purse, takes out all of her money, pockets it and exits.

SCENE 11

It is early in the morning. ANGEL is setting up her hut. She stumbles a little and sits on a chair to steady herself for a while.

NAOMI is looking for shells down by the beach. REEFIE is sat under the shade of a palm tree watching her. She turns, smiles and waves at him. He waves back.

MAGGIE approaches NAOMI.

MAGGIE: I'm all packed.

NAOMI: You don't look very well.

MAGGIE: Got the shits something chronic. Must've been something I ate. Taken some tablets to cork it all up. Now I'm feeling bloated.

NAOMI: Oh dear.

MAGGIE: Not looking forward to the plane journey… You'll be okay on your own?

NAOMI: Don't worry about me.

MAGGIE: Don't hang around here too long will you?

NAOMI: Stop fussing.

MAGGIE: Where's loverboy?

NAOMI: Getting dressed.

MAGGIE: You going to go all 'native' like your mum?

NAOMI: Don't…

MAGGIE: It won't last.

NAOMI: Never met a bloke like Andre back home.

MAGGIE: It's all an act.

NAOMI: It isn't.

MAGGIE: Only difference I see is that he's better at the game. Quite clever cos he's got you eating out of the palm of his…

NAOMI: Stop it! Don't talk about him as if he's a conman.

MAGGIE: He's after your money.

NAOMI: No. He's not like the others.

MAGGIE: How d'you know?

NAOMI: Because Andre's a good man. We'll see each other. I'll come out here, maybe he'll come and visit me. Maybe it'll all die a death – I dunno. But right this minute, now – it feels right.

MAGGIE: He will always be financially beholden to you and eventually it drives men mad. They can't cope unless they are the breadwinners.

NAOMI: He's shown me laughter and love again.

MAGGIE: Euch – you are so soppy.

NAOMI: When did you get so mean-spirited?

MAGGIE looks at NAOMI, hurt.

MAGGIE: When I faced the truth.

MAGGIE clutches her stomach and groans.

You'll call me as soon as you get back?

NAOMI: Course I will. Have a safe journey.

MAGGIE hugs NAOMI briefly and hobbles off clutching her stomach.

NAOMI watches after MAGGIE and then continues to look for shells.

Eventually, REEFIE approaches her.

REEFIE: You find any nice shells?

NAOMI: Loads. Gonna decorate my bathroom with them.

NAOMI shows REEFIE her shells.

REEFIE: Dat one dere is coral – from de reef.

NAOMI: Oh!

REEFIE: You been snorkelling?

NAOMI: Yeah. Beautiful. Really stunning. Bit scared at first. But in the end – loved it.

REEFIE: Who tek you out?

NAOMI: Andre. Some friend's boat. We were out there for ages. It's another whole world down there.

REEFIE: You have a nice time here Naomi?

NAOMI: Fantastic.

REEFIE: You going back now?

NAOMI: Leaving Negril today but I thought I'd see a bit more of the island. Just another ten days. Want to see Kingston properly and the Blue Mountains and I never made it to the Mayfield Falls.

REEFIE: You must go. You can walk up de waterfall – but you have to be careful. Mek sure you tek a guide.

NAOMI: Where's Yolanda?

REEFIE: She go back home.

NAOMI: Never got to say goodbye. Didn't even get her email address.

REEFIE: Me can pass yours on.

NAOMI: Great – she was such fun. Here, I have a card. It's got my address and stuff on it.

NAOMI produces a card from her bag and hands it to REEFIE. REEFIE reads it.

REEFIE: *(Reads the card.)* You an architect!

NAOMI: Sounds more glamorous than it actually is. Only just finished training. Takes years to qualify.

REEFIE: You work in London?

NAOMI: Small firm – designing new homes. One day, I'll design something else – like a boat or a sky scraper or something like that.

REEFIE smiles.

REEFIE: So. You have a good time here.

NAOMI: This is where I was born.

REEFIE: Me hear.

Beat.

I got someting for you. A lickle present to remind you of Reefie.

NAOMI: For me?

REEFIE goes back to the palm tree and brings back a large conch shell which he hands over to NAOMI.

REEFIE: Me find it out in de sea when me go out in me boat.

NAOMI: Wow. It's stunning. Look at the colours! That's so kind of you. Thank you. I'll look at it and think of you and Negril.

ANDRE stands at some distance and waits for NAOMI. The two men clock each other warily.

REEFIE: You 'ave a safe journey now.

NAOMI: Thanks for this Reefie. I'll check you out when I come back.

REEFIE: Sure ting.

NAOMI touches fists with REEFIE. She walks up to ANDRE. He puts his arm around NAOMI's waist and kisses her. REEFIE looks at ANDRE and NAOMI together. He looks wistful.

ANDRE and NAOMI walk off together arm in arm. REEFIE watches them go.

REEFIE walks back up to ANGEL – tentatively approaching her. She looks at him haughtily.

Me sorry Angel – dat ting wid your byah – me get hot head.

ANGEL: You could hab kill him.

REEFIE: No mon…me jus' idiot…me no hurt your byah.

Beat.

ANGEL: Maybe dem hab a chance.

REEFIE is silent.

Why you not tell her? Why you hide de truth?

REEFIE looks away. He is close to tears.

REEFIE: Look at me Angel. What I am?

ANGEL: A man.

REEFIE: Me cyan admit to her…not want to disappoint her. What her fadder is. Me ashame of what I am. Me ashame.

ANGEL stands up, holds REEFIE. They stay like this for some time.

Eventually, they pull apart.

REEFIE: You okay Angel? You look tired.

ANGEL: Me jus' hear some news. Me need to sit a while.

ANGEL sits back down again.

REEFIE: Your man?

ANGEL: He die. Las' night. In him dirty room, on him own.

ANGEL looks out to sea sadly. REEFIE says nothing but goes round the back of her and massages her shoulders.

End.